REVISED

EXPERIENCING GOD

KNOWING *and* DOING
THE WILL OF GOD

HENRY & RICHARD
BLACKABY
CLAUDE KING

B&H
PUBLISHING GROUP

NASHVILLE, TENNESSEE

Copyright © 2008 by Henry Blackaby,
Richard Blackaby, and Claude King
All rights reserved.

978-1-4627-8685-5
International version

Published by B&H Publishing Group,
Nashville, Tennessee

Dewey Decimal Classification: 231
Subject Heading: GOD—WILL \ CHRISTIAN LIFE

Art on page 54 is used with permission from *Experiencing God: Knowing and Doing the Will of God* by Henry T. Blackaby and Claude V. King, published by LifeWay Press, 1990.

Henry and Richard Blackaby are represented by the literary agency of Wolgemuth & Associates, Inc.

Unless otherwise noted, Scripture quotations are from the Holman Christian Standard Bible®, copyright © 1999, 2000, 2002, 2003 by Holman Bible Publishers.

Printed in the United States of America
1 2 3 4 5 6 7 8 • 21 20 19 18 17

EXPERIENCING GOD

To my parents, Mr. and Mrs. G. R. S. Blackaby,
and parents-in-law, Mr. and Mrs. M. A. Wells, Sr.,
for their faithful example before me;

and to my wife Marilynn,
for her faithful companionship,

and my children, Richard, Thomas, Melvin, Norman, and Carrie,
as we have been experiencing God together.

—Henry T. Blackaby

To my amazing children, Mike, Daniel, and Carrie.
May you always enjoy experiencing God the way
your parents, grandparents, and great-grandparents have.

—Richard Blackaby

Contents

Preface	ix
Introduction	1
1. Knowing God by Experience	9
2. God Works According to His Nature	19
3. Doing God's Will	31
4. Being God's Servant	41
5. Seven Realities of Experiencing God	51
6. God Is at Work around You	65
7. God Pursues a Love Relationship with You	79
8. God's Invitation to Join Him in His Work	101
9. God Invites You to Join Him	119
10. God Speaks to His People	133
11. God Reveals Himself, His Purposes, and His Ways	155
12. God Speaks through the Bible	165
13. God Speaks through Prayer	173
14. God Speaks through Circumstances	183
15. God Speaks through the Church	199
16. God's Invitation Leads to a Crisis of Belief	207
17. Joining God Requires Adjustments	225
18. Joining God Requires Obedience	239
19. God Accomplishes His Work	253
20. Returning to God	263
21. Experiencing God as Couples	273
22. Joining God's Activity in Your Children's Lives	281
23. Experiencing God in the Church	289
24. Experiencing God in the Marketplace	299
25. Experiencing God in His Kingdom	307
26. Continuing to Experience God	315
Closing Remarks	319
About the Authors	321
Appendix: Names, Titles, and Descriptions of God	325

Preface

When I became a Christian, I couldn't have imagined all God intended to do in and through my life. I grew up in an isolated community on the west coast of Canada near the Alaska border. My father was a bank manager and a dedicated man of God. As a boy I came to a profound realization: God is God and I am not.

That seems straightforward enough, but that truth revolutionized my life. I came to believe that not only is God real, but He wants to take an active role in my life. I grew up to be a shy, introverted teenager. Then in a special worship service, God made it clear that He wanted exclusive access to my life, to use it for His purposes. I'll never forget the evening when I fully surrendered my life to God and told Him I would do whatever He instructed me to do. From that point on, I no longer attempted to set the agenda for my life. My only goal was to do God's will, whatever that might be.

When I was a young man, God did not reveal to me that I would one day be a pastor, or a denominational leader, or an author or mentor to corporate executives. God simply gave me one assignment at a time, and I sought to be faithful. Eventually I grew to realize that God is always actively at work around me and, if I look for it, I will recognize God's activity in the lives of the people around me. I also discovered that every time God told me to do something—no matter how difficult it might appear—He *always* enabled me to accomplish what He asked.

Over time, God led me to serve as a youth leader, worship director, education minister, senior pastor, Bible college president, denominational leader, author, and international speaker. Each new assignment took me well beyond what I felt comfortable or skilled to do. Yet each time, God proved to be more than just my Creator or Savior. He was also my sustainer, counselor, comforter, teacher, strength, protector, guide, and much more. Every time I obeyed

God, I came to experience Him in new and deeper dimensions than I had ever known.

I was occasionally asked to speak at conferences, especially student meetings, to tell others how I had learned to walk with God. My relationship with God seemed pretty ordinary to me—since it was the only one I had experienced—and I am extremely ordinary! Yet time and time again, people told me my sharing had convicted them that they had been religious, moral, and orthodox, but they had not been experiencing God the way I was describing.

I found that a growing number of people wanted to work with me in my church and then in the denominational association in which I was a leader. Pastors would leave strong churches and move to a mission setting, living on faith, to become involved in what God was doing in our midst. It seemed so simple. And yet every time we believed God, He would show us what He wanted us to do next. As we obeyed Him, we would experience a fresh demonstration of His power, love, and provision. This became such a natural part of how I and those around me walked with God that we scarcely realized it was not the way most Christians and churches were functioning.

In the midst of those exciting days—when I worked with churches in the city of Vancouver, Canada—Avery Willis approached me to ask if I would put into writing the lessons I had learned from my walk with God. That way, others could study and learn from them. I was keenly aware of how ordinary I was, so this was a humbling moment. I was not a writer. I had a full and hectic schedule, and attempting to put into a book what I had learned over a lifetime of relating to God seemed a daunting task.

Eventually, the publisher assigned an editor, Claude King, to work with me. Claude was and is a Spirit-filled, gracious man. He listened to me teach. He read over transcripts of my sermons. We spent many hours discussing how God walks with people and reveals His will. At one point the publisher suggested we call my work, "Knowing God," but I said absolutely not. My concern was that God's people were already immersed in Bible studies and Christian books that gave them an enormous amount of information about God. As a result, sincere Christians were coming to church every week and learning more and more about God, but they were not *experiencing* Him. To many, He was simply a faraway God to be believed in, a doctrine to affirm, an invisible deity to whom they recited their prayers. They needed to know He is a Person with whom Christians can enjoy an intimate, growing, loving fellowship.

I prayed that the result of our efforts would not merely be another course people could take. I asked God to somehow guide us in such a way that through our writing, people would experience a life-changing encounter with the living God. Claude and I enlisted prayer warriors from all over North America and asked them to pray every day that God would guide us to produce something He would be pleased to use to bless His people. Eventually, the material was published as an interactive study entitled *Experiencing God: Knowing and Doing the Will of God*.

The literary world was not standing in long lines to purchase copies of the book upon its release! No one had heard of Henry Blackaby. Interactive studies were not popular, and the publisher did not launch a major advertising campaign. Expectations were modest, to say the least. But something began to happen. A few small groups worked through the study, and they encountered God in a fresh, new way. They and their churches began to experience renewal. Word began to spread that this was unlike any other course people had taken. Before long, we were hearing of God doing amazing things across the country among various denominations, as well as internationally. Often, as people studied the material, they would sense God calling them into Christian ministry. I heard from mission agencies and seminaries that the number one reason people were listing for entering the ministry was that God had clearly spoken to them as they were studying *Experiencing God*. Many people expressed to us that the truths they encountered helped them become God-centered in their thinking and taught them how to recognize God's will for themselves, their families, their businesses, and their churches. A couple of years later, the material was developed into a trade book, the revised and expanded edition of which you are reading now.

Some of the most exciting testimonies have come from readers who are longtime Christians. They've said things like:

- "I wish I had known these truths forty years ago. My life and ministry would have been totally different."

- "This is the most wonderful time in my Christian life. I never knew I could have an intimate and personal relationship with my heavenly Father."
- "My whole life and attitudes have changed since I began this study."
- "I sensed God's call to missions while I was studying *Experiencing God*. That is how God led me to the mission field."
- "Our church is not the same. It has come alive again. We have started eleven new ministries in the past year."

I can't tell you how thrilling it has been for me to see the way God has used that material to impact His kingdom! *Experiencing God* has been translated into more than seventy languages. I have ministered in one hundred fourteen countries, and everywhere I have gone, people have tearfully related how God used the book to transform their lives. Countless individuals have told me they're serving in their church or on the mission field or in their current job because of what God said to them while they were studying *Experiencing God*.

I discovered there was a deep hunger in the hearts of Christians to know and do God's will. This has led me to incredible opportunities to serve the Lord. I've been invited on several occasions to minister at the United Nations as well as the Pentagon and the White House. Many fine Christian leaders, authors, and government leaders have told me that, as they were studying *Experiencing God*, God clearly guided them into their present position and gave them focus for their lives. I also became involved with a dynamic group of Christian CEOs who asked me to help disciple them and to teach them how to recognize God's activity in the marketplace. It has been truly amazing and humbling to be a part of what God has done over these years.

Since I first wrote *Experiencing God*, it has been deeply rewarding to see people discover practical ways to apply the spiritual truths to their lives. I have written, along with my wife and children, a number of related materials, including *A God Centered Church, Fresh Encounter, The Man God Uses, Experiencing God as Couples,*

Hearing God's Voice, Spiritual Leadership, Experiencing God Day by Day, God in the Marketplace, Called and Accountable, When God Speaks, and many more. I'll never forget listening to an immense choir singing the debut of the *Experiencing God Musical*. Words cannot describe the deep gratitude to God I felt as the truths I had experienced walking with Him were sung by ten thousand people that evening! I was also blessed to be able to establish Blackaby Ministries International (www.blackaby.org) to continue spreading the message contained in *Experiencing God* around the world for many years to come.

After seventeen years of seeing *Experiencing God* used to teach and challenge people around the world, we felt it was time to revise and update the course. While I've heard many marvelous testimonies from those who encountered God as they studied the material, I have also been asked numerous questions I didn't anticipate when we first put the course together. The result is the book you now hold—a completely revised and expanded edition more comprehensive than the original version.

In this new endeavor, I was pleased to have my oldest son, Richard, join Claude and me as a writer. Richard has served as a pastor and seminary president and is now the president of Blackaby Ministries International. He has coauthored numerous other works with me and is well qualified to join in the revision of this material. He coauthored the revision of *Experiencing God, Interactive Study* and was a field editor for the original material. Richard knows my heart and my message thoroughly, and he travels internationally sharing truths from *Experiencing God*. This book is written in the first person—from my perspective—because the biblical understandings and illustrations have come primarily from me. However, Claude and Richard have both made significant contributions to this work. I pray you will encounter your Lord in its pages and that, as a result, your life will never be the same.

INTRODUCTION

IN CHURCH BUT NOT IN CHRIST

While speaking in a series of meetings several years ago, I was approached by a man during a break. He appeared visibly shaken by what I had said and told me he was a professor at his denomination's Bible college. He explained that for years he had taught his students to treat the Bible like a classic piece of literature—a book to read and to enjoy its beauty but not something through which Almighty God would speak directly to the reader. Through tears, he confessed that he had done this because he had not personally experienced God communicating with Him. But during that conference, the Spirit of God had spoken clearly to the man and reminded him that Christianity is fundamentally an interactive relationship between God and people. When this man was younger, he had experienced God's guidance in his life. As he grew older, however, and entered the academic world, he had steadily grown more distant from God. Eventually, his estranged relationship with God seemed normal for him. Now he assumed it also should be normative for the students he taught.

Here was a man who had studied the Bible all his life. Yet for him, Scripture had become merely a collection of ancient writings that had little direct application to his life. Now that this man's heart had been awakened to the living God of those Scriptures, he realized he had been poisoning the minds of a generation of young people by teaching that God does not speak to His people. This man had experienced revival, and he was eager to re-enter the classroom to tell students that God is real, and that He wants to encounter every person.

Sadly, we experience this scenario regularly. There are far too many people who settle for practicing a sterile religion rather than enjoying a growing, vibrant, personal relationship with the living God.

God's Invitation

God is not a concept or a doctrine. He is a Person who seeks a close, one-on-one relationship with you and me. God does not want us to merely believe in Him, He wants to relate to us on a personal level. He does not just want to hear us recite prayers. He wants to converse with us. God's plan is not to abandon Christians once we are born again, leaving us to build the best life we can. He does not intend that we simply use our wits to "get by," to bravely "survive" until we are finally ushered into heaven. God wants to be actively involved in our lives each day.

God knows what your life can become. Only He understands your full potential as His child. He does not want you to miss out on anything He has for you. I believe that within the heart of every Christian is an innate desire to know God and to do His will.

When you became a Christian, you were immediately adopted as a child of the heavenly king. The king's business became your business. And now, as your Savior and Lord, Christ wants to bring your life into the middle of His activity, which offers salvation to every person on earth. God Himself will give you the desire to serve and obey Him. The Holy Spirit will create within you a longing to know the Father's will and to become involved in what God is doing around you. Yet God has far more in store for your life than merely giving you an assignment to accomplish for Him. He wants you to have an intimate love relationship with Him that is real and personal. Jesus said: "This is eternal life: that they may know You, the only true God, and the One You have sent—Jesus Christ" (John 17:3).

Eternal Life—Now

The essence of eternal life—and the heart of this book—is for you to personally know God the Father and Jesus Christ, His Son. Knowing God does not come through a program, a study, or a method. It is the result of a vibrant, growing, one-on-one relationship with God. Within this intimate connection, God will reveal Himself, His purposes, and His ways so you can know Him in deeper and profound dimensions. As you relate to Him, God will invite you to join in His activity where He is already at work. When you obey what God tells you, He will accomplish through you things only He can do. As the Lord works in and through your life, you will come to know Him ever more closely.

Jesus said, "I have come that they may have life and have it in abundance" (John 10:10). Would you like to experience life in its fullest and richest dimensions? You may, if you are willing to respond to God's invitation to enjoy an intimate love relationship with Him.

Prerequisite: A Saving Relationship with Jesus Christ

The pages that follow assume that you have already trusted Jesus Christ as your Savior and acknowledged Him to be the Lord of your life. If you have not made this most important decision, the rest of this book will have little meaning for you because spiritual matters can only be understood by those who have the Spirit of Christ dwelling within them. Scripture says: "The natural man does not welcome what comes from God's Spirit, because it is foolishness to him; he is not able to know it since it is evaluated spiritually" (1 Cor. 2:14).

Perhaps you were baptized as an infant. Or you may have regularly attended church since you were a child. You may even be a leader in your church. Baptism, worship attendance, and church involvement are all appropriate, obedient responses to a relationship with God. However, they do not *create* or *replace* the relationship. Was there an occasion when you repented to God for your sins and asked Christ to be your Savior and Lord? If not, then the most important thing you could possibly do right now is to obey what Scripture exhorts and settle this matter with God. Ask the Lord to speak to you as you read and consider the following Scriptures:

- Romans 3:23—All have sinned.
- Romans 6:23—Eternal life is a free gift of God.

- Romans 5:8—Because of His love, Jesus paid the death penalty for your sins.
- Romans 10:9–10—Confess Jesus as your Lord and acknowledge that God raised Him from the dead.
- Romans 10:13—Ask God to forgive your sins and trust Him to do so.

To place your faith in Jesus and receive His gift of eternal life you must:

- Recognize that God created you for a love relationship with Him. He wants you to love Him with all your being.
- Admit you are a sinner, and that you cannot save yourself.
- Believe Jesus paid the penalty for your sin by His death on the cross and that He rose from the dead in victory over death.
- Confess (agree with God about) your sins that separate you from Him.
- Repent (turn away from) your sins.
- Ask Jesus to save you by His grace, which is an undeserved gift.
- Turn over the control of your life to Jesus.

If you need help, call on a minister, a deacon, an elder, or a Christian friend. If you have just made this important decision, tell someone the good news of what God has done in your life. Then share your decision with your church.

Looking to Know God Better?

You may be frustrated as a Christian because you know God has a more abundant life for you than you are presently experiencing. Or you may earnestly desire God's directions for your life as you seek to serve Him. Perhaps you have recently experienced tragedy and now you stand bewildered in the middle of a broken life, not knowing what to do next. Whatever your present circumstances, my sincere prayer is that this book may help you to do the following:

- Believe and experience daily God's infinite love for you.
- Hear when God is speaking to you.
- Identify God's unmistakable activity in your life.
- Believe Him to be and to do everything He promises.
- Adjust your beliefs, character, and behavior to Him and His ways.
- Identify a direction He is taking in your life, and recognize what He wants to do through you.
- Know clearly how to respond to what He shows you.
- Experience God doing through you what only He can do.

These are not things that *I* can do or that *this book* can do for you. *Only God can accomplish these things.* I can serve as your guide, encourager, and, hopefully, as a catalyst to help you enjoy a deeper walk with God. I will share with you the biblical truths by which God has guided my life. I will recount for you some of the amazing works the Lord has done when God's people have applied biblical truths to following Him.

I invite you to interact with God as you read this book, asking Him to reveal the ways He wants you to apply these truths in your own life, family, ministry, job, and church. But take your time! Many people have told me that as they were reading this book, they suddenly encountered God face-to-face and He changed their lives forever. That is my prayer for you. As you read, take time to pause and pray, asking God to speak to you, to guide you, and to reveal how He wants you to respond. If God speaks clearly about something He wants to do in your life, don't move quickly on to the next chapter. Instead, camp out on what God said, and let Him show how He wants to implement that truth in your life. Once you feel you have processed what God wants you to understand, begin reading further to discover what else God has in store for you.

I have found that God always has a fresh and deeper truth He wants us to learn about Him. So once He has taught you one thing, get ready for the *next* marvelous truth God will soon introduce!

Where Are You?

People can be in many different places along their spiritual walk. I've noted below some of the ways you might describe your spiritual life. See if one or more of these descriptions matches your present relationship with God:

nonexistent	plateaued	in decline	confused
exciting	growing	miraculous	victorious
discouraging	powerful	bewildered	defeated
dynamic	contagious	hopeless	joyful
sinful	embarrassing	deepening	ashamed

This book is unlike most you will read. Repeatedly, God has used the truths it explains to initiate a profound encounter with those who read them. So before you go further, take a moment to ask yourself, *"What does God want to do in my life as I read this book?"* Pause now to pray, and ask God to accomplish His will in your life as you continue.

Your Teacher

Jesus said, "But the Counselor, the Holy Spirit—the Father will send Him in My name—will teach you all things" (John 14:26). God's Holy Spirit is your personal teacher. He will draw you into a closer walk with God as He reveals God's purposes and ways to you. Jesus said, "If anyone wants to do His will, he will understand whether the teaching is from God or if I am speaking on My own." (John 7:17).

That is the criteria for this and any book. The Holy Spirit, who resides within you, will always confirm in your heart the truth of Scripture. When I share in this book what I perceive as a biblical principle, you can depend on the Holy Spirit to affirm whether that teaching comes from God or not. You shouldn't automatically take my word for it! Always ask the Holy Spirit to verify—through Scripture—what I am teaching. As you read this book, be sure to nurture your relationship with God through prayer, meditation, and Bible study so you will be able to receive and obey everything God tells you.

Your Source of Authority

The Bible is God's Word to you. The Holy Spirit honors and uses God's Word as He speaks to you. The Scriptures will be your source of authority for how you live your Christian life and how you relate to God. You can't depend on human traditions, your experience, or the opinions of others to be accurate authorities on God's will and ways. While these can be helpful, they must always be evaluated in light of the teaching of Scripture.

Anything of spiritual significance that happens in your life will be a result of God's activity in you. He is infinitely more concerned with your life and your relationship with Him than you or I could possibly be. Let God's Spirit bring you into an intimate relationship with the Lord of the universe "who is able to do above and beyond all that we ask or think—according to the power that works in you" (Eph. 3:20). *Would you pray at the outset of your reading, and surrender your life to God so He may guide and instruct you in any way He pleases?* As you prepare to obey Him, trust that God who has already begun a good work in you will complete it in His time (Phil. 1:6).

I urge you to allow the Holy Spirit to take your life to a new, higher, dynamic level in your walk with God. You may be presently enjoying a vibrant Christian life. But I can assure you, there is still much more God wants you to experience of Him, for He is an infinite being. You may have been disappointed in the past. Perhaps you attempted other studies or made other commitments to grow spiritually, but your enthusiasm eventually waned and your growth fizzled. I encourage you: Don't let any previous failure or disappointment stop you from confidently moving forward with God. No matter where we are, why would any of us ever become satisfied with the current status of our walk with God when there is so much He wants to do in and through our lives?

Each chapter of this book includes a section featuring questions to ponder, set apart like the one on the following page. You might wish to keep a notebook nearby as you consider these issues and apply the book's message to your life circumstances.

QUESTIONS FOR REFLECTION

1. Are you certain you are a child of God, that He has forgiven you of your sin? If not, stop right now and settle that matter with the Lord.

2. What in particular would you like to see God do in your life as you study this book? Do you long for a deeper walk with Him? Do you need victory over a particular sin in your life? Do you desire more profound times in prayer and reading God's Word? Would you like to gain a deeper sense of joy in your life or to better understand God's will? Ask God to address these specific issues as you read.

3. Do you have questions regarding the Christian life or your own personal experience? If so, list them in the margin of this book or in a prayer journal, and then watch to see how God guides you into the truth of your circumstances.

1

KNOWING GOD BY EXPERIENCE

This is eternal life: that they may know You, the only true God, and the One You have sent—Jesus Christ. (John 17:3)

EXPERIENCING GOD'S PROTECTION

One day, I was travelling in a mini-van with my wife Marilynn and two men on an extremely busy freeway near Washington, D.C. It was rush hour, and the multi-lane expressway was jammed with vehicles as impatient drivers rushed to their destinations. Suddenly, our van swerved to the left and almost collided with an eighteen-wheeler in the next lane. We all braced ourselves, certain we were about to be crushed by the behemoth. The truck blasted its air horn, and our driver veered back into our lane. But before long our vehicle again drifted into the busy lane of traffic beside us. We asked the driver if he was OK, and he assured us he was. But his driving became increasingly erratic. Finally, we insisted that he pull over and eventually discovered this dear man was having a stroke. He barely knew what he was doing. It had been a miracle we had not had a serious accident.

I had known that God was my Protector since I was a little boy (Ps. 41:2; 121:7). Yet on that day, I *experienced* His divine safeguarding. There is a world of difference between knowing something to be true in your head and experiencing the reality in your life. When we finally arrived at our destination that evening, I had a profound new, *experiential* understanding of God as my Protector.

Scripture is filled with descriptions of God's character. You can read these accounts and believe them to be true about God. Yet God does not merely want you to read *about* Him, He wants you to *know* Him. For the Greeks, to know something meant you understood a concept in your mind. It was an academic process. For example, a Greek orphan might grow up and know the concept of a father. He could describe what fathers do and what it looks like to relate to one. He could conduct research and know all the nuances of the Greek word for father. Yet a small child who had a loving father would know much more about fatherhood than the expert who had studied the concept abstractly his entire life.

In contrast, for a Hebrew person—like Jesus—knowing something entailed experiencing it. In fact, you could not truly say you knew something unless you had dealt with it personally. The small child who had a father might not understand the various grammatical uses of the word "father," but he would know a great deal about what it was like to have one. So it is significant that, when Jesus spoke about knowing God, He was speaking as a Hebrew.

When Jesus said eternal life is knowing God—including God the Son, Jesus Christ—He did not mean that eternal life is knowing *about* God. He was not referring to someone who has read many books and attended numerous seminars about God. He was talking about a firsthand, experiential knowledge. We come to truly know God as we experience Him in and around our lives. Many people have grown up attending church and hearing about God all their lives, but they do not have a personal, dynamic, growing relationship with God. They never hear His voice. They have no idea what God's will is. They do not encounter His love firsthand. They have no sense of divine purpose for their lives. They may know a lot about God, but they don't really know Him.

Merely knowing about God will leave you unsatisfied. Truly knowing God only comes through experience as He reveals Himself to you through His word and as you relate to Him. Throughout the Bible, we can see that God took the initiative to disclose Himself to people through their life events.

KNOWING GOD THROUGH HIS NAMES

In biblical days, a Hebrew person's name represented his character or described her nature. Peoples' names gave insight into what they were like.

Similarly, biblical names, titles, and descriptions of God identify how men and women personally came to know Him. The Scripture is the record of God's revelation of Himself to people. Each of the many names for God represents a different aspect of His nature.

THE LORD WILL PROVIDE

Genesis 22:1–18 tells us that God was in the process of developing Abraham's character so he could be the father of a new nation. God put Abraham's faith and obedience to the test by asking him to sacrifice his only son, Isaac. This brought Abraham to a crisis of belief. He had to decide what he really believed about God. Until this time, Abraham had known God by experience as "God Almighty," for God had miraculously provided him with a son when he and his wife, Sarah, were old and beyond the human limits of childbearing. It was wonderful to know God as "Almighty," but God wanted to expand Abraham's understanding and his experience of who He is.

The command from God to kill Isaac seemingly contradicts everything we know about God. However, in Abraham's day, people sometimes would sacrifice children on altars dedicated to their idols. They believed that demonstrating such devotion to their gods would earn them divine pleasure and, in return, bring bountiful crops. Nowhere else does the Bible record God ever asking someone to sacrifice a child to Him. Clearly, God was testing Abraham to see if he was as devoted to the true God as his neighbors were committed to their false gods.

Of course, any such sacrifice would be horrendous, but putting to death your only child—for whom you had waited twenty-five years—would have been an agonizing assignment. Obeying such a command required Abraham to trust God at a new and deeper level of faith than he ever had before. On the way to the place of sacrifice, Isaac asked his dad, "Where is the lamb for the burnt offering?" (Gen. 22:7). Can you imagine how sobering this moment was for Abraham, knowing his beloved son Isaac was to be the sacrifice?

"Abraham answered, 'God Himself will provide the lamb for the burnt offering, my son'" (Gen. 22:8). We don't know all Abraham was thinking as he trudged up the mountain with his son, but clearly he trusted God to provide everything he needed for the imminent sacrifice. He acted on his belief that God was his Provider. He did what God told him to do. When God saw that Abraham did not merely claim to have faith in Him but that he was willing to act out his trust though obedience in this excruciating task, He stopped Abraham and provided a ram for the sacrifice instead. Abraham named that place after the characteristic of God he had just come to know by experience. This is the first time we see the name *Jehovah Jireh* in Scripture, meaning "The Lord Will Provide." Abraham came to an intimate knowledge of God that day through the experience of God as his Provider.

This is how we, too, grow to know God. As we experience God firsthand, we come to know Him in new and increasingly deeper dimensions. We can learn that God provides as we read this story about Abraham's walk, but we really know God as Provider once we experience Him providing something specifically for us.

God's Perfect Provision

For twelve years I served as a church pastor in Saskatoon, Saskatchewan, Canada. When we started our first mission church, we called Jack Conner as our mission pastor. Although the new congregation needed a full-time pastor, we had no money for moving expenses and no provision for his salary. But we knew God was asking us to invite Jack to come. He had three children in school, so we needed to pay him at least a modest salary with which to care for his family. We began to pray that God would provide for his moving expenses and his salary once he arrived.

Jack had a secure job as a senior pastor in California. Yet we were asking him to move his family to a new country with no guarantee of a steady paycheck. Jack and his wife Bonna prayed, and they, too, sensed God's hand at work. Jack began to take his family up a mountain just as Abraham had done, without knowing just how his need would be met when he arrived. I did not have an extensive list of contacts I could canvas for Jack's financial support. I felt the full weight of what I was asking Jack to do, and I began asking myself,

"How in the world will God make this provision?" Then it dawned on me that as long as God knew where I was, He could cause anybody in the world to help me. He could place my need on the heart of anyone anywhere.

Jack was approved by Canadian immigration and began his trek of faith. As he prepared to move, I received a letter from a church in Fayetteville, Arkansas. The pastor said, "God has laid it on our hearts to send one percent of our mission giving to Saskatchewan missions. We are enclosing a check to use however you choose." I had no idea how they became involved with us at that time, but a large donation was included with the letter.

Not long afterwards, someone called me and pledged to contribute funds every month for Jack's financial support. That promise brought the monthly financial package to the level we had hoped to pay Jack. When Jack drove into our driveway with his family, I asked, "Jack, what did it cost to move you?" The amount was almost exactly what the church in Arkansas had just sent us.

We began that step of faith by believing what the Bible teaches: that God can use anyone, anywhere, to be His instrument of provision for those who trust Him (Phil. 4:13). We had believed God, and we had followed through in obedience. We already knew *academically* that God was One who provides. But after that event, our whole church came to know *from experience* that God is, indeed, the Provider. Calling Jack by faith and seeing God provide for him led us to a deeper love relationship with an all-sufficient God.

The Lord Is My Banner

The Bible is filled with examples of God helping His people come to know the reality of who He is through their experiences. As Joshua and the Israelites were fighting their relentless enemies, the Amalekites, Moses oversaw the battle from a nearby mountain. While he held his hands up to God, the Israelites were victorious, but whenever he lowered his weary arms, the Israelites would begin to lose.

God gave Israel victory over the Amalekites that day, and Moses built an altar to commemorate the occasion. He named it "The Lord Is My Banner." A banner was a standard or flag that armies, tribes, or nations carried in their front ranks to identify who they were as they marched into battle. It could be difficult at times to recognize an army as it marched through dusty fields. But when you saw its banner held high in the air, you could immediately discern if the army was a friend or foe, and you could gain a sense of its strength by understanding which king or nation it represented. The title, "The Lord Is My Banner" indicated that the Israelites belonged to God and that to oppose them was to battle against the power of God.

Moses' uplifted hands gave constant glory to God, indicating the battle was His and that the people of Israel belonged to Him. Israel came to understand God in a fresh and powerful way that day as they realized anew that they were God's people and that He was their defender (Exod. 17:8–15).

I Am Who I Am

When Moses encountered God in a burning bush, he asked, "If I go to the Israelites and say to them: The God of your fathers has sent me to you, and they ask me, 'What is His name?' what should I tell them?" (Exod. 3:13).

"God replied to Moses, 'I AM WHO I AM. This is what you are to say to the Israelites: I AM has sent me to you.'" (Exod. 3:14). By this God was declaring, "I am the eternal One. I will be what I will be." In essence this declaration held a promise: "Whatever you need me to be in your life, that is what I will be. I am everything you will need." During the next forty years, Moses came to experience God as Yahweh, the Great I AM. God was everything Moses and Israel needed Him to be.

A Relationship—Not Just a Name

Whenever God reveals His nature in a new way, *it is always for a purpose.* He created you for a love relationship with Him. When He encounters you, He is allowing you to know Him by experience. Encounters with God are always an expression of God's love for you. Jesus said: "The one who has My commands and keeps them is the one who loves Me. And the one who loves Me will be loved by My Father. I also will love him and will reveal Myself to him" (John 14:21).

If you have a love relationship with God, you will experience Him actively working in and through your life. For instance, you could not truly know God as the "Comforter in sorrow" unless you experienced His compassion during a time of grief or sadness.

The various names of God found in Scripture can become a call to worship for you. The psalmist said: "Happy are the people who know the joyful shout; LORD, they walk in the light of Your presence. They rejoice in Your name all day long, and they are exalted by Your righteousness" (Ps. 89:15–16). Acknowledging God's name amounts to recognizing who God is. Calling on His name indicates we are seeking His presence. To praise His name is to exalt Him. God's name is majestic and worthy of our praise.

Summary

The names of God in Scripture reveal something of His nature, activity, or character. You come to know God by experience—at His initiative—as He allows you to learn something new about Him. As you experience God, you grow to know Him more intimately and personally. As you grow in your knowledge of Him, you will naturally want to express your praise, gratitude, and worship to Him. One of the ways to worship Him is to praise and honor Him by acknowledging His names.

Experiencing God Today

Watch for ways God may bring you to a deeper knowledge of Him through the experiences of your life. Then take time to worship God as you have come to know Him. To worship is to revere and honor God, to acknowledge Him as worthy of your praise.

The list below and on the next page may help you recall some ways you have come to know God better. As you review the many ways the Bible describes God, try to remember experiences in your life that similarly helped you to know God. Perhaps you will discover some characteristics of the Lord you have not yet acknowledged or experienced, but it may surprise and encourage you to realize the numerous facets of God's nature you have experienced.

Names God has revealed to me:

- ✓ my witness (Job 16:19)
- ✓ bread of life (John 6:35)
- ✓ Comforter in sorrow (Jer. 8:18)

- my hope (Ps. 71:5)
- Wonderful Counselor (Isa. 9:6)
- defender of widows (Ps. 68:5)
- the strength of my salvation (Ps. 140:7)
- Faithful and True (Rev. 19:11)
- our Father (Isa. 64:8)
- a sure foundation (Isa. 28:16)
- my friend (John 15:14)
- Almighty God (Gen. 17:1)
- God of all comfort (2 Cor. 1:3)
- God who avenges me (Ps. 18:47)
- God who saves me (Ps. 51:14)
- our guide (Ps. 48:14)
- our head (2 Chron. 13:12)
- head of the church (Eph. 5:23)
- our help (Ps. 33:20)
- my hiding place (Ps. 32:7)
- a great High Priest (Heb. 4:14)
- Holy One in your midst (Hos. 11:9)
- righteous Judge (2 Tim. 4:8)
- King of kings (1 Tim. 6:15)
- our life (Col. 3:4)
- light of life (John 8:12)
- Lord of lords (1 Tim. 6:15)
- Lord of the harvest (Matt. 9:38)
- mediator (1 Tim. 2:5)
- our peace (Eph. 2:14)
- Prince of Peace (Isa. 9:6)
- my Redeemer (Ps. 19:14)
- refuge and strength (Ps. 46:1)
- my salvation (Exod. 15:2)
- my help (Ps. 42:5)
- the Good Shepherd (John 10:11)
- Lord (Luke 2:29)
- my stronghold (Ps. 18:2)

Knowing God by Experience   17

- my support (2 Sam. 22:19)
- Good Teacher (Mark 10:17)

QUESTIONS FOR REFLECTION

1. What are some characteristics of God you have come to know by experience?

2. Which name of God currently seems most significant in your life? Why is that?

3. What is one aspect of God's nature you would like to experience more fully in the coming days?

2

God Works According to His Nature

Dear friends, let us love one another, because love is from God, and everyone who loves has been born of God and knows God. The one who does not love does not know God, because God is love.
(1 John 4:7–8)

My Daughter's Cancer

When one of my children couldn't get his own way, he used to say accusingly, "You don't love me." But was that true? No, of course not. At that moment, however, my love was expressing itself differently than he wanted it to. My actions might sometimes have been confusing to my children, but my love for them was constant and unchanging.

When our only daughter Carrie was sixteen, doctors told us she had Hodgkins Disease. The doctor had missed a spot in her chest cavity during an earlier x-ray, and now cancer had spread dramatically and was threatening her life. We had to take her through aggressive chemotherapy and radiation treatments from which she suffered terribly. It was extremely difficult for Marilynn and me to watch her endure the debilitating nausea and pain that resulted from the treatments. Some people face painful experiences like this and angrily blame God for their suffering, assuming He doesn't love them anymore. Carrie's cancer treatments certainly could have been devastating for us. We had never undergone anything so difficult. Yet did God still love us? Yes. His love for us had not changed. Our circumstances had altered, but God had not.

When you face situations like this, you may want to ask God to explain what is happening. We did that. We desperately wanted to know God's purpose in allowing our young daughter to suffer so terribly. We asked God to help us understand why He was allowing our family to undergo such a difficult ordeal. But we never concluded that God no longer loved us.

At times as I prayed about Carrie, I would see that behind her and her illness stood the cross of Jesus Christ. I said, "Father, don't ever let me look at my difficult circumstances and question Your love for me. Your love was forever settled on the cross. That has never changed and it will never change for me. After what You did for me, I will never question whether You love me." My love for God did not hinge on whether or not God healed my daughter. I believe with all my heart that my wife and I would still have loved God even if He had chosen in His sovereign will not to heal Carrie. I recognize that there are times in God's divine will and infinite wisdom that He chooses not to heal or to protect from harm. It was out of my love relationship with God that I was able to trust Him to walk with me through the situation, regardless of how it turned out.[1]

God created you for a love relationship with Him. He yearns for you to love Him and respond to His immeasurable love for you. God's nature is perfect, holy, total love. He will never relate to you in any other way although you may not always understand His actions. There will be times when you do not comprehend why He allows certain things to occur, and that is to be expected. He is the infinite God while we are limited human creatures. He sees the eternal ramifications of everything that happens. We don't.

There are many things God does that we will never understand this side of heaven. But God does invite us to come to know His nature, the essence of who He is and what He is like. As you think about knowing and doing God's will, you must first come to know who God is.

Let's look at three aspects of God's nature that dispose Him to act in certain ways. Each of these characteristics has special implications for how you relate to Him and how you understand and do His will.

God's Nature

> 1. God is love—His will is always best.
>
> 2. God is all-knowing—His directions are always right.
>
> 3. God is all-powerful—He can enable you to accomplish His will.

God Is Love—His Will Is Always Best

According to 1 John 4:16, "God is love." This does not say that God loves, though He does love perfectly and unconditionally. The Scripture says that God's essential nature is love. God will never act contrary to His nature. You will never experience God expressing His will except in a demonstration of perfect love. God's kind of love always seeks His best for each person. If we reject His best, He will discipline us. However, the discipline will come from a heavenly Father who loves us and who will do whatever is necessary to bring us to a place in our lives where we can receive what He wants to give us (see Heb. 12:5–11).

God does bring discipline, judgment, and wrath on those who continue to live in sin and rebellion against Him. Even this discipline, though, is based on love. "For the Lord disciplines the one He loves, and punishes every son whom He receives" (Heb. 12:6). Because His nature is love, I'm confident that however He expresses Himself to me is always best. Many other verses describe His love toward us. For example: "For God loved the world in this way: He gave His One and Only Son" (John 3:16), and "This is how we have come to know love: He laid down His life for us" (1 John 3:16).

Your confidence in the love nature of God is crucial. This has been a powerful influence in my life. I always view my circumstances against the backdrop of the cross, where God clearly demonstrated once and for all His deep love for me. I may not always understand my current situation or how things will eventually turn out, but I can trust in the love Christ proved to me when He laid down His life for me on the cross. In the death and resurrection of Jesus Christ, God forever convinced me that He loves me. I choose to base my trust in God on what I know—His love for me—and I choose to trust that in time He will help me understand the confusing circumstances I may be experiencing.

Trust Him!

Have you ever heard someone say: "I'm afraid to surrender my life totally to the Lord because He might send me to Africa as a missionary"? Or have you been cautioned, "Don't say what you don't want to do because, sure enough, that's what God will tell you to do"? Such statements indicate a lack of trust and understanding of God's love, for He would not call you to be a missionary in Africa unless He knew such a call was best for you. I know many people who serve the Lord in dangerous or impoverished nations, and they would not want to be anywhere else in the world. They love their adopted country and its people, and they know God gave them His best when He invited them to serve Him there.

One missionary couple came back to their home in the United States for a year with their two children before returning to Zimbabwe. Their schedule in the United States was so full and hurried, they declared, "We can't wait to get back to Africa. We love African time!" The place in Africa where they work has no electricity. They go to bed when it gets dark, and they rise with the sun. When they go to a village for a meeting, no schedule drives them. Upon arrival, they send word throughout the village by children. A crowd gathers, and they meet until they are finished. The pace is far less stressful than the frenetic schedule in America.

When you trust that God always gives His best, you will devote your heart to whatever assignment God gives because you know in that role you can experience everything God has in His heart for you. Those who are perennially unhappy and dissatisfied with God's assignments exhibit their lack of belief that God loves them and that He is expressing His love in His guidance of their lives.

Never allow your heart to question God's love. Settle it on the front end of your quest to know Him and experience Him: He loves you. Every dealing He has with you is an expression of His love for you. God would not be God if He expressed Himself in any way other than perfect love! What you believe about God's love for you will be reflected in how you relate to Him. If you really believe God is love, you will also accept that His will is always best.

God's Commands Are for Your Own Good

When you hear words such as command, judgment, statute, or law, your first impression may be negative. God's commands, however, are expressions of His love, as the following passages demonstrate:

> What does the LORD your God ask of you except to fear the LORD your God by walking in all His ways, to love Him, and to worship the LORD your God with all your heart and all your soul? Keep the LORD's commands and statutes I am giving you today, for your good. (Deut. 10:12–13)

> He said to them, "Take to heart all these words I am giving you today, so that you may command your children to carefully follow all the words of this law. For they are not meaningless words to you but they are your life, and by them you will live long in the land you are crossing the Jordan to possess." (Deut. 32:46–47)

The foundation for God's commands is His love relationship with you. When you come to know God by experience, you will be thoroughly convinced of His love. You will know you can believe Him and trust Him, and because you trust Him, you will readily obey Him. Those who love the Lord have no problem doing what He says. "For this is what love for God is: to keep His commands. Now His commands are not a burden" (1 John 5:3).

God loves you deeply and profoundly. Therefore, He has given you guidelines for living, lest you miss the full dimensions of the love relationship He seeks to have with you. Life has some "land mines" that could harm or destroy you. God does not want you to miss out on His best, and He does not want your life to be destroyed through foolish choices.

Avoiding Land Mines

Suppose you were in a war-torn country, and you had to cross a field full of land mines. If a local soldier knew exactly where every one of them was buried and offered to take you through the field, would you protest and say, "I don't want you to tell me what to do. I want to be free to make my own choices"? I don't know about you, but I would stay as close to that person as I could. I certainly would not go wandering off. His directions to me would not restrict me; they would preserve my life. As we walked together, he would say, "Don't go that way, because that path will kill you. Go this way and live."

The Purpose of God's Commands

God wants you to live an abundant life (John 10:10). When God gives you a command, it is to protect you and lead you toward His blessings. He does not want you to miss out on the fullness of life He wants you to experience. God's instructions do not restrict; they free you. God's purpose is that you prosper and live:

"When your son asks you in the future, 'What is the meaning of the decrees, statutes, and ordinances, which the LORD our God has commanded you?' tell him. . . 'The LORD commanded us to follow all these statutes and to fear the LORD our God for our prosperity always and for our preservation, as it is today. Righteousness will be ours if we are careful to follow every one of these commandments before the LORD our God, as He has commanded us'" (Deut. 6:20–21, 24–25).

Suppose the Lord says, "I have a gift for you—a beautiful, wonderful expression of what love is. I will provide you with a spouse who will love and cherish you. Your relationship with this person will bring out the best in you. It will give you an opportunity to experience some of the deepest and most meaningful dimensions of human love that are possible. That individual will walk alongside you to encourage, challenge, and strengthen you when you lose heart. Within that relationship, your mate will love you, believe in you, and trust you. Out of that relationship, I will bless you with children, and those children will grow up to love you with all their hearts."

But then He cautions, "Do not commit adultery" (Matt. 5:27). Is that command meant to limit your happiness? No! It is to protect you so you can experience love at its human best. What happens if you begin to view your marriage vows as restricting, choosing instead to ignore God's command and to be unfaithful to your spouse? The love relationship in your marriage will be ruptured. Trust will disintegrate. Guilt will set in and bitterness will fester. Your children will feel the pain as well. Emotional scars may severely limit the future dimensions of love you and your family could experience together. God knows what the horrific result of sin is, so He clearly warns you not to succumb to it.

God's commands are designed to guide you to the best He has to offer. You will struggle to obey Him, however, if you do not trust Him. You will not trust Him if you do not love Him. And you will not love Him unless you know Him. But if you come to know Him as He reveals Himself to you, you will love Him, trust Him, and obey Him. The Bible is crystal clear at this point: if you love God, you will obey Him! If you do not obey Him, you do not really love Him, regardless of what you may claim (see John 14:24).

GOD IS ALL-KNOWING—
HIS DIRECTIONS ARE ALWAYS RIGHT

By nature God is omniscient, or all-knowing. He is not limited by the dimension of time—He knows the past, present, and future. He created all things, so nothing is outside of His knowledge. Whenever God expresses Himself to you, therefore, His directions are always right. When God gives you a directive, you can be sure He has already considered every factor. You will never do God's bidding only to discover that God was somehow mistaken. You can have absolute confidence that when God tells you to do something, it is the right course of action.

As you seek to know and obey God's will, you must wait to proceed until you clearly understand what God wants you to do and how He wants you to do it. Human wisdom and knowledge are inadequate to determine what you should do. You must depend on God's wisdom and knowledge for the important decisions of your life. At times, you may not understand why God is asking you to do something. As you obey, however, you will come to understand why His guidance was the best possible counsel for your life.

Perhaps you have asked God to give you several alternatives so you could choose the one you thought was best. But how many options does God need to give you so you know the right one? God always gets it right the first time. You only need His one best option. Once you've heard God speak, you don't need to continue waiting to seek other alternatives. You need to proceed with confidence based on what God said.

Trusting in God's Direction

When I served as a denominational leader in Vancouver, one of our churches believed God was leading it to begin three new mission churches for different language groups. At that time, the church had only seventeen members. Human reason would have immediately ruled out such a large assignment for a small church. They were hoping to receive financial support from our denomination's Home Mission Board to pay the mission pastors' salaries. One pastor was already in the process of relocating to Vancouver when we unexpectedly received word that the mission board would be unable to fund any new work in our area for the next three years.

The church didn't have the funds to do what God had called it to do. When they sought my counsel, I suggested that they first go back to the Lord and clarify what God had said to them. If this was merely something they wanted to do for God, God would not be obligated to provide for them. After they sought the Lord, they returned and said, "We still believe God is calling us to start all three new churches." At this point, they had to walk by faith and trust God to provide for what He was clearly leading them to do. A few months later, the church received some surprising news.

Six years earlier, I had led a series of meetings in a church in California. An elderly woman had approached me and said she wanted to will part of her estate for use in mission work in our city. The associational office had just received a letter from an attorney in California informing them that they would be receiving a substantial check from that dear woman's estate. The association could now provide the funds needed by the sponsoring church. The amount was sufficient to firmly establish all three churches this faithful congregation had launched.

Did God know what He was doing when He told a seventeen-member church to begin three new congregations? Yes. He already knew the funds would not be available from the missions agency, and He was also aware of the generosity of an elderly saint in California. None of these details caught God by surprise. That small church in Vancouver had known in their minds that God could provide. But through this experience they developed a deeper trust in their all-knowing God. Whenever God directs you, you will never have to question His will. He knows what He is going to do.

God Is All-Powerful—
He Can Enable You to Accomplish His Will

Our all-powerful God created the universe out of nothing. He breathed life into creatures of dust. He can accomplish anything He purposes to do. In fact, He declared, "My plan will take place, and I will do all My will. . . . Yes, I have spoken; so I will also bring it about. I have planned it; I will also do it" (Isa. 46:10–11). If He ever asks you to do something, He Himself will work through you to do it. Think of these biblical examples:

- God enabled Noah and his sons to build an enormous boat that spared the lives of every animal species during the great flood (see Gen. 6–9).
- God used Gideon and three hundred men to defeat an army of one hundred twenty thousand (see Judg. 7–8).
- Christ Jesus empowered His twelve disciples to heal people and to cast out demons (see Matt. 10).
- God equipped Paul to carry the gospel to the Gentiles and to establish churches throughout Asia Minor, all the way to Rome (see Acts 9:13–28).

When your life is centered in God's activity, He will rearrange your thinking. God's ways and thoughts are so different from yours that they will often appear wrong, unloving, or impossible. You will often realize that the task He assigns is far beyond your power or resources to accomplish. As soon as you recognize that the job appears humanly unattainable, you need to be ready to believe God and to trust Him completely.

You must believe He will enable and equip you to do everything He asks you to do. Don't second-guess Him. Simply take Him at His word. Turn to Him for the power, insight, skill, and resources required. At times I hear Christians say things like, "My pastor asked me to give my testimony in church next Sunday, but I could never do that . . . I have been approached about leading a Bible study at work during the noon hour, but I have never done anything like that before, and I don't think I could . . . I sense God wants me to go on my church's mission trip to South America next summer, but I can't afford to . . ." When we announce what we think we *can't* do in response to God's initiative, we are actually saying more about our faith in God than we are about our own abilities. The fact is, either we believe God is all-powerful or we don't. When you declare it's impossible for you to do what God told you to do, you show your doubts about how powerful God really is. It is one thing to believe in God's power, it is quite another to live your life in obedient response to an all-powerful God.

As you set out on your walk with God, He will initially make Himself known to you quite simply. As you respond with a childlike trust, an entirely new way of viewing life will unfold. Your life will be fulfilling. You'll never have to live with a sense of emptiness or lack of purpose. He will always fill your life with Himself. When you have the Lord, you have everything you need. As He was to Moses, He will be to you the "I Am that I Am."

Summary

Knowing and doing God's will depends on how well you know Him and His nature. Because God is love, His will is always best. As you follow and obey Him, He will direct you in ways that are best for you and for the situation into which He calls you. Since God is all-knowing, you'll never have to question the wisdom of His directions—even when they don't make sense to you. His plans are always right. God is all-powerful, so you need not doubt your ability, strength, or resources to complete His assignments. He will equip you to accomplish all He calls you to do.

Experiencing God Today

Meditate on the truths in this chapter, and ask God to reveal His nature to you. Ask Him to develop in you a confidence to trust Him anytime He has an assignment for you.

QUESTIONS FOR REFLECTION

As you answer the questions below, ponder the following three characteristics of the Lord:

- God is love. His will is always best.
- God is all-knowing. His directions are always right.
- God is all-powerful. He can enable you to accomplish His will.

1. Describe the experience that most permanently settled your belief in God's love for you. What questions did you ask during that experience? Did God provide answers for your questions? How? Or why not? Did you ever doubt God's love during this experience? How can you be sure God loves you today?

2. When God has asked you to do something, what has your response typically been? If you struggled to obey, what hindered you? Did you lack trust in God's love? His wisdom? His power?

3. Has God ever asked you to do something that didn't make sense to you? If so, what happened? What did you learn about God and yourself through that experience?

---

1. In chapter 14, "God Speaks through Circumstances," I will tell you how God used the circumstance of Carrie's cancer to bring glory to Himself and renew prayer ministries around the world. Since then, Carrie has graduated from college and seminary, has married, had two beautiful children, and is a career missionary in Germany.

3

Doing God's Will

"My food is to do the will of Him who sent Me and to finish His work," Jesus told them. (John 4:34)

Doing Things for God

After Claude King graduated from seminary in 1984, he and his wife set out to fulfill their dream of becoming "tentmaking" church planters in Gwinnett County, Georgia. As a seminary student, Claude had taken all the church planting and evangelism classes he could. He spent eighteen months developing plans to begin churches all over the county. But everything went wrong. In a period of only 2 percent unemployment, Claude and his wife could not find jobs. Having exhausted their meager savings and with debts mounting daily, they had not even gathered a nucleus of interested people to start a church. Devastated, Claude moved his family back home to live with parents. He had wanted to reach people for Christ. He sought to expand the kingdom of God. He was willing to work hard. Yet the result was failure. For a while, he was bewildered as to why God had not blessed his efforts.

Then in 1986, God crossed my path with Claude's. He had taken a job as an editor for a Christian publisher, but his heart was still in church planting. As Claude and I talked, the Lord revealed that his efforts, though admirable, had been misdirected. Claude had been making his own plans and trying to enlist God to bless them. God had been waiting for Claude to surrender his life to Him, making himself available for God to accomplish His divine purposes. As Claude changed his perspective, he immediately began to see the difference between man-centered and God-centered activity. Claude volunteered to help his local association of churches in church planting. But this time Claude did not develop his own plan. He simply shared with the churches in his association the need for new church plants and then watched to see what God did next.

Within three months, Claude received word from fourteen communities requesting new churches. Two years later, there were six new congregations with full-time pastors and the beginnings of a seventh church underway.

Claude saw that God could do more in a week than he could accomplish in years of his own effort. He also came to realize that he had been so busy attempting to do things *for* God he had not spent time enjoying fellowship *with* God. As Claude coauthored *Experiencing God* with me, he experienced God using his life in ever-increasing measure. The more he drew into a close relationship with God, the more God began to accomplish through Claude's life.

The Wrong Question

Jesus considered God's will to be His highest priority (see John 4:32–34). Following God's will is also important for you. Often when people want to know God's will, they will ask, "What is God's will for my life?" As one of my seminary professors, Gaines S. Dobbins, used to say, "If you ask the wrong question, you are going to get the wrong answer."

"What is God's will for my life?" is not the best question to ask. The better inquiry is, "What is God's will?" Because people are naturally self-centered, we tend to view the whole world—even God's activity—in terms of our own lives. Of course, we want to know what we should do and how events will affect us. But that is actually an inverted life-perspective. Once I know God's will, then my life gains its proper perspective, and I can adjust my life to Him and to His purposes. In other words, what is it that God is purposing to accomplish where I am? Once I know what God is doing, then

I see what I should do. My focus needs to be outward on God and His purposes, not inward on my life.

Now, that does not mean God has no plans for your life. He certainly does. He created you, and He knows how your life can reach its maximum potential. The Bible says He wants you to live an abundant life and to be filled with divine joy. But the plans He has for your life are based on what He is doing in the world around you. He has a larger purpose in mind for all humanity. His desire is for you to become involved in what He is doing to bring salvation to others. Discovering God's greater plan helps you know what He wants to do through you.

Don't Just Do Something

We are an industrious people. We always want to accomplish something. The idea of doing God's will sounds exciting. Once in a while, someone says, "Don't just stand there—*do* something." Sometimes individuals or churches are so busy carrying out plans they think will help achieve God's purposes that they don't bother to find out what He actually wants. We often wear ourselves out and accomplish little for the kingdom of God.

I think God is crying out to us: "Don't just do something. Stand there! Enter into a love relationship with Me. Get to know Me. Adjust your life to Me. Let Me love you and teach you about Myself as I work through you." A time will come when action is required, but we must not short-circuit the relationship (Ps. 37:7). Your relationship with God must come first. Out of your walk with God, He accomplishes His plans for our world.

Jesus said, "I am the vine; you are the branches. The one who remains in Me and I in him produces much fruit, because you can do nothing without Me." (John 15:5). Do you believe that without Him you can do nothing? Sure, you can keep yourself busy. You can immerse yourself in activities, programs, meetings, and events, but they will not have any lasting value for God's kingdom. The apostle Paul warned that one day every person's work would be tested by fire to see if it was done according to God's will and divine power (1 Cor. 3:13). The activities God will commend in the final judgment will be those which He initiated. If you are experiencing a time of spiritual dryness in your life, you may be trying to do things on your own that God has not initiated. However, when you abide in Christ, you will be amazed at what God accomplishes through your life.

God wants you to gain a greater knowledge of Him by experience. That's what abiding in Him will do for you. He wants a love relationship with you, and He wants to involve you in His kingdom work. He alone can initiate His plans. He wants your involvement, but you cannot do it for Him. When you believe Him and do as He directs, then He will accomplish His work through you.

Jesus had advice for those who wearied themselves trying to do things in their own strength: "Come to Me, all of you who are weary and burdened, and I will give you rest. All of you, take up My yoke and learn from Me, because I am gentle and humble in heart, and you will find rest for yourselves. For My yoke is easy and My burden is light" (Matt. 11:28–30).

A yoke was an instrument built for two oxen to work together in tandem. Often farmers would pair up an experienced animal with a younger ox. Thus the younger one could learn from the seasoned animal. Jesus' invitation is for you to join up with Him—to walk alongside Him and follow His lead. When you labor where He is already at work, He accomplishes His purposes through you. The experience is not meant to be exhausting or burdensome, but exhilarating and fulfilling. Sadly, the chronic ailment of Christians today is burnout, particularly among pastors and those in Christian ministry. They grow weary doing things for God in their own strength. Yet Jesus promised that those who walk alongside Him and work with Him will find rest for their souls. God has more than enough knowledge, power, and resources to accomplish whatever He desires. Our involvement—at His invitation—is a privilege that should invigorate us and keep us close to Him. If you are worn out or stressed by your "Christian duties," perhaps you are not properly yoked to your Master.

God Pursues a Love Relationship

Some people have suggested that God gives us general directions and then turns us loose to work out the details of our lives. *I disagree.* God's intention is to have a love relationship with each of us. We get ahead of ourselves when we try to discern a life plan up front. Some folks want the security of deciding if they will be a businessperson, a school teacher, a preacher, or a nurse. They want to know if they should settle in their home country or go to Japan for decades or move to Argentina. But God doesn't necessarily lay everything out that way. He may place you in one job at one location for an extended time, but God's assignments come on a daily basis. You should always be open to whatever He has for you—even if it's not something you could have foreseen.

God calls you to a relationship in which He is Lord—where you are willing to do and be anything He chooses. If you respond to Him as Lord, He may lead you to do things you would never have dreamed of. If you don't follow Him as Lord, you may lock yourself into a job or an assignment and miss something God wants to do through you. I've heard people say things like: "God called me to be a _____, so this other opportunity couldn't possibly be His will." Or "My spiritual gift is _____, so this ministry couldn't be God's will for me." We tend to seek things that keep us comfortable, but God is not restricted by our fears. He sees beyond our current limitations and is constantly leading us to grow into the person He knows we can become.

Nowhere does the Bible teach that God gives us a life plan and then abandons us to work it out. Rather, the pattern and emphasis in Scripture is a daily walk with Him in which He gives new assignments and then works through us to accomplish them. That is what a spiritual gift is—a supernatural empowering to accomplish the assignment God gives you.

Don't focus on your talents, abilities, and interests to determine God's will. Instead, seek God's will and watch Him equip you for whatever assignment He gives. I have heard so many people say, "I am good at _____; therefore, it must be God's will." That kind of thinking is self-centered. Since Christ is Lord, your attitude should instead be: "Lord, I will do anything Your kingdom requires of me. Wherever You want me, I'll go. Whatever the circumstances, I'm willing to follow. If You want to meet a need through my life, I am Your servant, and I will do whatever you ask."

The Farmer Was My Map

For twelve years, I was the pastor of a church in a city surrounded by farming communities. One day a farmer invited me to visit him at his home. His directions went something like this: "Go a quarter mile past the edge of the city, and you will see a big red barn on your left. Go to the next road, and turn to your left. Take that road for three-quarters of a mile. You'll see a large poplar tree. Go right for about four miles, and then you will see a big rock. . . ." I wrote all of this down, and only by God's grace did I eventually manage to find the farm!

The next time I went to the man's house, he was with me in my vehicle. Because there was more than one way to get to his house, he could have taken me any way he wanted to. This time, I didn't need the written instructions. You see, he was my map. What did I have to do? I simply had to listen to him and do what he said. Every time he said "Turn," I did what he said. He took me a new way I would not have discovered on my own. I could never retrace that route by myself because the farmer—my map—knew the way.

Jesus Is Your Way

Often people approach knowing and doing God's will this way: They ask, "Lord, what do You want me to do? When do You want me to do it? How shall I do it? Where shall I do it? What will the outcome be?"

Isn't it typical of us to ask God for a detailed road map before we are willing to set out on the journey? We say, "Lord, if You would just tell me where I need to end up, then I'll be able to set my course and go." You might even decide you won't move forward until God tells you ahead of time the details of what you will face. But that is not the way God led people in the Scriptures.

The Lord doesn't send us off like an errand boy. He intends to accompany us on the journey. He wants us to continually heed His voice and go with Him one day at a time. As long as we walk daily with Christ, we will always know where to be—right beside Him—and will always end up where He wants us to be. Jesus did not say:

- "I will give you the entire plan."
- "I will give you a road map."
- "I will tell you which direction to go and send you off."

He did say, "I am the way" (John 14:6). Jesus knows the way; He is your way.

Can you trust God to guide you as the farmer led me, pointing out each turn along the route? You might say, "No, Jesus doesn't direct people specifically like that." But He does! The Bible is full of examples where God guided His people precisely. Perhaps you have been taught—or concluded—that you have to take control of your own life and do the best you can. But your life is too valuable to waste by trusting your own best thinking. You are human and prone to making mistakes. God alone is perfect and infinitely wise. He knows the future. He is all powerful. Your life is in far better hands when you surrender it to God and His leading.

When you get to the place where you trust Jesus to guide you one step at a time, you'll experience tremendous freedom. But as long as you rely on your own judgment, you'll worry every time you must make a decision that you might take a wrong turn. I know several people who were so immobilized with worry that they spent years in a limbo of indecision, all because they didn't believe God would really give them specific guidance. But God does not want us to live in anxiety (see Phil. 4:6; 1 Pet. 5:7).

When I focus on my relationship with God, out of that divine fellowship God shares His heart with me. When God speaks, I respond to everything He tells me daily, and He gives me plenty to do to fill each day with meaning and purpose. When I do what He says, I am in the center of His will, and He can use my life to accomplish His purposes. My primary concern should not be, "What should I do with my life tomorrow?" but rather, "What does God want me to do today?" *As you follow Jesus one day at a time, He will keep you in the center of God's will.*

Abraham Followed God One Day at a Time

Abraham walked by faith and not by sight. In the following passage, read about the call of Abram to do God's will. Watch to see how much detail he was given before God asked him to follow.

> The LORD said to Abram: Go out from your land, your
> relatives, and your father's house to the land that I will
> show you. I will make you into a great nation, I will bless

you, I will make your name great, and you will be a blessing. I will bless those who bless you, I will curse those who treat you with contempt, and all the peoples on earth will be blessed through you.

So Abram went, as the LORD had told him, and Lot went with him. Abram was 75 years old when he left Haran. He took his wife Sarai, his nephew Lot, all the possessions they had accumulated, and the people he had acquired in Haran, and they set out for the land of Canaan. (Gen. 12:1–5)

God said, "Get out of your country." How specific were the directions? He gave Abram this much detail: "to the land I will show you." That is all God asked Abram to do. God promised to do the rest. Abram had to move all of his possessions and family day by day waiting for God to show him where he was going. Would you be willing to follow God's directions for your life with so little detail?

Few Details at First

God often calls people to follow Him without giving them all the details at the beginning. That is certainly the pattern in Scripture. Many times, as with Abram, God invites people to follow Him step by step. If God were to give you a specific plan for your life, you would likely put your focus on the plan rather than on Him. God does not want your life to depend on a plan or an income or a person or anything else. He wants you to trust Him.

Throughout Scripture, God seldom gave the same amount of detail to each person as He revealed His will. God told Moses much of His plan before Moses returned to Egypt. On the other hand, God told Abraham to begin moving, and He would provide further details along the way. God gave extremely specific instructions to Ananias about where to find Saul and what to do to heal him (see Acts 9:10–19). Yet Jesus would not even tell Andrew where He was staying for the evening (see John 1:39). In every case, however, people had to remain close to God for their guidance.

For Peter, Andrew, James, John, and Paul (see Matt. 4:18–22; 9:9; Acts 9:1–20), God gave minimal details about their assignments. He simply said, "Follow Me." Jesus said: "But seek first the kingdom of God and His righteousness, and all these things will be provided for you. Therefore don't worry about tomorrow, because tomorrow will worry about itself. Each day has enough trouble of its own" (Matt. 6:33–34). God wants us to enter each day seeking Him. Out of that relationship, we will experience Him guiding our lives.

Summary

God is far more interested in a love relationship with you than He is in what you do for Him. His desire is for you to love Him. As He walks alongside you, He will guide you into specific activities. But even as you do those things, He will be the One working through you to accomplish His purposes. He is all you need. Christ in you is your way; He is your map. When you follow His leadership one day at a time, you will always be right in the middle of God's will.

Experiencing God Today

Are you anxious about the future, or are you content to walk with Jesus one day at a time? Take some time alone with God today, enjoying fellowship with Him without focusing on what you may need to do next.

QUESTIONS FOR REFLECTION

1. Have you struggled to know God's will? If so, what has been your biggest challenge?

2. Are you satisfied with your relationship with Christ, or do you constantly feel the need to be doing something for Him?

3. How have you experienced God working through your life as you have been abiding in Christ?

4. Are you content to follow God one day at a time, or do you become anxious if you do not know where God is leading you in the future? If so, why is that?

4

Being God's Servant

If anyone serves Me, he must follow Me. Where I am, there My servant also will be. If anyone serves Me, the Father will honor him. (John 12:26)

Back on Track

Once at a large convention, a man approached me, grasped my hand, and said, "I used to be a pastor." He went on to explain that in his first church some ungodly leaders bitterly opposed him and determined to run him out of the church. They hurt him and his wife deeply by their actions and their lies. The pastor eventually resigned in anger, vowing he would never serve in the ministry again. He took a job with a friend in a new company as its executive vice president.

The business became extremely successful, and the former pastor enjoyed financial prosperity like he had never imagined. Then one day, the church he attended began a study of *Experiencing God*. Those taking the course learned that God is at work to redeem a lost world and that He invites people to join Him in His work. The former pastor was struck deeply as he remembered the time God had invited him to join His work in the church. The man realized he had forsaken his divine calling by leaving the ministry. He resigned his lucrative position in the company and accepted the pastorate of a small church. "I'm a pastor again," he told me with tears in his eyes. This dear brother had lost sight of the fact that he was a servant and that his Lord had a right to assign him to any task He chose. After he regained a clear view of God, it put his bitter feelings in their proper perspective. Once again, he was fulfilled and content as a pastor.

The point is not that every businessperson should resign to enter the ministry, but that to participate in God's work you must be a servant. Many Scripture passages describe Jesus as God's servant. He came to earth to accomplish God's will in redeeming humanity. Paul described Jesus' humble attitude and commended it to us in this way:

> Make your own attitude that of Christ Jesus, who, existing in the form of God, did not consider equality with God as something to be used for His own advantage. Instead He emptied Himself by assuming the form of a slave, taking on the likeness of men. And when He had come as a man in His external form, He humbled Himself by becoming obedient to the point of death—even death on a cross. (Phil. 2:5–8)

We are to develop the servant attitude of Christ that requires humility and obedience. In His instructions to His disciples about servanthood, Jesus described His own role of service: "Whoever wants to be first among you must be your slave; just as the Son of Man did not come to be served, but to serve, and to give His life—a ransom for many" (Matt. 20:27–28).

Jesus also explained our relationship to Him, "As the Father has sent Me, I also send you" (John 20:21). When you respond to God's invitation to salvation, you join Him in His mission of world redemption. The salvation God offers comes with a corresponding summons to be on mission with Him. In this new relationship you move into a servant role with God as your Lord and Master.

The common understanding of a servant is someone who approaches the master and says, "Master, what do you want me to do?" The master tells him, and the servant goes off and does it. But that is not the biblical picture of a servant of God. Being God's servant is quite different from working for a human master. While an ordinary servant labors for his master, God works *through* His servants.

The biblical portrayal of God's servant is more like a potter and clay. God described the relationship with His people this way:

> This is the word that came to Jeremiah from the LORD: "Go down at once to the potter's house; there I will reveal My words to you." So I went down to the potter's house, and there he was, working away at the wheel. But the jar that he was making from the clay became flawed in the potter's hand, so he made it into another jar, as it seemed right for him to do.
>
> The word of the LORD came to me: "House of Israel, can I not treat you as this potter treats his clay?"—this is the LORD's declaration. "Just like clay in the potter's hand, so are you in My hand, house of Israel." (Jer. 18:1–6)

To be useful, clay has to be pliable. Once it is made into a vessel, its usefulness is still subject to the discretion of the potter.

DIVINE MASTER AND HUMAN SERVANT

This portrayal of our service to God is far different than the way people serve one another. When you offer yourself to God as His servant, He first expects to shape you into the instrument of His choosing. He will always work *in* you before He works *through* you. As you obey, He is the One who completes the work. We'll address this subject further when we look at Jesus' life in chapter 6.

As God's servants, we must do two things: (1) be moldable and (2) remain available for the Master's (Potter's) use. Then the Master will use us as He chooses. We can do nothing of kingdom value in our own power. As Jesus said, "The Son is not able to do anything on His own" (John 5:19) and "you can do nothing without Me" (John 15:5). When God works through His servant, that person can do anything God chooses to do through his or her life. The potential is unlimited. But servanthood requires obedience. Servants of God must do what they are told, and they must remember who is accomplishing the work—God.

If you have been operating from a disoriented approach to spiritual servanthood, this concept should change your perspective about serving God. You don't receive orders, then go and carry them out to the best of your knowledge and ability. You relate to God, respond to Him, and adjust your life to Him so He will do what He wants through you.

Expo '86

When the World's Fair was coming to Vancouver, our affiliation of churches was convinced God wanted us to reach out to the twenty-two million people who would visit our city. Yet the combined membership of all our Vancouver churches was only about two thousand. How could such a small group impact such a mass of tourists from all over the world?

Two years before the fair, we sought the Lord's guidance and began to do what we sensed He was telling us. The total income for our association was $9,000. The following year it grew to $16,000. The year of the World's Fair we set a budget of $202,000. Obviously we were attempting something only God could do. Often churches or denominations will establish a practical budget that represents what they can do. Then they might set a second "hope" or "faith" budget. The figures they really trust and use, however, are in the "real" budget—the funds they can manage themselves. The rest is more of a wish list that we do not make use of unless the funds materialize. But I suggest that is not faith at all.

As a group of churches, we knew God had definitely led us to a work that would cost $202,000. So that became our operating budget. Our people began to pray for everything we believed God was leading us to do during the World's Fair. At the end of the year, I asked our treasurer how much money we had received. We had taken in $264,000.

People from all over North America assisted us. And, of course, money was not the goal. It was a means to accomplish what God told us to do. During the fair we were a catalyst, seeing almost twenty thousand people accept Jesus Christ as Savior and Lord! Only God could have done that. He accomplished it with a small group of people who had determined to be servants and who made themselves available for their Master's use. Today our world does not need to see what we can do, but people desperately need to witness what God wants to accomplish through us.

Elijah the Servant

Elijah was one of the great Old Testament prophets of Israel and a servant of God (see 1 Kings 17:1) during the time when King Ahab and his wife Jezebel, through their wicked leadership, led the people of Israel away from God to worship Baal, a Canaanite fertility god. We read in 1 Kings 18:16–39 that Elijah challenged the prophets of Baal to a public showdown to prove definitively who was the true God. This was an extremely bold move since Elijah was outnumbered eight hundred and fifty to one.

Elijah proposed that the prophets of Baal prepare a sacrifice and ask their god to send fire to consume it. He would similarly appeal to the God of Israel for fire. Of course, Baal—who was no god—did not answer the prophets' pleas, even when they wailed and pleaded. When it was Elijah's turn, he repaired the altar of the Lord and laid out his sacrifice. God answered with fire, consuming the sacrifice—and even the stone altar—as Elijah had proposed. If God had not displayed His own work by sending fire, Elijah would have utterly failed, and that would have cost him his life. It's crucial to understand that this test was not Elijah's idea but God's.

Throughout the process, Elijah had to remain close to God and do whatever the Lord commanded. Elijah acted in obedience to God's command. He went where God told him, when God told him, and he did what God told him to do. In his prayer Elijah said, "Let it be known that You are God in Israel and I am Your servant, and that at Your word I have done all these things" (1 Kings 18:36). Then God accomplished His purposes through Elijah who attributed the work back to God when he said, "You have turned their hearts back" (1 Kings 18:37). Elijah wanted the people to identify the Lord as the true God, and that is exactly how the people responded.

So to review: Did Elijah bring down fire from heaven, or did God do it? God did. What was Elijah's role? Obedience.

Elijah had no ability to bring fire down from the sky, but God did. Elijah did not have the strength to overcome eight hundred and fifty hostile idol worshippers, but God did. When God did something only He could do, all the people knew He was the true God. God did this mighty work, but He acted through His servant Elijah. Because Elijah made his life available for God's use, God did a powerful work that impacted the nation.

Ordinary People

When you think about working with God in His mission to redeem a lost world, you may ask, "What can one ordinary person do?" One of the wonderful Scriptures that has helped me on this point describes Elijah: "Elijah was a man with a nature like ours; yet he prayed earnestly that it would not rain, and for three years and six months it did not rain on the land. Then he prayed again, and the sky gave rain and the land produced its fruit" (James 5:17–18).

This mighty man of God was an ordinary person just like you and me. But when he prayed, God responded miraculously. Elijah did not have any unusual giftedness or power. He simply humbled himself in the role of a servant. He obeyed everything God instructed him to do, and God worked through Elijah to influence an entire nation to return to God.

Peter and John

Peter and John were two of the first disciples Jesus called to follow Him. After Jesus' resurrection, God healed a crippled beggar through Peter. Peter and John were called before the Sanhedrin—the highest court in the land—to give an account of their actions. Filled with the Holy Spirit, Peter spoke fearlessly to the religious leaders. Notice the peoples' response: "When they observed the boldness of Peter and John and realized that they were uneducated and untrained men, they were amazed and knew that they had been with Jesus" (Acts 4:13).

Most of the people we read about in the Scriptures were ordinary men and women. Their relationships with God and God's activity in their lives made them extraordinary. Did you notice the statement—the leaders recognized that Peter and John "had been with Jesus"? Peter and John were common fishermen, but their association with Jesus made them world changers. Anyone who enters into an intimate relationship with God can see God do exceptional things through his or her life. The outcome does not depend upon a person being unusually gifted, educated, or wealthy. The key is the indwelling presence of God doing unusual things through a willing servant.

D. L. Moody: A Common Shoe Salesman

Dwight L. Moody was a poorly educated shoe salesman who felt the call of God to preach the gospel. While visiting the British Isles, Moody attended an all-night prayer meeting with some friends. The next morning, his friend Henry Varley said, "The world has yet to see what God will do with a man fully consecrated to Him."

Moody was deeply moved by those words. Later, he listened to the famous pastor Charles H. Spurgeon preaching in his massive church in London. Moody's biographer described how he responded:

"The world had yet to see! With and for and through and in! A man!" Varley meant any man! Varley didn't say he had to be educated, or brilliant, or anything else! Just a man! Well, by the Holy Spirit in him, he'd [Moody] be one of those men. And then suddenly, in that high gallery, he saw something he'd never realized before—it was not Mr. Spurgeon, after all, who was doing that work: it was God. And if God could use Mr. Spurgeon, why should He not use the rest of us, and why should we not all just lay ourselves at the Master's feet, and say to Him, "Send me! Use me!"

Soon afterward, God began to use Moody in powerful ways. Moody had come to realize that his effectiveness did not depend on his own eloquence, charisma, or intelligence but on his surrendered life to Christ. Moody could not make himself more talented, but he could choose to be more surrendered. As he yielded his life to God, he immediately began to experience God using him in ways he could never have imagined. Moody became one of the greatest evangelists of modern times. During much of the nineteenth century he preached in revival services across Britain and America where thousands upon thousands of people came to faith in Christ.

Could God work in extraordinary ways through your life to accomplish significant things for His kingdom? You might say, "Well, I am not D. L. Moody." You don't have to be. God wants you to be the person He created you to be and to let Him do through you whatever He chooses. When you believe that nothing consequential can happen through you, you have said more about your belief in God than you have indicated about yourself. The truth is that God can do anything He pleases through an ordinary person who is fully dedicated to Him.

John the Baptist

It probably does not surprise you that God's standard of excellence is different from ours. The public ministry of John the Baptist lasted perhaps six months, but what was Jesus' estimate of John's life? "I tell you, among those born of women no one is greater than John" (Luke 7:28).

Don't measure excellence by the world's standards. Many denominations are doing it. Many pastors and churches are doing it. Many business people are doing it. By the world's assessment, a person or church may look pretty good yet in God's sight be totally unacceptable (see Rev. 3:17). Similarly, a person or a congregation may be wholly yielded and pleasing to Him yet in the world's eyes appear insignificant. Could a pastor who faithfully serves God in a small rural community be pleasing to the Lord? Of course—if that is where God placed him. Could a homemaker or shoe salesman bring great glory to God through the seemingly ordinary tasks they accomplish? Yes. God will look for and reward faithfulness, whether the person has been given responsibility for little or much (see Matt. 25:14–30).

God delights in using ordinary people to accomplish His divine purposes. Paul said God deliberately seeks out the weak and the despised things because it is from them that He receives the greatest glory (see 1 Cor. 1:26–31). When God does exceptional things through unexceptional people, then others recognize that only God could have done it. If you feel weak, limited, and ordinary, take heart! You are the best material through which God can work!

Summary

The call to salvation carries with it a summons to be on mission with God as He reconciles a lost world to Himself. This calling requires you to be a servant of God. Jesus provided the best model of servanthood, which is both humble and obedient. As a servant you must be moldable and remain available for the Master's use. Even though you may consider yourself ordinary, God will prepare you. Then He will do His work through you, revealing Himself to a watching world.

Experiencing God Today

Consider what kind of servant you are for God. Today, make a special effort to serve your Lord in anything He prompts you to do.

QUESTIONS FOR REFLECTION

1. Do you prefer to see yourself as a servant or as a manager? What kind of servant are you for God? *Servant, weak*

2. Do you ever feel as if you are too ordinary or that you have failed too many times to be of use to God? If so, what does the Bible say about that? *Yes — That God uses ordinary people.*

3. Have you set conditions for how or where or when you will serve God? How do you think God views your conditional obedience? *No, not very disciplined*

4. How have you been experiencing God working powerfully through your life in ways only He can? *Trying to be a kinder, more understanding person.*

5. Do you need to make a fresh surrender of your life to Christ and His service? If so, take the next few moments and offer yourself to God in a sincere, wholehearted act of submission to Him. *✓ Yes*

5

SEVEN REALITIES OF EXPERIENCING GOD

*Indeed, the Lord God does nothing without revealing
His counsel to His servants the prophets. (Amos 3:7)*

GOD IS AT WORK!

Angola Prison in Louisiana is one of the largest and most formidable maximum security institutions in the United States. The vast inmate population serving life sentences has no hope for the future. Several years ago, the prison hired a new warden who was a Christian. As he assumed his new position, he had no idea what God intended for that dismal, hopeless place. One day, a prisoner was executed for his crimes. The Holy Spirit convicted the warden that he did not know if the convict had been a Christian, but he had assisted in ushering the man into eternity.

The warden sensed God wanting to use him to bring hope and salvation to the prison residents. His church had been going through *Experiencing God*, and he decided to make the study available to any inmate who wanted to take the course. It was also offered to all those on death row.

God began to transform lives through the study. Many of those awaiting execution became Christians. In fact, so many prisoners were becoming Christians that seven different congregations were begun throughout the prison with inmates serving as pastors. Violence and drug use in the prison was dramatically curtailed. As the inmates completed *Experiencing God*, they began to do other Bible studies. Some of the men even sensed God calling them into Christian ministry!

Ultimately, a theological seminary began to provide training to the inmates and made the prison an official satellite campus. Some of the residents felt called to missions. As a result, these prisoners asked to be transferred to other prisons where they began leading Bible studies and leading fellow convicts to faith in Christ. These inmates were making such a positive impact on the prison population that wardens from across the country began asking Angola Prison to transfer some of their transformed prisoners to them! God had been working in the midst of one of the most demoralizing places in the country, and He had been looking for someone to join Him in His work. When God invited the warden to join in, this man could not possibly have imagined all God was prepared to do. Such is the case every time God comes to one of His children and invites that person to join Him in His mission.

The Scriptures testify that when God prepares to do something in our world, He reveals to His people what He is about to do. Then God accomplishes His purposes through His people. This is also the way God will work with you. The Bible is designed to help you understand the ways of God. Then, when God starts to use your life in the same way He worked in the Scriptures, you'll recognize that it is God.

When God Speaks

In examining the Bible for ways God involved men and women in His work, I recognized the three characteristics outlined below. When God spoke:

1. They knew it was God.

2. They knew what God was saying.

3. They knew what they were to do in response.

In examining Scripture, I also see common experiences that I call the seven realities of experiencing God. They do not comprise a formula for knowing God's will. You can't accomplish these steps on your own. They do, however, identify ways God works with a person or group to involve them in His activity. The remainder of this book will focus on these realities to help you understand how God works in and through a person's life. In this chapter, I will give an overview. Reading through the seven realities may raise several questions. For example:

- What is involved in a love relationship with God?
- How can I know when God is speaking?
- How can I recognize where God is at work?
- What kinds of adjustments does God require me to make?
- What is the difference between adjustment and obedience?

As I have worked with groups and individuals in many settings, I have been asked questions like these. I will try to answer them during the remaining chapters of this book.

Moses' Example

The experience of Moses beautifully portrays how God works in a person's life. His early life and call to ministry are described in chapters 2, 3, and 4 of Exodus. You may want to read those chapters as a background for the discussion that follows. Other passages show how Moses came to know and follow God's will. Moses' experience at the burning bush clearly illustrates the way God invites people to join Him in His work. I could have chosen any number of other people, such as Noah, Abraham, Esther, David, Mary, the disciples, or Paul.

The diagram of "The Seven Realities of Experiencing God" on the next page describes the way God worked with Moses. Notice that key words for each of the seven realities are on the diagram. Let's take a look at this process and see how Moses experienced each reality.

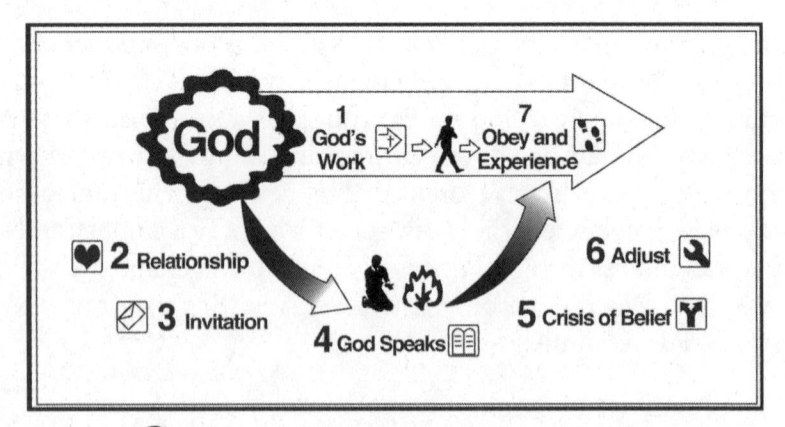

Reality 1: God is always at work around you.

God did not create the world and then abandon it to function on its own. He has been actively involved in human affairs throughout history. In fact, He is orchestrating history. Because of sin, humanity has been separated from a close relationship with God. God is working in His world to bring about the redemption of those who are alienated from Him and facing imminent judgment and destruction. The Father is working through Christ to reconcile the world to Himself. In God's sovereignty, He has chosen to accomplish His work through His people. As He carries out His mission, He seeks to move people into the mainstream of His activity.

God was already at work around Moses' life when He encountered Moses at the burning bush. God had a purpose He was steadily working out in Moses' world. Even though Moses was an exile in the desert, he was right on God's schedule, in the fullness of God's timing, in the middle of God's will for that moment.

Years earlier, God told Abraham his descendants would be in bondage, but that He would deliver them and give them the Promised Land. God was watching and waiting for the right time to carry out His purposes for Israel. The time came when: "The Israelites groaned because of their difficult labor, and they cried out; and their cry for help ascended to God because of the difficult labor. So God heard their groaning, and He remembered His covenant with Abraham, Isaac, and Jacob. God saw the Israelites, and He took notice" (Exod. 2:23–25).

At the time God was about to deliver the children of Israel, the overriding concern was God's will for Israel, not God's will for

Moses. God was at work with Israel, and He was preparing to bring Moses into the mainstream of His activity to redeem His people. This truth also applies to your life. God is actively working in the lives of people around you. Even when you do not recognize it or see God at work, He is active. However, unless God opens your spiritual eyes to recognize what He is doing, you will remain blind to His presence and work.

REALITY 2: GOD PURSUES A CONTINUING LOVE RELATIONSHIP WITH YOU THAT IS REAL AND PERSONAL.

God created humanity for a love relationship with Him. More than anything else, God wants us to love Him with our total being (see Mark 12:30). He is the One who pursues the love relationship with us. We do not naturally seek God on our own initiative. Everything we are experiencing from God comes in response to His invitation. In fact, He reached out to us dramatically by sending His Son Jesus (see John 3:16). God clearly demonstrated how valuable the love relationship is to Him when He permitted Jesus to die an excruciating death on a cross in order to make a relationship with us possible (see Rom. 5:8).

This intimate love relationship with God is both extremely personal and practical. This is probably the most important factor in knowing and doing the will of God. *If your love relationship with God is not as it should be, nothing else will be in order.*

God took the lead in inviting Moses into a personal and dynamic relationship with Him. Moses had led the sheep he was tending to "Horeb, the mountain of God" (Exod. 3:1). Moses may have come to the mountain for a time of worship, but God interrupted Moses' plans by encountering him at the burning bush. God told Moses that He would go with Moses into Egypt. Many texts throughout Exodus, Leviticus, Numbers, and Deuteronomy illustrate how God pursued a continuing love relationship with Moses. Here is one example:

> The LORD said to Moses, "Come up to Me on the mountain and stay there so that I may give you the stone tablets with the law and commands I have written for their instruction.". . . When Moses went up the mountain, the cloud covered it. The glory of the LORD settled on Mount

Sinai . . . Moses entered the cloud as he went up the mountain, and he remained on the mountain 40 days and 40 nights. (Exod. 24:12, 15–16, 18)

Time and time again God invited Moses to talk with Him and to be with Him. God initiated and maintained a growing relationship with Moses. This fellowship was based on love, and God daily fulfilled His purposes through Moses. The relationship with God was extremely practical as God guided and provided for His people under Moses' leadership. (For other examples of the love relationship, you may want to read Exod. 33:7–34:10 or Num. 12:6–8.)

Reality 3: God invites you to become involved with Him in His work.

God is the sovereign ruler of the universe. He has been working throughout history to accomplish His purposes. He does not ask us to dream our dreams for Him. He does not invite us to set magnificent goals and then pray that He will help us achieve them. He already has His own agenda when He approaches us. His desire is to get us from where we are to where He is working. He leads us from being self-centered to being God-centered. When God reveals to you where He is working, that becomes His invitation to join Him in His activity. When God reveals His work to you, that is the time to respond to Him.

In Moses' story, God's purpose was to rescue the Israelites out of slavery in Egypt and to establish them as a nation in their own land. Moses was the one through whom God intended to accomplish His plans. God invited Moses to become involved with Him in His work: "I have come down to rescue them from the power of the Egyptians and to bring them from that land to a good and spacious land. . . . Therefore, go. I am sending you to Pharaoh so that you may lead My people, the Israelites, out of Egypt" (Exod. 3:8, 10). It would never have crossed Moses' mind to do something like this had God not invited him. Yet suddenly Moses was being summoned to join in a work that God had been preparing centuries for.

Reality 4: God speaks by the Holy Spirit through the Bible, prayer, circumstances, and the church to reveal Himself, His purposes, and His ways.

The testimony of the Bible from Genesis to Revelation is that God speaks to His people. In our day, God communicates to us through the Holy Spirit. The Holy Spirit will use the Bible, prayer, circumstances, and the church (other believers) to guide us. When you hear God speak to you through a verse of Scripture, it's always best to verify what you heard through prayer, other believers, and your circumstances. If you hear God say the same thing through each of these sources, you can proceed confidently.

God will draw you into a deeper and closer walk with Him so you can trust Him and have faith in Him. He will reveal His purposes to you so you can become involved in His work rather than merely pursuing your own goals and dreams. He reveals His ways so you can accomplish His purposes in a manner that glorifies Him. God's ways are not our ways (see Is. 55:8–9). You cannot discover these truths about God on your own. Divine truth must be revealed.

God spoke to Moses through the unique experience at a burning bush to reveal Himself, His purposes, and His ways.

> Then the Angel of the LORD appeared to him in a flame of fire within a bush. . . . God called out to him from the bush, "Moses, Moses!"
>
> "Here I am," he answered.
>
> "Do not come closer," He said. "Take your sandals off your feet, for the place where you are standing is holy ground." Then He continued, "I am the God of your father, the God of Abraham, the God of Isaac, and the God of Jacob."
>
> Then the LORD said, "I have observed the misery of My people in Egypt, and have heard them crying out because of their oppressors, and I know about their sufferings. I have come down to rescue them from the power of the Egyptians and to bring them from that land to a good and spacious land." (Exod. 3:2–8)

> "If there is a prophet among you from the LORD, I make Myself known to him in a vision; I speak with him in a dream. Not so with My servant Moses; he is faithful in all My household. I speak with him directly, openly, and not in riddles; he sees the form of the LORD." (Num. 12:6–8)

God came and talked to Moses about His will. God wanted Moses to go to Egypt so He could deliver the Israelites. He revealed to Moses His holiness, His mercy, His power, His name, and His purpose to keep His promise to Abraham and to give Israel the Promised Land, as well as many other things not described in the Scriptures above. When God spoke, Moses knew it was God. He knew what God said, and he knew what he had to do in response.

Reality 5: God's invitation for you to work with Him always leads you to a crisis of belief that requires faith and action.

God wants a watching world to come to know who He truly is. He does not call you to get involved in His activity merely so people can see what you can do. He will call you to an assignment that you cannot accomplish apart from His divine intervention. God's assignments have God-sized dimensions. This does not mean God does not ask us to undertake mundane, seemingly ordinary tasks. But when God is involved in anything, there are always eternal, divine dimensions, implications, and possibilities.

When God asks you to do something you cannot do, you will face a crisis of belief. You'll have to decide what you really believe about God. Can He and will He do what He has said He wants to do through you? Can God do the seemingly impossible through your ordinary life? How you respond to His invitation reveals what you truly believe about God, regardless of what you say.

This major turning point is where many people miss out on experiencing God's mighty power working through them. If they cannot understand exactly how everything is going to happen, they won't proceed. They want to walk with God by sight, not faith. To follow God, you'll have to walk by faith because without faith, it is *impossible* to please Him (see Heb. 11:6). Faith is more than just belief. Biblical faith always requires action (see James 2:14). God does not want you merely to *believe* what He says. He wants you to *obey* what He commands (see Luke 6:4). All of God's promises and invitations will be meaningless to you unless you believe Him and obey Him.

God's invitation for Moses to work with Him led to a crisis of belief that required faith and action. Moses expressed this crisis of belief in the following statements to God:

- "Who am I, that I should go to Pharaoh and that I should bring the Israelites out of Egypt?" (Exod. 3:11)
- "If I go to the Israelites and say to them: The God of your fathers has sent me to you, and they ask me, 'What is His name?' what should I tell them?" (Exod. 3:13)
- "What if they won't believe me and will not obey me but say, 'The LORD did not appear to you'?" (Exod. 4:1)
- "Please, Lord, I have never been eloquent—either in the past or recently or since You have been speaking to Your servant—because I am slow and hesitant in speech." (Exod. 4:10)
- "Please, Lord, send someone else." (Exod. 4:13)

Moses offered God numerous objections. He questioned whether God could accomplish such an enormous task through him (see Exod. 3:11), whether the Israelites would believe God had appeared to him (see Exod. 4:1), and whether he was capable of speaking eloquently enough to convince Pharaoh and the people of what he said (see Exod. 4:10).

In each case, Moses doubted God's power more than he was questioning his own ability. He faced the crisis of belief: Is God really able to do what He says? God finally convinced Moses to become involved in delivering Israel from slavery. Moses' faith is described in Hebrews, however, as a model of self-sacrifice and trust in Almighty God. Once God let Moses know what He was about to do, that revelation became Moses' invitation to join Him. The writer of Hebrews describes Moses' faith and action:

By faith Moses, when he had grown up, refused to be called the son of Pharaoh's daughter and chose to suffer with the people of God rather than to enjoy the short-lived pleasure of sin.... By faith he left Egypt behind, not being afraid of the king's anger, for he persevered, as one who sees Him who is invisible. By faith he instituted the Passover and the sprinkling of the blood, so that the destroyer of the firstborn might not touch them. By faith they crossed the Red Sea as though they were on dry land. When the Egyptians attempted to do this, they were drowned. (Heb. 11:24–29)

Reality 6: You must make major adjustments in your life to join God in what He is doing.

This is a second point at which many miss out on experiencing God. To get from where you are to where God is requires significant adjustments in your life. These adjustments may relate to your thinking, circumstances, relationships, commitments, actions, and beliefs. I have been asked if every adjustment God asks us to make is significant. My response is always: To move from your way of thinking or acting to God's way of thinking or acting will require fundamental adjustments. You can't stay where you are and go with God at the same time.

Moses had to make major changes in his life to join God in what He was doing. Moses couldn't stay in the desert and stand before Pharaoh at the same time. God said: "'Return to Egypt, for all the men who wanted to kill you are dead.' So Moses took his wife and sons, put them on a donkey, and set out for the land of Egypt." (Exod. 4:19–20).

Moses made the required adjustments to orient his life to God. He had to become convinced God could do everything He said He would do. Then he had to leave his job and extended family and move to Egypt. When Moses fled from Egypt forty years earlier, he had been a fugitive. Returning to the court of Pharaoh could have been tantamount to turning himself over to the authorities who wanted to punish him severely. Moses had to believe God could do what He said or else Moses' life was in grave danger. After determining to move forward, he was in a position to obey God. That did not mean he was going to do something all by himself for God. It meant he was going to be where God was working. Then God would do what He had purposed through Moses. Moses was a servant who was moldable, and he remained at God's disposal to be used as God chose. God accomplished His enormous purposes through the ordinary shepherd, Moses.

Reality 7: You come to know God by experience as you obey Him and He accomplishes His work through you.

Once you have determined to follow God by faith and you have made the adjustments, you must obey Him. When you do what He tells you, no matter how impossible or bewildering it may seem, God carries out what He purposed through you. Not only do you experience God's power and presence, but so do those who observe your life.

Moses came to know God by experience as he obeyed God, and God accomplished His work through him. Many Scripture passages in Exodus, Leviticus, Numbers, and Deuteronomy illustrate how God spoke to Moses and brought him into a deeper understanding of who He is. As Moses obeyed God, God accomplished through him what Moses could not do on his own. Here is one example where Moses and the people came to know God as their Deliverer: The people were on their way out of Egypt when they approached the Red Sea. They couldn't go forward, and the Egyptian army was blocking their retreat. The people could see no way out. It seemed as if by following God's guidance Moses had inadvertently led his people right into a horrific bloodbath. But then God spoke:

> The LORD said to Moses, "Why are you crying out to Me? Tell the Israelites to break camp. As for you, lift up your staff, stretch out your hand over the sea, and divide it so that the Israelites can go through the sea on dry ground. I am going to harden the hearts of the Egyptians so that they will go in after them, and I will receive glory by means of Pharaoh, all his army, and his chariots and horsemen. . . ."
>
> Then Moses stretched out his hand over the sea. The LORD drove the sea back with a powerful east wind all that

night and turned the sea into dry land. So the waters were divided, and the Israelites went through the sea on dry ground, with the waters like a wall to them on their right and their left. The Egyptians set out in pursuit . . .

Then the LORD said to Moses, "Stretch out your hand over the sea so that the waters may come back on the Egyptians, on their chariots and horsemen." So Moses stretched out his hand over the sea, and at daybreak the sea returned to its normal depth. . . .

But the Israelites had walked through the sea on dry ground, with the waters like a wall to them on their right and their left. That day the LORD saved Israel from the power of the Egyptians, and Israel saw the Egyptians dead on the seashore. When Israel saw the great power that the LORD used against the Egyptians, the people feared the LORD and believed in Him and in His servant Moses. (Exod. 14:15–17, 21–23, 26–27, 29–31)

Moses must have felt humbled and unworthy to be used in such a significant way. Yet Moses obeyed and did everything God told him. Then God accomplished through Moses all He intended. Every step of obedience brought Moses (and Israel) to a greater knowledge of God (see Exod. 6:1–8).

Summary

God is at work reconciling a world to Himself. Because He loves you, He wants to involve you in His activity. He begins by pursuing a love relationship with you. He then invites you to become involved with Him in His work. As He relates to you, He discloses Himself, His purposes, and His ways. If you want to experience God's mighty power at work in and through you, you must walk by faith, make major adjustments, and obey whatever God tells you to do.

Experiencing God Today

Spend some time with your heavenly Father. Pray through the "Seven Realities of Experiencing God," and ask the Father to help you understand how He works with His people.

> ## SEVEN REALITIES
> 1. God is always at work around you.
> 2. God pursues a continuing love relationship with you that is real and personal.
> 3. God invites you to become involved with Him in His work.
> 4. God speaks by the Holy Spirit through the Bible, prayer, circumstances, and the church to reveal Himself, His purposes, and His ways.
> 5. God's invitation for you to work with Him always leads you to a crisis of belief that requires faith and action.
> 6. You must make major adjustments in your life to join God in what He is doing.
> 7. You come to know God by experience as you obey Him, and He accomplishes His work through you.

QUESTIONS FOR REFLECTION

1. Do you believe God is at work around you right now? If so, what do you sense He is presently doing?

2. What has God done lately that provided you an opportunity to come to know Him more personally than you had before?

3. Is God inviting you to join Him in His activity? If so, what is He asking you to do?

4. Have you heard God speak to you recently? If so, what did He say? What have you done in response?

5. Are you presently experiencing a crisis of belief? If so, why?

6. What adjustments in your life is God asking you to make?

7. How have you come to know God more personally as a result of obeying what He told you to do?

6

God Is at Work around You

My Father is still working, and I am working. . . . I assure you: The Son is not able to do anything on His own, but only what He sees the Father doing. For whatever the Father does, the Son also does these things in the same way. For the Father loves the Son and shows Him everything He is doing. (John 5:17, 19–20)

An Inner City Church

A California inner city church had suffered years of decline as its neighborhood went through a transition and church members moved to the suburbs. When only a remnant was left, they determined to disband their congregation. As a final activity, the members decided to study *Experiencing God*. At the conclusion of the course, they would close their doors for the last time. As they studied the first units, the people learned that God is always at work around them. They chuckled at the thought, since nothing unusual had happened in their church for many years. Nevertheless, they decided to watch and pray during the week to see where God might be working.

That week an apartment manager approached one of the church members and asked if her congregation could do anything about the children in the apartment block nearby. Most were latchkey kids with nothing to do when they were out of school. The apartment manager offered free use of the apartment building's common room if the church would provide some activities. The church decided to offer a children's program during the final few months of its existence. This soon brought several unwed mothers to their attention. Through their new relationships with the children's families, church members began to meet drug addicts as well as gang members who were living in the community. Before long, this little group had launched several new ministries and were seeing people come to faith in Christ almost every week. At the close of the thirteen-week study, instead of disbanding, the church, now revitalized, began to minister powerfully to its community. Rather than remaining discouraged, the people realized they were in the center of God's activity. He had been working in their neighborhood all along.

When you want to learn how to know and do the will of God, you should always look to Jesus. We can find no better model than the way He conducted His earthly life. Although Jesus was God, He was also completely human. During His life on earth, Jesus perfectly fulfilled every assignment the Father gave Him. He never failed to do His Father's will. He never sinned. He demonstrated what absolute surrender to God and obedience to His will looks like. Possibly the clearest statement Jesus made about carrying out His Father's will is found in John 5, quoted at the beginning of this chapter. Let's take a closer look at the relationship between Jesus and the Father.

The Trinity

Although we may have difficulty understanding it, God the Father, Christ the Son, and God the Holy Spirit are all three persons of one Godhead. They are not three separate gods. They are all one God. Our finite minds may struggle to comprehend such a majestic and infinite existence.

The Scriptures reveal that whenever God encountered people, He did it in one of three ways: in the person of the Father, the Son, or the Spirit. Whenever God is working, all three persons of the Trinity are involved.

This is a profound truth that Jesus' twelve disciples had difficulty grasping. After three years with Jesus, Philip asked, "Show us the Father," and Jesus responded, "Have I been among you all this time without your knowing Me, Philip? The one who has seen Me has seen the Father.... Don't you believe that I am in the Father and the Father is in Me? The words I speak to you I do not speak on My own. The Father who lives in Me does His works" (John 14:9–10).

God Involves Us

Jesus recognized that His Father is always working on earth to accomplish His divine purposes. God did not create the world and then abandon it to run itself. He is not sitting in a heavenly throne room passively observing the activity on earth. God is orchestrating history. He is present and in the middle of human activity. God is actively at work redeeming a lost world, and He chooses to involve His servants in carrying out His redemptive plans.

Paul explored this truth in a letter to the church at Corinth:

> Therefore if anyone is in Christ, there is a new creation; old things have passed away, and look, new things have come. Now everything is from God, who reconciled us to Himself through Christ and gave us the ministry of reconciliation: that is, in Christ, God was reconciling the world to Himself, not counting their trespasses against them, and He has committed the message of reconciliation to us. Therefore, we are ambassadors for Christ; certain that God is appealing through us. (2 Cor. 5:17–20)

Therefore, since the Father is at work reconciling the world to Himself and since He has chosen to carry out that reconciliation through His people, what are we to do? How are we to respond to that commission? If we go back to Christ's words in John 5, we find a clear model in the way the Lord Jesus approached knowing and doing the Father's will. We could outline Jesus' example like this:

- The Father has been working all along.
- Now the Father has Me working.
- I do nothing on My own initiative.
- I watch to see what the Father is doing.
- I do what I see the Father is doing.
- The Father loves Me.
- He shows Me everything that He, Himself, is doing.

The Father's Work through Jesus

Jesus often spoke about His relationship with the Father and His dependence on the Father to show Him what to do. Jesus made it clear that the Father initiated the relationship and invited the Son to be involved in His activity. The Father revealed His plan and the Son joined the Father where He was at work. Jesus spoke several times about this relationship:

- "My teaching is not Mine but is from the One who sent Me." (John 7:16)
- "When you lift up the Son of Man, then you will know that I am He, and that I do nothing on My own. But just as the Father taught Me, I say these things." (John 8:28)
- "If I am not doing My Father's works, don't believe Me. But if I am doing them and you don't believe Me, believe the works. This way you will know and understand that the Father is in Me and I in the Father." (John 10:37–38)
- "For I have not spoken on My own, but the Father Himself who sent Me has given Me a command as to what I should speak." (John 12:49)
- "The words I speak to you I do not speak on My own. The Father who lives in Me does His works." (John 14:10)
- "The words that You gave Me, I have given them." (John 17:8)

Later, Peter affirmed that the heavenly Father worked through His Son. He described the Son: "This Jesus the Nazarene was a man pointed out to you by God with miracles, wonders, and signs that God did among you through Him" (Acts 2:22). God the Father accomplished His work through Jesus the Son.

Jesus realized that He could do nothing by Himself. Yet with the Father at work in Him, He could do anything. This is particularly significant for you and me because Jesus was the Son of God. Yet He never took the initiative to dream a dream or launch a new ministry. He lived His life in absolute dependence upon His Father. If Jesus was that dependent on the Father, then you and I should realize how ludicrous it is for us to set out on our own without any direction or guidance from the Father.

Watching for God at Work on the Campus

While I was a pastor, my congregation began to sense God leading us to reach out to the city's college campus. I had never done student ministry before, nor had our church. We were advised by experts in collegiate ministry that to reach the campus we needed to begin Bible studies in the dormitories. So for almost two years we tried to start a Bible study in the dorms on campus, but very little came of that. Yet we were convinced that the university campus with its thousands of young people was a field "ripe unto harvest."

One Sunday, I pulled our students together and said, "This week I want you to go to the campus and watch to see where God is working. If God shows you where He is working, immediately join Him!" They asked me to explain. God had impressed on my heart two Scriptures: "There is no one righteous, not even one; there is no one who understands, there is no one who seeks God" (Rom. 3:10–11) and "No one can come to Me unless the Father who sent Me draws him" (John 6:44).

I explained, "According to these passages, people do not seek God on their own initiative. People don't ask questions about spiritual matters unless God is at work in their lives. When you see someone seeking God or asking questions about Christianity, you are witnessing God at work. That is something only God does in people's lives."

An obvious biblical example of this truth is found in the book of Luke. When Jesus passed through a crowd, He always looked for where the Father was at work. The crowd was not the harvest field. The harvest field was within the crowd. As Jesus walked through the busy streets of Jericho, He was intent on reaching Jerusalem where He knew the cross awaited Him. Although Jesus was only passing by, He noticed Zacchaeus in a tree. It must have been evident to Jesus that for a man to seek Him so earnestly, the Father must be at work in his heart. So Jesus turned aside and said, "Zacchaeus, hurry and come down, because today I must stay at your house" (Luke 19:5). Salvation came to that household that day. Jesus always looked for the activity of the Father and joined Him. Salvation came as a result of Jesus adjusting His life to the work of His Father. Jesus was so in tune with His Father's activity that He could spot it even in the midst of crowded city streets.

That Sunday, I told the students, "If during the course of your day attending class, someone starts asking you spiritual questions, whatever else you may have planned, don't do it. Cancel what you had planned and spend time with that individual to discover what God is doing." That week our students went onto the campus, watching to see where God was at work so they could join Him.

On Wednesday, one of our female students excitedly reported, "Pastor, a girl who has been in classes with me for two years approached me after class today. She said, 'I think you might be a Christian. I need to talk to you.' I remembered what you said. I had a class in a few minutes, but I skipped it. We went to the cafeteria to talk. She said, 'Eleven of us girls in the dorm have been studying the Bible, and none of us are Christians. Do you know someone who can lead us in a Bible study?'"

As a result of that contact, we started three Bible study groups in the women's dorms and two in the men's. For almost two years we had tried to do something for God and failed. Then for three days we looked to see where God was working, and what a difference that made! Over the following years, hundreds of students trusted Christ as Savior and Lord through that student ministry. Many of those surrendered to full-time ministry and are now serving as pastors and missionaries all over the world.

God Is Always Active

Right now, God is working all around you. One of the greatest tragedies among God's people is that even though they long to experience Him, they do not know how to recognize Him at work in their midst. If this has been true of your Christian experience, I pray that this book will help you learn how to clearly recognize God's activity in and around your life. These are extremely exciting days to be walking with the Lord! You don't want to miss out on what He is doing. The Holy Spirit will instruct you and help you know when and where God is working. Once you know where He is working, you can adjust your life to join Him in His divine purposes.

I've heard stories from people all around the world who suddenly discovered God had been present and active in their workplace or church or family or neighborhood all along, but they had not recognized it. When God revealed where He was at work, suddenly they were able to start a noon hour Bible study at their job site, see revival come to their church, help a spouse draw closer to the Lord, or lead a neighbor to faith in Christ. Before, these Christians had assumed God was not doing anything significant around them. After God revealed to them what He was doing, they realized they had been missing out on God's great work.

A Love Relationship

Many people long for God to do a significant work in their life. However, they try to bypass the love relationship. The love relationship is why God created you. That is far more important to Him than what you do for Him. Anticipate that the first thing God will do in your life is to draw you into an intimate love relationship with Himself. When your relationship with God is as it should be, He will begin giving you assignments at His initiative. Whenever it seems that God is not doing anything fresh in your life, focus on the love relationship and stay there until God gives you a new assignment.

Focus on the Call, Not the Gift

I believe many people today are taking an unbiblical approach to spiritual gifts. A common teaching is that people should "discover" their spiritual gifts and then find a ministry or activity that specifically utilizes their gifting. But this assumes Christians will always keep the same gift, and that once they discern their gifts, they should accept ministry opportunities that match the gift and decline any ministry that is not supported by their particular gift. This teaching has been frustrating to some who have attempted to find their gift. At times they will be asked to perform a ministry they do not feel gifted to do, or they may not be able to find a ministry that makes adequate use of their gifts.

It is important to understand that a spiritual gift is a manifestation of the Holy Spirit working in people's lives to enable them to obey what God asks them to do. Biblically, God always gives the assignment first. Then God equips the person by the Holy Spirit to accomplish what He assigns. We must remember that when we became Christians, God placed His Holy Spirit within us. We did not merely receive a spiritual gift; we received the Spirit Himself. When the Spirit resides in us, we have all the power of God and the resources of heaven at our disposal. When God gives us a task and we obey, God will carry out what He intended through our lives. The evidence of God's activity in our lives is what we usually identify as a spiritual gift. But a person who has never accepted an assignment from God does not need to be spiritually equipped because that individual is not undertaking a divine task.

Focusing on identifying gifts instead of determining what God's assignment is can also be severely limiting for believers who base their future usefulness for God only on their past effectiveness. The way many people teach about spiritual gifts is that God will always use your life in similar ways, according to whatever gift He has built into you. For example, if God previously equipped someone to teach His word, then he will assume his spiritual gift is teaching and will decline opportunities later that involve different gifts such as administration or mercy. Consequently, some people receive a fresh invitation from God, but they assume, "That couldn't possibly be from God since it is not in the area of my giftedness." Or "This can't be of God because He has never asked me to do that in my entire life!" However, when you recognize that God is inviting you to join Him, and you respond obediently—even when it is to do something you believe is outside your giftedness—you will experience God working in and through your life in an entirely new dimension than you imagined possible.

The common approach to spiritual gifts can easily become self-centered rather than God-centered if you are the one who is taking the initiative to decide on a ministry that you think suits you. God does not ask us to find ministries we think match our giftedness. Often when people focus solely on what they perceive to be their spiritual gifts, they assume that any ministry in their church or life that matches their gifting is something they should undertake. Yet only God can tell us what He wants to do through our lives. We can't figure that out on our own. We can't discover God's activity; God must reveal it to us. We don't choose what we will do for God; He invites us to join Him where He wants to involve us.

Since this perspective on spiritual gifts is contrary to much that is taught today, if you are uncertain at this point, pause and pray right now that the Holy Spirit will be your teacher. Ask God to help you understand the relationship between a God-given assignment and a spiritual gift. It will be helpful to consider some biblical examples in which the Lord called His servants and then equipped them to do what He commanded.

The Old Testament Pattern

The Old Testament lays the foundation for our understanding of the Holy Spirit's work in the New Testament. In the Old Testament, the Holy Spirit did not continually reside within believers. Rather, the Spirit would come upon individuals to enable them to achieve a specific assignment God had given them. Moses had an assignment as an administrator and national religious leader. Moses, however, was quite certain he was unqualified for this assignment, so he argued at length with God (see Exod. 3:11–4:17).

But God knew exactly what He was doing when He called Moses. Moses' success did not depend on his skills, abilities, likes, preferences, or past successes. First, God gave Moses an assignment, and then God equipped him with His Holy Spirit to administer and to lead. When Moses obeyed God, God enabled Moses to do what He had commanded. The results revealed that God was working through Moses doing things Moses could never have done in his own strength.

When David was a young shepherd boy, God called him to be a king. How could he possibly govern Israel in a tumultuous and dangerous time when he was only an inexperienced young shepherd? Even David's father thought David was the least likely of his sons to shoulder this enormous responsibility. However, the Holy Spirit came upon David and equipped him to be his nation's greatest king.

In the book of Judges, God gave each judge a specific assignment. Then the Spirit of God rested upon him or her and equipped that judge to accomplish the divine task. Deborah could never have liberated her people from the harsh oppression of their enemies. Yet God spoke through her to encourage Barak and the army to utterly defeat their foes (see Judg. 4–5). Ezekiel was called to be a prophet. How could he prophesy in such a discouraging and confusing time? The Scripture says the Spirit of God came upon him and caused him to do everything God asked of him (see Ezek. 2–3).

Here is the pattern we see in the Old Testament:

- God gave an assignment to a person.
- The Holy Spirit equipped that person to perform the assignment.
- The proof of the Spirit's presence was that the person was able to complete the assignment effectively through the enabling of the Holy Spirit.

The workmen constructing the tabernacle in the wilderness are a clear example of how the Holy Spirit equipped people. God gave Moses specific details about how to build the tabernacle (see Exod. 25–30), and God wanted it done exactly as He had instructed. Then God said, "Look, I have appointed by name Bezalel son of Uri, son of Hur, of the tribe of Judah. I have filled him with God's Spirit, with wisdom, understanding, and ability in every craft . . . I have also selected Oholiab son of Ahisamach, of the tribe of Dan, to be with him. I have placed wisdom within every skilled craftsman in order to make all that I have commanded you" (Exod. 31:2–3, 6).

How could Moses confirm that the Spirit of God was upon those men? He would watch them at work. If they were divinely enabled to carry out God's assignment, Moses would recognize the Holy Spirit's presence in their lives and labors.

The Old Testament bears witness that the Spirit of God was always present to equip individuals to carry out His assignments. God didn't give a person a thing, such as a permanent skill at administration. Rather, He placed His Holy Spirit within people so they had access to the Spirit's ability to administer. The Holy Spirit was the gift. The Spirit manifested His presence by equipping people to function where God had assigned them.

Sincere but Not Equipped

When I was a pastor, I had a sincere church member who longed to serve the Lord in her church. She had a tender heart for those who were suffering illness, so she volunteered to be the church's official hospital visitor. Every time someone from our congregation entered the hospital, the church secretary would call this woman, and she would immediately go and visit. I would often arrive at the hospital after this woman had already been there. Inevitably, I would find the patients distressed and even weeping because of something she had said. Although she meant well, she would inevitably upset the one she was there to encourage. She would mention someone she knew who had a similar condition and how the poor soul ultimately died. Or she would warn them of the dire symptoms that were sure to come as a result of their condition.

I finally had to have a talk with her. I thanked her for her willingness to encourage those in the hospital, but I added that it did not seem God was equipping her to be effective in that ministry. Then I mentioned that what I had witnessed in her life was an unusual effectiveness to pray. It seemed that God had given her a passion for intercession and that God regularly answered her prayers. I told her that the church was seeking someone who would intercede for those connected to the church who were not yet believers in Christ, and I asked her to pray about whether God was leading her to serve in this new position. She contacted me several days later and told me she sensed this was, indeed, what God was asking her to do. I gave her a list of seventy-five names of people connected to our church who were not yet believers. She began to pray fervently, and soon we began to see these people come to faith in Christ.

Later, when her health declined and she could not attend church services, she would call me and ask if certain people had made public professions of faith that Sunday. Inevitably, they had. As she had been praying that morning, God had given her a sense of peace for particular people for whom she was praying and, sure enough, I would later report that they had received Christ as their Savior that day.

Even after I left that church and began doing mission work in Canada, I would call and enlist her to pray for serious needs that I and my church were facing. When my wife, Marilynn, almost died from complications in childbirth, I instinctively called this faithful intercessor from my former church. Here was a wonderful woman who wanted to serve her Lord. She had seen a need and had attempted to meet it in her own strength, but the results were disastrous! When she recognized how God was equipping her, however, and placed her life into the corresponding ministry, the Holy Spirit enabled her to have one of the most important ministries in the church. I believe one of the most significant roles of a church staff is to help people understand where God is assigning them to serve in the body so they can experience the joy of God working powerfully through them to accomplish what only He can do.

The Equipping of the Holy Spirit

First Corinthians 12:7 says: "A manifestation of the Spirit is given to each person to produce what is beneficial." The Holy Spirit does not give believers a gift. The Holy Spirit *is* the gift! (see Acts 2:38). The Spirit reveals Himself to each member for the common good of the body.

The church is the body of Christ. Christ adds members to local churches. Each member has the Holy Spirit's active presence in his or her life. The Holy Spirit does not work in people's lives merely for their own personal edification but so the body of Christ can be built up and strengthened. That is why we need each other. Without a healthy and functioning body, a church will miss much of what God intends for it. When members refuse to serve or they leave the church because of broken relationships, church members suffer because part of God's provision for them is now missing.

Jesus said: "The Father who lives in Me does His works." (John 14:10). Throughout Jesus' earthly ministry, the Father manifested Himself through His Son. The Father was in Jesus, and He worked through Jesus to accomplish His purposes. Then Jesus informed His disciples, "You can do nothing without Me" (John 15:5).

A spiritual gift is a manifestation of God at work through you. God works in and through you to bear spiritual fruit. Your focus should be on God living His life through you to accomplish His purposes. When you concentrate on a particular gift you receive in order to do something for God, your attention is usually on self rather than on God.

Many Christians have made use of what is called a "spiritual gifts inventory." They will answer a series of questions and then determine what their spiritual gift is. Those who advocate such instruments suggest Christians use them to determine what their spiritual gifts are so they can find a ministry that matches their gifts.

When a person takes a spiritual gifts inventory and it identifies a particular gift in his or her life, the reason may well be because God previously equipped this person in that area to accomplish a divine assignment. This does not mean, however, that this is the only means by which God expects the person to serve in the future. If God gives a different assignment, He will provide an equipping to match the new task. That is why there are people who, over the years, have discovered that their "spiritual gift" seemed to change. The reason? Their assignment shifted, so the Holy Spirit equipped them to accomplish their new task.

If God merely provided us with a gift, we would tend to place our confidence in the gift rather than in Him. But since the Holy Spirit does the work through us, we must continually rely upon our relationship with Him if we are to be effective in the ministry He gives us. Conversely, if we refuse to obey what God asks us to do, the Holy Spirit will not equip us. We don't need to be equipped for something we refuse to do. Our divine enabling always comes as we obey what God tells us to do—never before our obedience.

Focus your attention on hearing God's call to an assignment which is His invitation for you to join Him. When you adjust your life to Him and obey Him, the Holy Spirit will work in you, enabling you to accomplish what God desires.

Summary

God is always at work in His world. He seeks to bring every person into a personal relationship with Himself through Jesus Christ. Jesus described the way He knew and did the will of His Father. Because the Father loved His Son, He showed the Son what He was doing. Jesus watched to see where the Father was working and joined Him. You can follow that same pattern by watching to see where God is at work around you. When He shows you, join Him in His work. Keep your attention on God's call to an assignment rather than on your spiritual gifts, personal desires, skills, abilities, or resources. Once you understand God's call to an assignment, obey Him, and He will work through you to accomplish His divine, eternal purposes.

Experiencing God Today

Take some time to reflect on the ways God has enabled you to serve Him in the past. Has it always been in the same way, or has He given you a variety of assignments? How have you come to rely upon Him as a result of the way He has led you?

Trust the first reality: God is always at work around you.

QUESTIONS FOR REFLECTION

1. Reflect on your experiences with God. Can you identify times when God was at work around you—and you knew it? Was there a time when God was working around you in past situations but you did not recognize it as God's activity at the time?

2. Have you recently been asked to be involved in a ministry for which you feel inadequate? Could it be that God is inviting you to a new level of ministry with Him for which He will equip you?

3. Has your service for God in the past been centered more on you and what you felt comfortable doing, or on listening to God's voice and doing whatever He asked? How might your service for God be more God-centered in the future?

7

GOD PURSUES A LOVE RELATIONSHIP WITH YOU

He said to him, "Love the Lord your God with all your heart, with all your soul, and with all your mind. This is the greatest and most important commandment." (Matthew 22:37–38)

PURSUED BY LOVE

While registering at a national conference in a large city, I gave the woman working at the registration table my name, and she screamed, "It's you! You saved my life!" Needless to say, I was intrigued.

She told me that when she had been a university student, she had faced a series of devastating events and had descended into a pit of despair, finally resolving to end the pain. As she was walking across the campus lawn to the place where she intended to take her life, she heard her name being called. Trying to ignore the voice, she pressed on at a faster pace, but the person calling her would not be deterred. A friend finally caught up to her and grabbed her arm. The friend said she was on her way to a new Bible study and that she *must* attend, too. The woman made an excuse, claiming she had another appointment, but her friend would not take no for an answer and literally dragged her by the arm all the way to the room where the study was to be held.

The group was studying *Experiencing God*. That night, they examined how God pursues each person in order to have a love relationship with them. Suddenly, this woman felt her heart flooded with the loving presence of God. It dawned on her that God had been relentlessly pursuing her, even as her world had been crumbling around her. She gave her life to Christ, and God transformed her and her situation. Cheerfully, she told me how God had used this biblical material to save her life. Oh, that all people would realize God is inviting them into a loving, transforming, forgiving, empowering relationship with Him!

God created you for intimate fellowship with Him. A life spent walking closely with the Lord is both exciting and rewarding. God does not want you to miss out on what He has intended for you from eternity. Sin causes us to follow our own selfish desires, but in doing so we reject God's best for our lives. So God takes the initiative to draw us closer to Himself.

This love relationship, however, is not one-sided. As you accept His love and forgiveness, He wants you to know and worship Him. Most of all, He wants you to love Him. Jesus said, "The one who has My commands and keeps them is the one who loves Me. And the one who loves Me will be loved by My Father. I also will love him and will reveal Myself to him" (John 14:21).

Obedience and Love

Your love for God and your obedience to His commands go hand in hand. Jesus declared, "If you love Me, you will keep My commandments" (John 14:15). When you obey Jesus, you demonstrate that you trust Him. Obedience is the outward expression of your love for God.

Jesus set an example in His life. He said, "I am going away so that the world may know that I love the Father. Just as the Father commanded Me, so I do" (John 14:31). Jesus demonstrated His love for the Father by obedience. Obeying God out of love does not merely mean following the letter of the law; it also includes obedience to the spirit of God's command.

If you have an obedience problem, you have a love problem. Focus your attention on God's love. Could you stand before God and describe your relationship to Him by saying, "I love You with all my heart and all my soul and all my mind and all my strength"? Jesus said He would take those who respond to His love into an ever-deepening experience of love and fellowship with Him.

Difficulty with the Relationship

One of our church members was suffering chronic difficulties in his personal life, in his family, at work, and in the church. One evening during a church business meeting, he grew so furious at the decisions being made that he angrily declared he was resigning from all his offices in the church. Then he stormed out of the building in the middle of the meeting. Later that week, I went to see him and asked, "Can you describe your relationship with God by sincerely saying, 'I love You with all of my heart'?"

The strangest look came over his face. He said, "Nobody has ever asked me that. No, I could not describe my relationship with God that way. I could say I obey Him, I serve Him, I worship Him, and I fear Him. But I cannot say that I love Him."

As we talked, I learned that he had never felt that his father loved him. His dad had constantly criticized him. Nothing he did ever measured up to his father's impossibly high standards. And, as often happens, he had grown up to view God just like his earthly father. Even as the man continued to be angry and hurt at the rejection of his earthly father, he also had anger and confusion in his life because of his estrangement from God. Everything in his life was out of order because God's basic purpose for his life was missing.

Sadly, this man is like many people who have regularly attended church all their lives. They are respected members of their congregation and serve in leadership positions. But when pressed, they would admit they do not love God. They serve Him, worship Him, believe in Him, and fear Him, but their relationship with God is not characterized by genuine, heartfelt love.

God created us for a love relationship with Him. When you are not living your life in the overflow of God's love for you and your love for Him, then you cannot live the Christian life as it is intended.

If you cannot describe your relationship with God by saying that you love Him with all your being, then before you do anything else, you need to entreat the Holy Spirit to bring you into that kind of relationship today.

If I were to summarize the entire Old Testament, it would be expressed in this verse: "Listen, Israel: The LORD our God, the LORD is One. Love the LORD your God with all your heart, with all your soul, and with all your strength" (Deut. 6:4–5).

The Greatest Commandment

This heart cry of God is expressed throughout the Old Testament, and the essence of the New Testament is the same. Quoting from Deuteronomy, Jesus said the greatest commandment in the Old Testament law was: "Love the Lord your God with all your heart, with all your soul, with all your mind, and with all your strength" (Mark 12:30). Everything in your Christian life, everything about knowing God and experiencing Him, everything about knowing His will depends on the quality of your love relationship with God. If this relationship is not right, nothing in your life will be in order. Notice what God says about a love relationship:

> I call heaven and earth as witnesses against you today
> that I have set before you life and death, blessing and curse.
> Choose life so that you and your descendants may live,
> love the LORD your God, obey Him, and remain faithful to Him. For He is your life. (Deut. 30:19–20)

> For God loved the world in this way: He gave His One and Only Son, so that everyone who believes in Him will not perish but have eternal life. (John 3:16)

> The one who has My commands and keeps them is the one who loves Me. And the one who loves Me will be loved by My Father. I also will love him and will reveal Myself to him. (John 14:21)

> Who can separate us from the love of Christ?
> Can affliction or anguish or persecution or famine or

nakedness or danger or sword? . . . No, in all these things we are more than victorious through Him who loved us . . . [Nothing] will have the power to separate us from the love of God that is in Christ Jesus our Lord. (Rom. 8:35, 37, 39)

This is how we have come to know love: He laid down His life for us. We should also lay down our lives for our brothers. (1 John 3:16)

God's love was revealed among us in this way. God sent His One and Only Son into the world so that we might live through Him. Love consists in this: not that we loved God, but that He loved us and sent His Son to be the propitiation for our sins . . . We love because He first loved us. (1 John 4:9–10, 19)

Do you realize that the Lord does not just *give* you life—He *is* your life? He does not grant you things and comforts so you have a "good" life. He brings you into a relationship with Him so out of that relationship you have everything you could possibly need. You did not initiate a love relationship with God; He initiated a love relationship with you. Long before you began your life on earth, God demonstrated His love for you on the cross of Christ.

Because God loves you, He wants you to love Him in return. The preceding Scriptures indicate some of the ways you can express your devotion to Him: you can choose life, listen to His voice, hold fast to Him, believe in His only Son, obey His commands and teachings, and be willing to lay down your life for your Christian brothers and sisters.

When you love God, He promises to respond with His blessings. You and your children will live under His favor. By trusting in Jesus, you have eternal life. God's Spirit will reside within you. He will make you more than a conqueror over every difficulty you face. Nothing will separate you from God's love.

What is the foremost thing God wants from you? He wants you to love Him with all your being. Your experiencing God depends on your love for Him.

Loved on Death Row

At 3:00 a.m. on June 13, 1983, Karla Fay Tucker and her boyfriend, Danny Garret, both high on drugs, committed a brutal double homicide while trying to steal a motorcycle. Thirty-five days later they were arrested and ultimately sentenced to be executed for their heinous crime. In many ways, this tragic event in Tucker's life was simply the lowest point in a disturbing life story. She grew up in a home with parents who constantly fought and eventually divorced. She used drugs for the first time when she was seven. By the time she reached the seventh grade she was using drugs heavily and dropped out of school. By the age of fourteen, she had followed her mother into prostitution. She married and divorced and continued her life in a downward spiral until that fateful June night.

While awaiting her trial, Karla Fay finally met Christ and realized that despite her horrendous deed, immoral lifestyle, and hardened heart, God still loved her. She began a fourteen-year odyssey on death row at the Mountain View Prison in Gatesville, Texas. During her time in prison, she began to study her Bible and took the course *Experiencing God*. Prison officials credited her with saving two inmates from committing suicide and encouraging numerous other people.

Tucker's case gained national attention, and she was interviewed by Larry King on national television. At the close of their interview, King said, "Finally, you remain up." Tucker said "Yes." Then King asked, "Can you explain that to me a little more? It can't just be God." She smiled and replied, "Yes, it can. It's called the joy of the Lord. When you've done something like I have done and you've been forgiven for it and you're loved—that has a way of so changing you. I have experienced real love. I know what forgiveness is, even when I've done something so horrible. I know this because Jesus forgave me when I accepted what He did on the cross. When I leave here, I'm going to be with Him."

Ultimately, Tucker's appeals ran out and she was executed on February 3, 1998, the first woman to be executed in Texas in more than a hundred years. To the very end, she remained true to the God who had forgiven her. Her last words were: "I love you all very much. I will see you all when you get there. I will wait for you."

Tucker realized that even when everything else is taken from you, you have all you need when you have Christ. Even when you are in the darkest, most hopeless situations, the love of God is more than sufficient to give you hope and life. Fortunately, Tucker saw that the most important thing in life was her relationship with Christ. Even as her executioner injected lethal drugs into her system, Tucker hummed praise songs to God. Unfortunately, many people spend their lives and never come to realize the profound truth that God loves them.

Your First Love

Picture in your mind a tall ladder leaning against a wall. Now think about your life as a process of climbing that ladder. Wouldn't it be tragic to reach the top and find you had inadvertently placed it against the wrong wall? One life to live—and you went the wrong way with it!

Your relationship to God is the single most important aspect of your life. If that is not in order, nothing else will be. If you knew that all you had in your life was a relationship with God, would you be totally satisfied? If everything else were removed from you, could you be content having nothing but your relationship with God? Many people would say, "Well, I would like to have that relationship, but I would also like to do something." Or "I would want a relationship with God, but I would also want a spouse and children, a good career, a nice home, and friends."

As good as all of these things are, they cannot provide you what God intends to give you: Himself. If your relationship with God is at the deepest level He intends, you will find enormous satisfaction and joy in your walk with Him. God alone can fulfill the deep longing in your soul that we try to satisfy with things, activities, and human relationships. Karla Fay Tucker, though confined to prison and facing execution, could still experience divine joy and peace because no one could take away her relationship with God.

Most of us in our culture feel worthless or useless if we are not busy accomplishing something. Scripture indicates that God is saying, "I want you to love me above everything else. When you are in a love relationship with Me, you have everything you need" (see Ps. 37:4; Matt. 6:33). To be loved by God is the greatest relationship, the highest achievement, and the noblest position in life.

That does not mean you will never do anything to express your love for Him. God will call you to obey Him and do whatever He asks. However, you do not need to be doing something to feel fulfilled or to be a person of worth in God's eyes. You are completely fulfilled in a relationship with God.

No Competitors

Do you really want to love the Lord your God with all of your heart? He will allow no competitors. He declares:

> No one can be a slave of two masters, since either he will hate one and love the other, or be devoted to one and despise the other. You cannot be slaves of God and of money. (Matt. 6:24)

> When the LORD your God brings you into the land He swore to your fathers Abraham, Isaac, and Jacob that He would give you—a land with large and beautiful cities that you did not build, houses full of every good thing that you did not fill them with, wells dug that you did not dig, and vineyards and olive groves that you did not plant—and when you eat and are satisfied, be careful not to forget the LORD who brought you out of the land of Egypt, out of the place of slavery. Fear the LORD your God, worship Him, and take your oaths in His name. Do not follow other gods, the gods of the peoples around you, for the LORD your God, who is among you, is a jealous God. (Deut. 6:10–15)

> Therefore do not worry, saying, "What will we eat?" or "What will we drink?" or "What will we wear?" For the idolaters eagerly seek all these things, and your heavenly Father knows that you need them. But seek first the kingdom of God and His righteousness, and all these things will be provided for you. (Matt. 6:31–33)

Out of His love for you, He will provide everything you need. But the Lord makes it clear that He wants first place in your heart.

The Pursuit

God always takes the initiative in this love relationship. This is the testimony of the entire Bible. He came to Adam and Eve in the garden of Eden. In love, He fellowshipped with them. He came to Noah, Abraham, Moses, and the prophets. God took the initiative so each person in the Old Testament would experience Him in a personal fellowship of love. This is true of the New Testament as well. Jesus chose the disciples to be with Him and to experience His love. He came to Mary, Martha, and Lazarus. He encountered Paul on the Damascus Road.

Sin has marred us so deeply that we do not seek after God of our own accord. Scripture explains: "There is no one righteous, not even one; there is no one who understands, there is no one who seeks God. All have turned away, together they have become useless; there is no one who does good, there is not even one" (Rom. 3:10–12). If God did not approach us, we would never find Him:

> No one can come to Me unless the Father who sent Me draws Him . . . Everyone who has listened to and learned from the Father comes to Me . . . This is why I told you that no one can come to Me unless it is granted to him by the Father. (John 6:44–45, 65)

> The LORD has appeared to me of old saying: "I have loved you with an everlasting love; therefore, I have continued to extend faithful love to you." (Jer. 31:3)

> I led them with human cords, with ropes of kindness. To them I was like one who eases the yoke from their jaws. (Hos. 11:4)

God showers everlasting love on your life. Out of His compassion for you, He lovingly drew you to Himself when you were not His friend but His enemy (Eph. 2:1–5). To firmly anchor your relationship with God and to know His will, you must be absolutely convinced of God's love for you.

Saul

Saul, later known as the apostle Paul (see Acts 9:1–19), violently opposed God by persecuting the followers of Jesus. Then the risen Christ encountered Paul and revealed the Father's loving purpose for him. This incredible reality is also true in our lives. Though we may reject God—or even oppose Him—He has chosen us, loved us, and revealed His eternal purposes for our lives.

The Disciples

Jesus said to His disciples: "You did not choose me, but I chose you . . . you are not of the world, but I have chosen you out of it." (John 15:16, 19). Didn't Peter elect to follow Jesus? No. Jesus chose Peter. Peter's decision to follow Jesus was a response to Jesus' invitation. God took the initiative.

> When Jesus came to the region of Caesarea Philippi, He asked His disciples, saying, "Who do people say the Son of Man is?"
> And they said, "Some say John the Baptist; others, Elijah; still others, Jeremiah or one of the Prophets."
> "But you," He asked them, "who do you say that I am?"
> Simon Peter answered, "You are the Messiah, the Son of the living God!"
> And Jesus responded, "Simon son of Jonah, you are blessed because flesh and blood did not reveal this to you, but My Father in heaven." (Matt. 16:13–17)

When Peter responded to the Teacher's question by confessing the truth that Jesus was the Christ, Jesus recognized the Father's activity in Peter. But Jesus made it clear that Peter did not figure this out on his own. The revelation of Jesus' identity had come directly from the Father.

Do you realize that God determined to love you? Apart from that, you never would have become a Christian. He had something in mind when He called you. He began to work in your life, and as He took the initiative, you began to experience a love relationship with God. He enlightened your understanding of spiritual matters and drew you to Himself.

When you responded to His invitation, He brought you into a love relationship. But you would never know and experience that love or enjoy the benefits of that love if God had not taken the initiative. The following Scriptures describe some of the ways God initiates a love relationship:

> The LORD your God will circumcise your heart and the hearts of your descendants, and you will love Him with all your heart and all your soul, so that you will live. (Deut. 30:6)

> All things have been entrusted to Me by My Father. No one knows who the Son is except the Father, and who the Father is except the Son, and anyone to whom the Son desires to reveal Him. (Luke 10:22)

> You did not choose Me, but I chose you. I appointed you that you should go out and produce fruit and that your fruit should remain. (John 15:16)

> For it is God who is working in you, enabling you both to will and to act for His good purpose. (Phil. 2:13)

> Listen! I stand at the door and knock. If anyone hears My voice and opens the door, I will come in to him and have dinner with him, and he with Me. (Rev. 3:20)

CREATED FOR ETERNITY, NOT FOR TIME

God did not create you for time; He created you for eternity. Your lifetime on earth provides the opportunity for you to become acquainted with Him and to choose to enter a relationship with Him. Time is a period during which God wants to develop your character into His likeness. Then eternity will have its fullest dimensions for you.

If you merely live for time, you will miss the ultimate purpose of creation. If you live for time, you will allow your past to control and limit your life today. Your life as a child of God ought to be shaped by the future (what you will ultimately be). God uses your present to mold and shape your future here on earth and throughout eternity.

You may have experienced things in your past that have a strong, limiting influence on your life. These may include handicaps, a troubled family background, failures, shame, poverty, pride, success, fame, excessive wealth, and so forth. You may realize you're being shaped primarily by your past rather than your future. You may also fear that because of past failures, you have little hope for the future.

A Hardened Heart

At the conclusion of a speaking engagement one evening, a serious-looking man approached me and said he desperately needed my help. He had served in the army during the Vietnam War. His experiences there (as well as later upon his return) had left him emotionally wounded and bitter. Even after seeing various specialists and receiving extensive counseling, he could not get over what he had experienced during the war. As a result, his marriage was falling apart. His heart had grown so hardened that he could not bring himself to do what was necessary to preserve his family. He realized if he did not get help soon, his life would end in disaster.

I opened my Bible and read to him Ezekiel 36:26: "I will give you a new heart and put a new spirit within you; I will remove your heart of stone and give you a heart of flesh." I told him that no matter how painful and devastating his experiences had been, God had been pursuing him with love, and He could free him from his hardened, bitter heart. Suddenly, the man cried out, "It's gone! It's gone! My hardened heart is gone!"

God set him free. He and I have become good friends, and he continues to experience the joy of the Lord in his life and in his home. What was impossible for him to do in his own strength and wisdom was more than possible for God.

Paul's Past

Paul had to deal with the problem of his past. Here was his approach:

God Pursues a Love Relationship with You

> I once had confidence in the flesh too. If anyone else thinks he has grounds for confidence in the flesh, I have more: circumcised the eighth day; of the nation of Israel, of the tribe of Benjamin, a Hebrew born of Hebrews; as to the law, a Pharisee; as to zeal, persecuting the church; as to the righteousness that is in the law, blameless.
>
> But everything that was a gain to me, I have considered to be a loss because of Christ. More than that, I also consider everything to be a loss in view of the surpassing value of knowing Christ Jesus my Lord. Because of Him I have suffered the loss of all things and consider them filth, so that I may gain Christ and be found in Him, not having a righteousness of my own from the law, but one that is through faith in Christ—the righteousness from God based on faith. My goal is to know Him and the power of His resurrection and the fellowship of His sufferings, being conformed to His death, assuming that I will somehow reach the resurrection from among the dead.
>
> Not that I have already reached the goal or am already fully mature, but I make every effort to take hold of it because I also have been taken hold of by Christ Jesus. Brothers, I do not consider myself to have taken hold of it. But one thing I do: forgetting what is behind and reaching forward to what is ahead, I pursue as my goal the prize promised by God's heavenly call in Christ Jesus.
> (Phil. 3:4–14)

A faithful Jew from the tribe of Benjamin, Paul was faultless in keeping the laws of the Pharisees. He had a distinguished education and reputation. He was zealous for God. Yet when Paul met Christ, he came to view his past successes as rubbish. More than anything else, Paul wanted to know Christ and to become like Him, attaining eternal life. In order to focus on the future, he set aside the past. He pressed toward the goal of a heavenly prize. There was nothing he could do to reorder his past. But now that he walked with the risen Christ, there were no limits to what God could do in and through Paul in the future.

Paul's compelling desire was to know Christ and become like Him. You, too, can so order your life under God's direction that you come to know Him, love Him, and become like Christ. Let your present be molded and shaped by what you are to become in Christ, not by what sin did to you in the past. You were created for eternity!

You can begin right now by orienting your life to the purposes of God. Because His plans go far beyond time and into eternity, God values eternal things. Make sure you are investing your life, time, and resources into that which is lasting, not in things that will soon pass away. If you don't recognize that God created you for eternity, you'll invest your life in the wrong things. Jesus said:

> Don't collect for yourselves treasure on earth, where moth and rust destroy and where thieves break in and steal. For where your treasure is, there your heart will be also. . . . But seek first the kingdom of God and His righteousness, and all these things will be provided for you. (Matt. 6:19–21, 33)

Only God—who loves you with an unfathomable devotion—knows what is best for you. Only He can guide you to invest your life in worthwhile ways. This guidance will come as you walk with Him and listen to Him.

A Sanctified Alcoholic

Over the years, I've had the continual privilege of hearing stories of many, many people who testified to how a love relationship with Christ had transformed them and their families. I know of a man in Brazil who grew up with a father and grandfather who were alcoholics. Not surprisingly, he became addicted to alcohol himself and cared only for drinking with his friends. He completely neglected his wife and children, and because he spent everything he had on liquor, his wife would labor and save to provide meager meals for the children. They lived in a tiny hut made out of little more than cardboard. This man's wife and family feared him, but they did not respect him.

The man's wife was invited to a Bible study being held in a home near theirs. Desperate for friendship and hope, she began attending. There she heard about God and His love for her. Earnestly wanting to experience God's love, she gave her life to Christ. Her new friends joined in praying daily that her errant husband would come to Christ, but this man had no interest in God or religion. He steadfastly refused to attend any Bible study or church service. But she kept praying, and God kept reaching out to him in love.

One day, when the man reached the bottom of his life, He discovered God was there, waiting for him. He became a Christian and began attending the Bible study with his wife. He gave up drinking. He began to share his new faith with his friends, and one by one, they, too, came to faith in Christ. He brought so many people with him to the Bible study that the sponsoring church eventually started a new study group and appointed him as its leader. That group grew so rapidly, they split his group in two and gave him supervision over both small groups. The man began to care for his wife and children as a godly man should.

Eventually, the couple saved enough money to purchase a modest brick house in a newer neighborhood. Within a year, he had led all but one of his neighbors to faith in Christ, and they were all attending his church. His church hired him on the pastoral staff, and today that church has more than twelve thousand people attending every week. The man and his wife now lead marriage enrichment seminars each year. Their children are wholesome young adults who sing on the church's worship team and obviously love and respect their father.

As this man told his story, his face glowed when he spoke of the way God had never given up on him. Even though his life raced toward destruction, God kept pursuing and reaching out to him. Ever since that glorious day when he entered into a personal relationship with Christ, he has devoted his life to helping others experience the forgiveness and freedom that he received.

Walking with God

God created the first man and woman, Adam and Eve, for a love relationship with Himself. After Adam and Eve sinned, they heard God walking in the garden, but they hid from Him because of their fear and shame. Try to sense the heart of a loving Father when He asked the piercing question, "Where are you?" (Gen. 3:9). God knew what had happened to the love relationship.

When your relationship with God is as it ought to be, you will always be in fellowship with the Father. You will enjoy being in His presence and having close fellowship with Him. When Adam and Eve were no longer coming to meet with God, something had gone wrong.

Devotional Times

When God sought to meet with His people during the prophet Jeremiah's day, God declared: "I have spoken to you time and time again but you wouldn't listen, and I have called to you, but you wouldn't answer" (Jer. 7:13). I have always tried to meet with my Lord each morning. I keep that time alone with God, not *in order* to have a relationship but because I *do have* a relationship. Because of my love for Him, I look forward to meeting with Him. I enjoy spending time with Him. Time with Him enriches and deepens the relationship He and I already share.

I have heard people say, "I really struggle trying to make that time alone with God." If that is a problem for you, let me suggest something. Don't merely discipline yourself to read your Bible and to pray as if it is a life sentence you must carry out. Instead, approach your times with God as an opportunity to get to better know someone who loves you with an infinite love. Simply making yourself read a chapter of the Bible each day and then reciting a prayer will not lead you into a deeper walk with God.

Make it the priority in your life and devotional times to love Him with all your heart. That will solve most of the problem with your quiet time. Read in Scripture of God's vast love for you. Recall what He has done to demonstrate His love. Share your heart, your concerns, and your burdens with Him in prayer. Remain silent before Him, and allow Him to share His love with you. The better you know God, the more you will love Him. The more you love Him, the easier it will be for you to spend time with Him. It is never a chore to spend time with someone you love, although it can be tedious to spend time with a stranger!

Suppose you were engaged to a person you loved and intended to marry. What would be your primary reason for spending time with him or her? Is it because you want to find out about his likes and dislikes or family background? Is it because you want to ascertain her knowledge and education? When two people love each other, they naturally are interested in finding out about each other. That is not, however, the primary reason why they spend time together. It is because they love each other and feel refreshed every time they are together.

Similarly, you will learn much about God, His Word, His purposes, and His ways when you spend time with Him. But learning about Him is not why you should want to have time with Him. You should desire fellowship with Him because of what you already know about Him, and as you interact with Him, you will learn even more about Him that will inevitably deepen your devotion. Everything we do with and for God should stem from our love relationship with Him.

Real, Personal, and Practical

The relationship God desires with you will be dynamic and personal. Some ask, "Can a person actually have a real, personal, and practical relationship with God?" They view God as someone who is distant and serenely unconcerned about their day-to-day living. But this is not the God presented in the Scriptures! From Genesis to Revelation, we see God relating to people in personal, intimate, practical ways. Pick up your Bible, and read the stories described below. Watch to see how each person's relationship with the Lord was extremely intimate and practical.

Adam and Eve. God had intimate fellowship with Adam and Eve, walking in the garden with them. When they sinned, God came after them to restore the love relationship. He met their practical need by providing clothing to cover their nakedness (see Gen. 3:20–21).

Hagar. Hagar had been used, mistreated, and abused by Sarai. Finally, she fled for her life. When she reached the end of her own resources and had nowhere else to turn, she heard from God. In her relationship with God, she learned that He saw her, knew her needs, and would lovingly provide for her (see Gen. 16:1–13).

Solomon. Solomon's father, David, had sought the Lord with his whole heart, so Solomon had a heritage of faith and obedience to follow. When he had the opportunity to ask and receive anything he wanted from God, Solomon demonstrated his love for God's people by asking for a discerning heart. God not only granted his request,

He gave him wealth and fame as well. Solomon found his relationship with God to be immensely practical (see 1 Kings 3:5–13).

The Twelve Disciples. The disciples had a real, personal, and practical relationship with Jesus, the Son of God. What a pleasure it must have been to walk so closely with Jesus! When Jesus gave the disciples a difficult assignment, He didn't send them out to meet the challenges in their limited strength. He gave them authority they had never known before to overcome whatever they faced (see Mark 6:7–13).

Peter in prison awaiting execution. In some places of the world, obedience to the Lord results in imprisonment and even execution. This was Peter's experience (see Acts 12:1–17). In answer to prayer, the Lord miraculously delivered him from captivity and imminent death. His deliverance was so dramatic that Peter first assumed it was a dream. When Peter went to tell fellow Christians his good news, they thought he was an angel. Soon they all discovered that the miracle was real. God's practical intervention saved Peter's life.

John in exile on the island of Patmos. John was spending the Lord's Day in communion with God (see Rev. 1:9–20). During this time of fellowship in the Spirit, the risen Christ came to John to "show His slaves what must quickly take place" (Rev. 1:1). This message has been both a challenge and encouragement to Christians from John's day to this.

Do you sense, as you read Scripture, that people came to experience God in real and personal ways? Did you notice how practical their relationships with God were? Both the Old and New Testaments are brimming with examples of God's personal involvement in the lives of men and women from all walks of life. And God has not changed! You, too, can experience a real, personal, and practical relationship with the Father as you respond to God's working in your life.

A New Walk of Faith Required

In the summer of 1992, I asked Claude King to work with me on a new course entitled *Fresh Encounter: God's Pattern for Revival and Spiritual Awakening.* As we began to work on the message God was giving concerning revival, we developed a sense of urgency that we needed to complete the work as quickly as possible. Claude already carried a heavy load as an editor, and he did not see how he could possibly work on the revival material and still fulfill his normal job requirements.

Two years before, God had spoken to him through His Word that a time would come when he would need to release his life and schedule completely to God. Claude began to pray and ask God if this was the time he needed to leave his job and walk by faith. He reviewed how God had led him to that point, and he sought the counsel of godly friends. By Labor Day weekend, Claude felt convinced that he should resign from his job and devote himself to completing the new project. With no source of income in sight, Claude's family joined him in this adventure with God.

After Claude announced his resignation and began wrapping up his job assignments, he received a call from a group of people who had formed a nonprofit group in Texas. They had been involved in renewal efforts for churches. Each of the directors of this ministry had studied the course *Experiencing God* and had witnessed the renewal God was bringing to His people through that material. They said, "We heard about your decision to leave your job to write *Fresh Encounter*. We have prayed and believe God wants us to support you financially."

They hired Claude to be their executive director and to serve as a catalyst for spiritual renewal. They agreed to provide him a full-time salary and said, "We will take care of raising the finances. You do whatever God tells you to do." This allowed Claude to work full-time on *Fresh Encounter*. When the Lord asked Claude to take a step of faith, Claude obeyed. God responded immediately to take care of Claude's needs.

The whole process of developing the revival materials called *Fresh Encounter* would normally have been placed on a five-year planning cycle by our publisher. But God gave Claude and me a sense of urgency, and as a result, we produced the materials in only eight months.

Claude clearly heard God speaking to him. But what God asked him to do seemed impractical! How does someone with a family to support and a mortgage to pay quit a job in mid-career to work on a project with no known source of income? Apart from God, doing such a thing would be foolish and irresponsible. But when you do something like that as a result of your love relationship with God, nothing could be more practical! I could tell you story after story of people who trusted God for the most pragmatic aspects of their lives and how God met every need, right on time.

Loving God

Love must be expressed in tangible ways. A person cannot love without another "someone" to love. A love relationship with God takes place between two persons. A relationship with God is personal and interactive. God is a person who wants to fill your life with His presence.

If you can't remember a time when your relationship with God was real, personal, and practical, you need to evaluate your walk with Him. Go before the Lord in prayer, and ask Him to reveal the true nature of your relationship. Ask Him to bring you into genuine intimacy with Him. If you realize you have never entered a saving relationship with God, return to the introduction for help in settling that most important issue now.

Some people say to me, "Henry, what you are suggesting about doing God's will is not sensible today." I disagree. God is extremely practical. He was that way in biblical times and He is the same today. When He provided manna, quail, and water for the children of Israel, He was being practical. When Jesus fed five thousand hungry people, He was being practical. The God revealed in biblical times is real, personal, and practical. I trust God to relate to me in that same way, too.

The daily presence of God should be the most practical aspect of a believer's life. His plan for the advance of His kingdom on earth includes working in real and tangible ways through relationships with His people.

Knowing and experiencing God through a real and personal relationship was exceedingly practical for people in Scripture, and I believe you'll find such a walk with God highly effective in your life as well. God can make a dramatic difference in your relationships, your home, your church, and your workplace. His involvement in your life should be visible and evident to you and to those around you, like it was in the lives of countless others revealed in the Scriptures.

SUMMARY

People do not seek God on their own initiative. God always takes the lead in pursuing a love relationship with you. This love relationship is real, personal, and extremely practical. More than anything else you might do, God wants you to love Him with your total being. He created you for that purpose. If your love relationship with Him is not close, everything else related to knowing and doing the will of God will be out of focus. When you find God is not working through your life to accomplish His purposes, focus on your love relationship with Him. God may be waiting until you respond to His loving invitation to a relationship before He works through your life to bless others.

EXPERIENCING GOD TODAY

Adam and Eve walked with God in the cool of the day. Take some time to walk with God and cultivate a more intimate relationship with Him this week. If possible, find a place outside to walk. Use this time to get out of your routine. You may even want to plan a special outing for part of a day just to be alone with God. Spend the time talking with Him. If the location permits, you may even want to talk to Him out loud. Praise Him for His love and mercy. Thank Him for expressions of His love to you. Be specific. Express to God your love for Him. Take time to worship Him. Then simply spend time with Him. Talk to Him about your concerns, and listen to what He wants to say to you.

QUESTIONS FOR REFLECTION

After spending time alone with God, reflect on your feelings. Consider some of the following questions:

1. How did you feel as you walked and talked with God?

2. What aspects of your love relationship with God became clear to you?

3. If this was a difficult or an emotionally uneasy time, why do you think it was?

4. What happened that was especially meaningful or joyful?

5. Would this be the kind of experience you might want to repeat regularly?

8

God's Invitation to Join Him in His Work

For it is God who is working in you, enabling you both to will and to act for His good purpose. (Philippians 2:13)

Invited to Canada

I had been a pastor for almost a decade in California when through a series of events, God made it clear to Marilynn and me that He was calling us to relocate to Saskatoon, Canada. Our assignment? To become involved in starting mission churches across western Canada. The church God called us to had suffered grievous decline and now only had ten members attending. The disheartened members had seriously considered disbanding the church and selling the property before I agreed to come as their pastor.

When we arrived at the church after the long drive from Los Angeles, we could see there was much work to be done. The church building desperately needed repair, but the remnant of people were too discouraged and tired to face that task. After a light lunch at the church, we made our way to the humble parsonage and began to unpack.

A thousand thoughts about what needed to be done to get that church back on track flooded my mind. Suddenly, a car pulled up in front of our house, and six men got out. Having just driven from Prince Albert, ninety miles away, they told me they had been praying God would send a pastor who would begin a new church in their city. When they heard I was coming to Saskatoon, they sensed I was God's provision for them as well. From a human perspective this seemed ludicrous. My church could not afford to pay my salary, let alone sponsor a mission ninety miles away. There was so much to do at my own church, it seemed impossible for me to make a three-hour round-trip commute twice a week to a mission church as well. But I discovered that what is impossible with people is possible with God!

As I sought the Lord's guidance, I was profoundly aware that I had received a divine invitation. God had called me to come and plant churches in Canada, and He was not wasting any time! On my first day in the country, He invited me to begin my first mission church!

For two years, I commuted twice a week to Prince Albert to minister to that wonderful group of people. God eventually led us to call Jack Conner, my prayer partner from seminary, to be the mission pastor. He used that church to start many other missions all over that spiritually needy area, reaching far into northern Canada. I have always been deeply grateful that when the Prince Albert carload arrived at my house that spring day, I did not merely see the work, the expense, the effort, and the difficulties. I also saw God. God was inviting me to join in a great work He was about to accomplish. My life and the lives of many others would never be the same again.

Part of the book of Genesis is the record of God accomplishing His purposes through the life of Abraham. Although through the story we see Abraham's growth, it is not primarily the record of Abraham's walk with God. Can you see the difference in focus? The attention of the Bible is always on God.

While the essence of sin is a shift from a God-centered to a self-centered life, the essence of salvation is a denial of self and a return to a God-centered outlook. We must come to a place where we renounce our self-focused approach to life and turn the attention and control over to God. When this happens, God orients us to Himself and to the purposes He is accomplishing around us.

God-centered Living

God-centered living is characterized by:

- confidence in God;
- dependence on God, on His abilities and provision;
- a life focused on God and His activity;
- humility before God;
- denial of self;
- seeking first the kingdom of God, His righteousness;
- seeking God's perspective on our circumstances;
- holy and godly living.

Consider the following biblical examples of God-centered living.

Joseph. Potiphar's wife daily attempted to seduce Joseph. He resisted her bold and persistent advances, refusing to sin against God. When she tried to force herself on him, he fled the house. Ultimately, he went to prison rather than yield to temptation (see Gen. 39). Joseph kept his focus on God rather than his fleshly appetites.

Joshua and *Caleb.* When God was ready for Israel to enter the Promised Land, Moses sent spies to survey the land. Unlike ten of the spies, Joshua and Caleb said, "If the LORD is pleased with us, He will bring us into this land . . . don't be afraid of the people of the land" (Num. 14:8–9). They were willing to trust the word from God and to proceed with confidence rather than trusting in their own strength and resources.

King Asa. In his earlier years King Asa lived a God-centered life. Facing Zerah the Cushite's army in battle, Asa said, "LORD, there is no one besides You to help the mighty and those without strength. Help us, LORD our God, for we depend on You, and in Your name we have come against this multitude. LORD, You are our God. Do not let a mere mortal hinder You" (2 Chron. 14:11). God delivered the enemy into his hand, and the nation experienced peace.

Self-centered Living

In contrast to God-centered living, self-centered living is characterized by:

- life focused on self;
- pride in self and personal accomplishments;

- self-confidence;
- depending on self and one's own abilities;
- affirming self;
- seeking to be acceptable to the world and its ways;
- looking at circumstances from a human perspective;
- selfish and materialistic living.

I've outlined below some biblical examples of self-centered living.

Adam and Eve. God placed Adam and Eve in a luxuriant garden. He made the entire garden and all it contained available to them for their comfort and pleasure. God warned them, however, not to eat from the tree of the knowledge of good and evil. But Eve couldn't resist the temptation to gain the wisdom she was led to believe God was withholding from her, so she ate the fruit (see Gen. 2:16–17; 3:1–7). She shared with Adam, and he also ate the forbidden fruit. Their self-centered decision violated the Lord's command and led to a broken love relationship with their Creator.

Ten Spies. Moses sent twelve men into Canaan to explore it and bring back a report of the land God had promised to Israel. The land was abundant, just as God had said it would be, but the people living there looked like giants to the scouts (see Num. 13–14). Though Joshua and Caleb were prepared to trust God, the other ten spies protested, "We can't go up against the people because they are stronger than we are" (Num. 13:31). Rather than looking to God and His power, they focused on themselves and their weaknesses. They couldn't imagine how they could conquer the enemy. Little did they know how God had prepared the way. Forty years later Rahab, an inhabitant of Jericho, described what God had done. She explained that when the people heard about God's deliverance of Israel from Egypt, "we lost heart, and everyone's courage failed because of you, for the LORD your God is God in heaven above and on earth below" (Josh. 2:11). The self-centered conclusion of the ten spies cost Israel forty years of needless waiting in the wilderness.

King Asa. King Asa and Judah were being threatened by Baasha, king of Israel. Once before when facing an enemy army, King Asa had led the people to trust in the Lord. This time, however, instead of turning to God for help, Asa sent gold and silver from the temple and his own palace to Ben-Hadad, king of Aram, asking for his help in the conflict (see 2 Chron. 16:1–3). Though once God-centered and trusting, King Asa became self-centered and dependent on himself and his own resources. God rebuked Asa and said, "You have been foolish in this matter, for from now on, you will have wars" (2 Chron. 16:9). Because of his self-centeredness, war—the very thing Asa had mainly attempted to avert by his scheming—would plague him the rest of his life.

Self-centeredness is a subtle yet common trap. The world praises self-reliance, and trusting God may make no sense from a human perspective. On the other hand, it makes perfect sense to Almighty God. So be careful. Like King Asa, you can trust God one time and fall right into self-reliance later.

God-centeredness requires a daily denial of self and a submission to God. Jesus said, "Unless a grain of wheat falls into the ground and dies, it remains by itself. But if it dies, it produces a large crop. The one who loves his life will lose it, and the one who hates his life in this world will keep it for eternal life" (John 12:24–25).

A Self-denying Doctor

I once urged the attendees of a conference to deny themselves and obey whatever God told them to do. During a break, a man told me his story. As a college student, he had felt God calling him to be a medical missionary. In obedience to God's call, he entered medical school. Because he excelled in his studies, his professors urged him to do advanced work. Ultimately, he became an expert in the study of immune diseases and was invited to join the staff of a prestigious hospital.

His friends and family praised him for his accomplishments and told him how much good he could do by accepting that position. For several years, he worked at the hospital and became a leading expert in immune diseases. But during the conference at which he and I met, God convicted him that he had neglected to obey his call to missions. Now, well established in his career and supporting a family, he wondered if it was too late. I cautioned him that the world urges us to protect, pamper, promote, comfort, and prosper ourselves. But God tells us to deny ourselves. Well-meaning family and friends want us to live close to them. They hope we'll earn a comfortable salary and build a prestigious reputation, but all of that may only be nurturing the very self Christ commanded us to deny. I advised the doctor to spend time with God and ask Him to clarify exactly what He wanted him to do at this stage of his life.

Later, I heard that this physician had resigned his distinguished position and had become a missionary in Africa, in an area ravaged by AIDS. His expertise in immunology would now be used to build the kingdom of God. He had denied himself, and now he was walking in fellowship with God, experiencing God at work in his life in ways the Lord had always intended.

God's Purposes, Not Our Plans

To live a God-centered life, you must focus on God's purposes, not your own plans. Try to see things from God's perspective rather than from your distorted human view. When God starts to do something in the world, He takes the initiative to tell someone what He is doing. Out of His grace, God involves His people in accomplishing His purposes.

God warned Noah when He was about to bring divine judgment on the earth through a devastating flood (see Gen. 6:5–14). When God prepared to obliterate the debased cities of Sodom and Gomorrah, He revealed His plan to Abraham (see Gen. 18:16–21; 19:13). Likewise, God approached Gideon when He wanted to deliver the Israelites from the oppression of the Midianite nation (see Judg. 6:11–16). When God was preparing to send the long awaited Savior to the earth, He told the teenage girl, Mary (see Luke 1:26–38). God appeared to Saul on the road to Damascus when He was about to send the gospel message to Gentiles around the known world (see Acts 9:1–16). The most important factor in each situation was not what the individual wanted to do for God. The critical factor was what God was about to do.

Let's look closer at the example of Noah. What about all the plans he had made to serve God? What if Noah had planned to conduct a door-to-door evangelistic survey of his neighborhood or start a ministry to homeless people? These would have been noble intentions, but they would have been completely irrelevant in light of God's imminent plans. Noah did not call on God to help him accomplish what he was dreaming of doing for God. In Scripture, you never find

God's Invitation to Join Him in His Work

God asking people to dream up what they want to do for Him. He never urges His people to set impressive goals and generate grand visions for Him and His kingdom.

In the Bible, God rebukes those who propose their own best thinking over His commands. Those in the Bible who received praise from God were not brilliant planners. They were humble "heroes of faith" (Heb. 11). God commended them for their compliance, not for their performance.

Who delivered the children of Israel from Egypt? Moses or God? God did. God chose to bring Moses into a relationship so He—God—could deliver His people through him. Did Moses ever try to take matters into his own hands? Yes, he did. Read this account of Moses' attempt to assume a leadership role for God's people:

> Years later, after Moses had grown up, he went out to his own people and observed their forced labor. He saw an Egyptian beating a Hebrew, one of his people. Looking all around and seeing no one, he struck the Egyptian dead and hid him in the sand. The next day he went out and saw two Hebrews fighting. He asked the one in the wrong, "Why are you attacking your neighbor?"
>
> "Who made you a leader and judge over us?" the man replied. "Are you planning to kill me as you killed the Egyptian?" Then Moses became afraid and thought: What I did is certainly known.
>
> When Pharaoh heard about this, he tried to kill Moses. But Moses fled from Pharaoh and went to live in the land of Midian. (Exod. 2:11–15)

Why did Moses assert himself on behalf of his own people? The sight of their suffering may have pricked his conscience because he was living in Egyptian comfort and luxury. Having been trained in the best schools of Egypt, he used his ingenuity and strength to help a fellow Israelite. Surely his intentions were commendable, but he failed miserably and as a result, spent forty years as a fugitive. What might have happened if Moses had tried to deliver the children of Israel through this same human approach? If he had used his own wisdom to mobilize the Israelites to cast off the yoke of bondage through military force, thousands of his people would have been killed. The Egyptians were a world power with a mighty army. Untrained, unarmed slaves would have been decimated by the dreaded Egyptian army with its seemingly invincible chariots. God sent Moses into exile in Midian to work as a shepherd so he could learn God-centered thinking and living.

When God delivered the Israelites from slavery, there were zero casualties. None. In the process, God even led the Egyptians to give the Israelites their gold, silver, and clothes. Egypt was plundered, the Egyptian army was destroyed, and the Israelites did not lose a single person.

Why don't we realize that doing things God's way is always best? We cause a great deal of pain in our relationships and division in our churches because we act the way Moses did in his youthful zeal. *We* decide what *we* think is best for our family or business or church. *We* develop *our* plans. *We* implement *our* strategies, at times imposing them on others and then experiencing the meager—or even destructive—results of our limited knowledge, reasoning, and power. Oh, that we would discover the difference when we acknowledge Christ as Head of His body, the church. He will accomplish more in six months through a people yielded to Him than we could in sixty years in our own strength and wisdom.

God's Ways

God wants us to know more than His character; He also wants us to learn His ways. You see, God's ways are not our ways (see Isa. 55:8–9). We cannot know how God acts unless He teaches us. God is infinitely wise. He sees the future. He understands our world and everything that takes place in it. God knows the eternal consequences of every action, of every act of obedience or disobedience to His word. God's ways lead to life. His ways bring joy. They are holy and perfect.

Doing things God's way is always best. When God's people do not follow His ways, the consequences can be extremely painful and discouraging. God promised the people of Israel joy and fulfillment if they would live according to His ways, but their failure to follow Him ultimately cost them everything. He said to Israel: "I am Yahweh your God, who brought you up from the land of Egypt. Open your mouth wide, and I will fill it. But My people did not listen to Me; Israel did not obey Me. So I gave them over to their stubborn hearts to follow their own plans" (Ps. 81:10–12). One of God's most devastating acts of discipline is when He allows us to experience the natural consequences of doing things our way instead of His.

God's ways would have been infinitely better than the life Israel chose for herself. God said, "If only My people would listen to Me and Israel would follow My ways, I would quickly subdue their enemies and turn My hand against their foes!" (Ps. 81:13–14).

God wants us to align our lives with Him so He will accomplish His divine purposes in and though us. God is not our servant to bless our plans and desires. He is our Lord, and we must adjust our lives to what He is doing and to the ways He chooses to accomplish His work. If we will not submit to God and His ways, He will allow us to follow our own devices. But be sure of this: we will miss God's activity, and we will not experience what God wants to do through us to bless others. As Christians, it is not only important *what* we do but *how* we do it.

BUILDING PROGRAMS THE WRONG WAY

I see this happen many times as churches try to serve God. A congregation believes God is leading them to build a new auditorium. However, once they know what to do—build a new auditorium—they don't seek Him to determine *how* He wants them to raise the money and construct the facility or *when* He wants them to begin. As a result, many church leaders have their feelings hurt, numerous families leave the church, and project costs skyrocket, leaving the diminished congregation with crippling, long-term debts. Bewildered, the people wonder how things could have gone so wrong since they believed God wanted them to undertake the project. What they did not understand is that with God, *how* you do something is as important as *what* you do. It is possible to do the right thing in the wrong *way* or at the wrong *time*. It is possible to perform a task God assigns but to do it in such an ungodly manner that it actually harms the cause of Christ rather than supporting it. Doing things God's way is critical.

Israel was delivered from bondage in Egypt by many miraculous signs and wonders. They walked through the sea on dry ground and saw the seemingly invincible Egyptian army destroyed by the Red Sea. They saw God provide bread from the sky, flocks of quail to eat when they needed meat, and fresh water spouting from a rock. Wouldn't you think they could trust God to do anything after all that? Yet when they arrived at Canaan, they did not trust Him to deliver the Promised Land to them. For that reason, they spent the next forty years wandering in the wilderness. Psalm 81 expresses God's reminder to Israel that He would have conquered their enemies quickly if they had only followed His plans rather than relying on themselves. God's ways were more than sufficient to conquer the land of Canaan, but the people trusted in their own thinking and chose to attempt only what they thought they could accomplish themselves. Because of that, they missed God's blessing.

Our Plans and God's Activity

One year, a group of missions leaders from our denomination visited our city to help churches make long-range plans for the metropolitan area. These leaders were going to work with us to develop and fund many new ministries. We studied various graphs and charts and discussed our plans when I suddenly had the thought, "But what if God has called our nation to judgment before that time?" I realized that the future might unfold much differently than we were anticipating. The economy could take a nosedive, or a major catastrophe could strike the city. Obviously, we needed to know what God had in mind for our city. If God was already planning to do one thing, our plans to do something else could be totally irrelevant. It became obvious to me that the most important thing we could do in planning was to find out what God wanted us to do.

When God commissioned the Old Testament prophets, He often gave them a two-fold message. God's first desire was: "Call the people to return to Me." If the people chose not to respond, they would receive a second message: "Let them know that judgment is imminent." Think about it. When God was about to bring a devastating judgment upon Jerusalem and destroy the city, was it important to know what He was up to? Certainly! Understanding God's plans for the world around you is far more important than telling God what you are planning to do for Him.

What good would Abraham have done by telling God that he was planning to conduct a series of evangelistic services in Sodom and Gomorrah the day after God intended to destroy the cities? What good would it do for you to make long-range plans for your church if, before you have the chance to implement them, God does something entirely different? The only way for us to make useful plans is first to understand what God's purposes are.

God is seeking to bring people in your community and nation to Himself. He wants to use your life and church in the process. While we know Christ has given us the Great Commission (see Matt. 28:18–20), we do not automatically know the specific ways He wants to use us to accomplish this purpose. For example, we know God wants us to be witnesses wherever we go (see Acts 1:8), but does He want us to begin a prison ministry so we can share the gospel with inmates? Or should we start a basketball league to share Christ with school kids? We must know how God intends to use us and our churches in His redemptive work. Then we can adjust our lives to God, so He will move us into the mainstream of His activity. Though God likely will not give us a detailed schedule of all He is planning, He will let us know what our next steps should be so we can respond to what He is doing.

If you study great movements of God in church history, you'll notice God repeatedly invited people to surrender to Him. As they adjusted their lives, God accomplished His purposes through those people.

JOHN AND CHARLES WESLEY, GEORGE WHITEFIELD

When God began to speak to John and Charles Wesley, He was preparing to bring a sweeping revival across England that would save the nation from a bloody revolution like the one France had experienced. Through the Wesleys, along with George Whitefield and others, God turned England around morally and spiritually. The Wesleys and Whitefield could not possibly have realized the magnitude of what God intended to do through their lives. Yet as we look back, we see that because of their obedience to what God told them, God did an enormous work in their land and across the world that continues to have an impact on people to this day.

God knows what is going to happen in your community. People are going to experience temptation, crises, disappointments, and hardship. God wants to intercept those lives and bring salvation and blessing to them. Suppose He chose to do that through your life. What if, when He came to you and invited you to join Him in His redemptive activity, you responded in a self-centered way? Suppose you said, "I don't think I can do that. I don't have enough formal education. I'm afraid to speak in public. I don't think I have the experience."

Do you see what happens? The focus is on self. The moment you sense God wants to do something in and through your life, you present Him with an extensive list of reasons why He has chosen the wrong person or why His timing is not convenient. That's what Moses did. But we need to seek God's perspective. God knows we can't do it! He wants to accomplish His purposes through us anyway. God's achieving anything in our life hinges on His presence and activity in us.

God's Purposes

Throughout Scripture, we see God taking the initiative in people's lives. He would encounter a person and reveal what He desired of them. The revelation was always an invitation for people to adjust their lives to God. No one to whom God spoke remained the same. All had to make major adjustments in order to walk with God. As they responded obediently, they experienced His character in different dimensions—such as Counselor or Provider or Redeemer.

What often happens when God begins to work around us is that we become self-centered. We begin trying to manage what is happening or to expand upon and administer it. We must reorient our lives to God, to see life from His perspective. We must allow Him to develop His character in us and let Him reveal His thoughts to us. Only then can we gain a proper perspective on life. When you're God-centered, even the desires to do things that please God come from God's stirring in your heart. The Bible says, "It is God who is working in you, enabling you both to will and to act for His good purpose" (Phil. 2:13).

If you keep your life God-centered, you will immediately want to participate in His activity when He reveals His plans to you.

God's Invitation to Join Him in His Work

When you see God at work around you, your heart will leap inside and say, "Thank You, Father. Thank You for letting me be involved where You are." When I'm surrounded by God's activity and God opens my eyes to recognize His work, I always assume He wants me to join Him.

You must be careful to identify God's initiative and distinguish it from your desires. A self-centered person tends to confuse his or her personal agenda with God's will.

Moreover, circumstances can't always be a clear direction for God's leadership. Christians often talk about "open" and "closed doors," asking God to close a door if they are not headed the right way. While it is admirable to seek indications of God's desires, the danger in this thinking lies in assuming that God's will is always the path of least resistance (i.e., the open door).

For example, many people have told me God led them to leave their current job or ministry position after having been there only a short time. Often, when I ask them to explain the process they went through, they tell me they sensed God leading them to the first position but, after they arrived, problems and difficulties arose. They assumed God would not want them to remain under such difficult circumstances. So when a new door "opened," they seized it as God's deliverance.

At times, I challenge them, "What do your difficult circumstances have to do with obeying God's will?" If you're focused on self, you'll always seek to protect yourself and pursue what is most comfortable and what most builds you up. When times get hard, "self" immediately urges you to quit or flee or find another position. To the children of Israel, the Red Sea certainly appeared to be a "closed door." But if you are God-centered, your focus remains on Him alone. Storms may rage around you, but as long as you have God in your sight, you'll stay the course.

Often things do become more difficult after we obey God. You cannot determine if you're in God's will by whether or not things are going well in your current circumstances. "Open" and "closed" doors are not always indications of God's directions. In seeking God's guidance, make sure that prayer, the Scriptures, and circumstances all confirm the direction you sense God leading.

A Praying Pastor

You may be thinking, "That all sounds good, but how do I actually apply these concepts?" In every situation, God demands that you depend on Him, not on a method. The key is not a formula but a relationship with God.

Perhaps I can help you grasp how to apply this way of thinking by telling the story of a man who learned to walk with God by prayer and faith. George Mueller was a pastor in England during the nineteenth century. He observed that God's people were discouraged, that most believers no longer expected God to do anything unusual in their lives or churches. They no longer trusted God to answer their prayers. In short, Christians were not living by faith.

God began leading Mueller to pray for God to guide him into a ministry that could only be explained as a work of God. George wanted people to learn that God is faithful and that He answers prayer.

Mueller came upon the verse in Psalm 81:10 that you read earlier: "Open your mouth wide, and I will fill it." Mueller began to seek God's provisions for his work in a way that God would be pleased to provide, and God took him on a journey of faith that became an outstanding testimony to all who hear his story.

When Mueller felt God leading him to undertake a project, he prayed for the resources needed but told no one of the need. He wanted everyone to know that God had provided for the need in answer to prayer and faith, not in response to fund-raising. During his ministry in Bristol, he started the Scriptural Knowledge Institute for the distribution of Scripture and for religious education. He also established an orphanage.

By the time of his death, George Mueller had been used by God to build four orphanages that cared for two thousand children at a time. In all, more than ten thousand children had been provided for through the orphanages he started. In addition, Mueller had distributed more than $8 million that had been given to him in direct answer to prayer. Yet when he died at ninety-three, his personal possessions were valued at only $800.

How did he know and do the will of God? The following is George Mueller's own explanation:

I never remember . . . a period . . . that I ever sincerely and patiently sought to know the will of God by the teaching of the Holy Ghost, through the instrumentality of the Word of God, but I have been always directed rightly. But if honesty of heart and uprightness before God were lacking, or if I did not patiently wait upon God for instruction, or if I preferred the counsel of my fellow men to the declarations of the Word of the living God, I made great mistakes.

What helped George Mueller know God's will?

- He sincerely sought God's direction.
- He waited patiently until he had a word from God in the Scriptures.
- He looked to the Holy Spirit to teach him through God's Word.

What led him to make mistakes in knowing God's will?

- Lacking honesty of heart;
- Lacking uprightness before God;
- Impatience about waiting for God;
- Preferring the counsel of men over the declarations of Scripture.

Here is how Mueller summed up the way to a heart relationship with God:

1. I seek at the beginning to get my heart into such a state that it has no will of its own in regard to a given matter. Nine-tenths of the trouble with people generally is just here. Nine-tenths of the difficulties are overcome when our hearts are ready to do the knowledge of what His will is.

2. Having done this, I do not leave the result to feeling or simple impression. If so, I make myself liable to great delusions.

3. I seek the will of the Spirit of God through, or in connection with, the Word of God. The Spirit and the Word must be

combined. If I look to the Spirit alone without the Word, I lay myself open to great delusions also. If the Holy Spirit guides us at all, He will do it according to the Scriptures and never contrary to them.

4. Next, I take into account providential circumstances. These often plainly indicate God's will in connection with His Word and Spirit.

5. I ask God in prayer to reveal His will to me aright.

6. Thus, through prayer to God, the study of the Word, and reflection, I come to a deliberate judgment according to the best of my ability and knowledge, and if my mind is thus at peace, and continues so after two or three more petitions, I proceed accordingly.[1]

Summary

Your love relationship with God prepares you to be involved in His work by developing in you a God-centered life. Focusing your attention on God's plans, purposes, and ways—rather than your own—is essential. With any other focus, you will be misguided in your involvement in God's work. Like George Mueller, you need to reach a point where you have no will of your own. Then the Holy Spirit will cause you to desire God's will above everything else.

God Himself is the One who initiates your involvement in His work. He does not ask you to dream up something you can do for Him. You need to know what He is doing—or is about to do—where you are. In the next chapter, we will discuss how God shows you what He is doing.

Experiencing God Today

Take an inventory of where your life efforts are being spent. How are you investing your time? What are your priorities? Then ask yourself, "What am I presently doing that can only be explained by God's activity in my life?" If you cannot think of anything, spend time with your Lord and ask Him why.

QUESTIONS FOR REFLECTION

1. Take a few minutes to review George Mueller's approach to knowing and doing God's will. Then pray and ask God to help you come to the place that you have no will of your own. If you have a set of self-made plans for what you want to do for God, surrender it, and let God reveal His plans instead.

2. Do you desire more than anything else to know and do the will of God? If your honest answer is "no," what must happen before you can reach the place where your will is replaced by God's?

3. Do you have some plans that God has not been blessing? If so, why might that be?

4. Have you been experiencing difficult times lately? Have they caused you to grow discouraged in doing what God told you to do? How might God interpret your current circumstances? Are your difficulties indicating that God wants you to quit what you are doing?

5. Have you been faithfully waiting on the Lord? Are you good at waiting for God? Why or why not?

---

1. For further reading on George Mueller, see *Answers to Prayer from George Mueller's Narratives*, compiled by A. E. C. Brooks, Moody Press, and *George Mueller by Faith*, Coxe Bailey, Moody Press.

9

God Invites You to Join Him

*In Christ, God was reconciling the world to Himself . . .
and He has committed the message of reconciliation to us.
Therefore, we are ambassadors for Christ; certain that
God is appealing through us. (2 Corinthians 5:19–20)*

Invited to Africa

I have had the privilege of ministering in Africa on a number of occasions, but one trip was particularly meaningful. While there, I met a wonderful African-American missionary who told me with deep emotion about the millions of AIDS orphans across Africa and their heartbreaking suffering. As I prepared to return home, this missionary told me he was burdened that African-American churches in North America take on the challenge of helping those in Africa who were suffering and in need.

I was deeply moved by what he shared and promised if there were any way I could help, I would. But, I added, I had not spoken in many African-American churches, and I didn't have a large platform from which to urge them to join the work in Africa. It seemed a bit strange that God would place a burden such as this on me when it lay beyond my expertise or sphere of influence. So I determined to pray and watch to see what God revealed next.

I had not been home two full days when my telephone rang. The call came from a pastor of one of the largest African-American churches in the United States. He explained that his church was hosting a national gathering of African-American church leaders, and he wanted me to speak to them. I instantly recognized I had just been handed my next set of divine instructions!

Not long after that, I received another unusual invitation. This time it was to address a group of African ambassadors at the United Nations. After I spoke to them about being spiritual leaders in their homelands, many of them gave me their business cards and asked when I could come and visit their nations and respective presidents. Since then, God has steadily revealed to me His great love for the people of Africa and especially for the millions who suffer there daily. As I responded to God's invitation through that one missionary, I had no idea God had so much He intended to do through me. Every invitation from God has limitless possibilities because of Him "who is able to do above and beyond all that we ask or think—according to the power that works in you" (Eph. 3:20).

God's Invitations

The Bible reveals that God has always been involved in the world to reconcile people to Himself. He is in the center of all that takes place. When we read the Bible, we read how God has accomplished this divine work in our world. We see that He always takes the initiative to involve His people in His activity.

When God wanted to save people from a severe famine, He helped the young man Joseph understand that a drought was coming. When God wanted to save His people from a widespread massacre, He raised up a young woman, Esther, to the royal throne. When He was preparing to send the Messiah into the world, God first commissioned John the Baptist to prepare the way. As Jesus lay His life down for the sins of humanity, the Father prompted a businessman, Joseph of Arimathea, to make his own tomb available for Jesus' body. Whenever God was about to accomplish a new work, He invited people to join Him in His activity.

God's Timing

As God's obedient child, you are in a love relationship with Him. In His timing, He will show you where He is working so you can join Him. Don't be in a hurry to be constantly engaged in activities for God. He may spend years preparing your character or developing your love relationship with Him before He gives you a large assignment. Don't get discouraged if the task or "call" does not come immediately. Remain faithful in what He *has* told you to do, no matter how small or seemingly insignificant it may appear. God knows what He is doing. Focus on deepening your communion with God, and out of that fellowship will inevitably flow effective service for God.

Jesus was twelve when He went about the Father's business in the temple. Yet, He was thirty before He began the public ministry God had prepared Him for. The Son of God spent several years as a carpenter, waiting until the Father was ready for Jesus to begin His public ministry.

In this process of knowing and doing God's will, you may ask: "Why doesn't God give me a big assignment?" Be patient and learn to trust Him. God will first build some basic foundations into your life before He gives you a larger role in service to Him.

The Next Level

Have you ever said something like, "Lord, if You will just tell me what you want me to do, I will serve You to the best of my ability"? If God *were* to put you in that kind of assignment, could He trust you to handle it? Are you ready to go to the next level of faith in God?

On the night before Jesus' crucifixion, Peter said to the Lord, "I'm ready to go with You both to prison and to death!" In response, Jesus warned him, "The rooster will not crow today until you deny three times that you know Me" (Luke 22:33–34). God also knows the exact limits of *your* faith. He knows what you can handle.

Our own hearts can deceive us (see Jer. 17:9). We can often have a higher estimate of our faithfulness and trust in God than we should. God is never fooled. He always matches His assignments with our character and faith in Him. So trust Him. Don't insist that God put you in a position you think you should have. Don't strive to gain a position you think you deserve or can handle. That could lead to your ruin. You might inadvertently manipulate yourself right into a position or responsibility that is beyond what your character can manage. Rather, trust Him and obey wholeheartedly where He has put you, and watch to see where He leads you next.

Remember: God is far more interested in accomplishing His kingdom purposes than you are. He will move you into every assignment He knows you are ready to take on. Let God orient you to Himself. The servant does not tell the Master what kind of position he or she wants. Servants wait on the Master for whatever instruction they may be given. So be patient and wait.

Waiting on the Lord should not be an idle time for you. Let God use times of waiting to mold and shape your character. Let Him purify your life and make you into a clean vessel for His service.

As you obey Him, God will prepare you for the assignment that is just right for you. Any responsibility that comes from the Maker of the universe is important. Do not use human standards to measure the significance or value of your assignment. Whatever mission God gives, do it with all your heart.

Reviewing Jesus' Example

To clarify how God invites us to be involved with Him, let's review Jesus' example from John 5:17, 19–20 (see chapter 6). "My Father is still working, and I am working also . . . I assure you: The Son is not able to do anything on His own, but only what He sees the Father doing. For whatever the Father does, the Son also does these things in the same way. For the Father loves the Son and shows Him everything He is doing, and He will show Him greater works than these so that you will be amazed."

Pay attention to these principles modeled by Jesus:

- The Father has been working right up until now.
- Now God has Me working.
- I do nothing on My own initiative.
- I watch to see what the Father is doing.
- I do what I see the Father is already doing.
- The Father loves Me.
- He shows Me everything that He is doing.

God has been active in our world from the beginning, and He is still working. Jesus announced that He had come, not to do His own will, but the will of the Father who had sent Him (see John 4:34; 5:30; 6:38; 8:29; 17:4). To know the Father's will, Jesus watched to see what the Father was doing. Then Jesus joined Him and did the same work.

The Father loved the Son and took the initiative to reveal to Jesus what He (the Father) was doing or was about to do. The Son kept watching for the Father's activity around Him so He could unite His life with the Father and His work.

God's Revelation Is Your Invitation

For Jesus, the revelation of where the Father was working was His invitation to join in that activity. When you see the Father accomplishing His purposes around you, that is your invitation to adjust your life to Him and join Him in that work.

Elisha's Servant. Is it possible for God to be active around you and you not to recognize it? Yes. Elisha and his servant were in the city of Dothan, which was surrounded by an enemy army that was intent on capturing them. The servant was terrified, but Elisha remained calm. "Then Elisha prayed, 'LORD, please open his eyes and let him see.' So the LORD opened the servant's eyes. He looked and saw that the mountain was covered with horses and chariots of fire all around Elisha" (2 Kings 6:17). Only when the Lord opened the servant's eyes did he see God's activity all around him. God had gathered a great host of His heavenly forces in that location and yet the servant was unaware of the divine activity that was occurring dramatically all around him.

Jerusalem's Leaders. Jesus wept over Jerusalem and its leaders as He prophesied the horrific destruction that would occur in A.D. 70. Jesus declared, "If you knew this day what would bring peace—but now it is hidden from your eyes" (Luke 19:42). God was in their midst performing amazing signs and miracles, yet His own people were oblivious to the Father's work. They had not developed their love relationship with the Father, even though they had been diligent students of Scripture. Now, with the Son of God Himself among them, they could not see that God had come to them. In fact, they were so out of touch with God that they actually put to death the very Messiah they had been looking for all their lives.

Jesus condemned many of the religious leaders of His day for missing the most important part of life—a love relationship with God. He said to them, "You pore over the Scriptures because you think you have eternal life in them, yet they testify about Me. And you are not willing to come to Me that you may have life" (John 5:39–40).

Two factors are important if you are going to recognize God's activity around you:

1. You must be living in an intimate love relationship with God.

2. God must open your spiritual eyes so you can see what He is doing. Unless God allows you to see where He is active, you will not recognize what God is doing even though He may be working mightily all around you.

Working Where God Is at Work

When some people want to start a new church, they begin by surveying the demographics of the target community. Then they apply human logic to decide where the most promising and productive places might be. By now, you know that I would take a different approach, and I have seen repeatedly that what makes sense to people is not necessarily what God has on His agenda.

The church of which I was the pastor in Saskatoon sensed that God wanted us to start new churches across Western Canada. Since there were hundreds of communities that had no evangelical church, we first tried to find out what God was already doing in the towns and cities around us. We believed He would show us where He was at work, and that revelation would be our invitation to join Him. We began praying and watching how God would answer.

Allan was a small town forty miles from Saskatoon, and one of our members felt led that our church should conduct a Vacation Bible School for the children in Allan. So we said, "Let's find out if God is at work there." We conducted the VBS, and at the end of the week, we hosted a "parents' night." We told the group, "We believe God may want us to establish a church in this town. If any of you would like to begin a regular Bible study group and become part of a new church, would you come and talk with one of us?"

An older lady came from the back of the hall, weeping. She said, "I have prayed for thirty years that there would be a church in this town, and you are the first people to respond."

From behind her came an elderly man known as "T.V. George" (he was a TV repairman). He, too, was deeply moved. Through tears, he explained, "For years I was active in a church. Then I became addicted to alcohol. Four-and-a-half years ago I came back to the Lord. I promised God then that I would pray every day until God brought a church to our town. You are the answer to my prayers."

We didn't have to take a survey. God had just shown us where He was at work! And that was our invitation to join Him. We went back and joyfully shared with our church what God was doing. The congregation immediately voted to start a new church in Allan. That congregation has now sponsored several mission churches of its own.

There may have been times when God has given you opportunities to join Him by revealing where He's at work. But perhaps when you saw the evidence of His activity, you failed to identify it as God's work. You say to yourself, "Well, I don't know if God wants me to get involved here or not. I had better pray about it." By the time you pray, the opportunity to join God may pass. On the other hand, a tender, sensitive heart, prepared through a love relationship with the Father, will be ready to respond to God at the slightest prompting.

Things Only God Can Do

If you are going to join God, you obviously need to know where He is working. Scripture tells us there are some things only God can do. So when you learn to identify these things and when you see them happening around you, you will immediately recognize God's activity.

The Bible declares that no one can come to Christ unless the Father draws him (see John 6:44). People will not seek God or pursue spiritual matters unless the Spirit of God is at work in their lives. Suppose a neighbor, a colleague, or one of your children begins to inquire about spiritual issues. You do not have to question whether God is drawing that individual. He is the only One who can do that. If they're asking, God is at work.

Many people who have applied this understanding to their witnessing have found great freedom. They pray and watch to see how God is working in the lives of others. When they see or hear someone seeking God, they recognize this as their invitation to bear witness to the God they know and serve. We do not have to pressure or manipulate people into a discussion about Christ or a decision for Christ. We cannot assume the role of the Holy Spirit. However, when we discern that the Spirit is working in someone, we can confidently share our faith because we know the Holy Spirit has gone before us.

An Unbelieving Spouse

I have known many a Christian who was deeply concerned because a husband or wife is an unbeliever. As a result, the believer would continually speak to his or her partner about the need for God. However, this persistence at times actually frustrated the nonbeliever and drove the spouse further from God. When the Christians come to me and tearfully share that they have done all they know to do but the mate seems more resistant than ever, I suggest they might be attempting to do what only the Holy Spirit can do. "Instead of trying to convict your spouse of sin," I say, "pray for your spouse daily and then watch to see when the Holy Spirit prepares him or her for a spiritual conversation."

Invariably, once the Christians back away from browbeating the spouse into a decision for Christ and instead began watching to see how God draws the partner to Himself, everything changes. Suddenly, the nonbelieving spouse will one day declare he or she wants to go to church, or the person will begin reading the Bible or a Christian book. When Christians watch to see where the Holy Spirit is working—even in an unbelieving spouse!—they are often surprised to see how God has gently but persistently been working toward the spouse's salvation.

The following Scriptures describe how the Holy Spirit works in our lives:

- "If you love Me, you will keep My commandments. And I will ask the Father, and He will give you another Counselor to be with you forever. He is the Spirit of truth. The world is unable to receive Him

God Invites You to Join Him

because it doesn't see Him or know Him. But you do know Him, because He remains with you and will be in you." (John 14:15–17)
- "But the Counselor, the Holy Spirit—the Father will send Him in My name—will teach you all things and remind you of everything I have told you." (John 14:26)
- "When He comes, He will convict the world about sin, righteousness, and judgment." (John 16:8)

When you are born again, you enter a love relationship with Jesus Christ—God Himself. At that point the Counselor, the Spirit of truth, takes up residence in your life. He is always present to teach you. The Holy Spirit also convicts you of guilt regarding sin. He convicts the world of righteousness and judgment.

Here is a summary of some things only God can do:

- God draws people to Himself.
- God causes people to seek after Him.
- God reveals spiritual truth.
- God convicts the world of guilt regarding sin.
- God convicts the world of righteousness.
- God convicts the world of judgment.

IDENTIFYING GOD'S ACTIVITY

God is at work when you see someone coming to Christ, asking about spiritual matters, beginning to understand spiritual truth, experiencing conviction of sin, being convinced of the righteousness of Christ or of God's judgment. When I was speaking in a series of meetings, Bill, a plant manager, said, "You know, I have not been looking on the job to see the activity of God." He mentioned Christian people in key positions in his plant, and he wondered if God had placed them in those jobs for a purpose. He decided to gather his believing coworkers together and suggest, "Let's see if God wants to reach our unbelieving colleagues in this plant through us."

Does that sound like something God might want to do? Yes! Your job is not merely a place to earn a paycheck. It is an arena in which God wants to use you to influence others for the kingdom. Suppose you were in Bill's place and planning to bring these Christians together. How would you proceed?

1. *Start by praying.* Only the Father knows what He has purposed for the people in your workplace, and He knows the best way to accomplish His will there. He knows why He brought these particular Christians together and put them in their current positions. If God impresses on these Christians that they need to reach out to their colleagues, then this is clear evidence God is at work. After you pray, watch to see what God does next. Take note of what people are saying when they approach you.

2. *Make the connection.* Suppose someone in the plant approaches a Christian employee and says, "My family is really having a tough time financially." Or, " I am having a really difficult time with my teenager." You have just prayed, "Oh God, show me where You are at work." Make the connection between your prayer and what happens next. If you do not pay attention to what follows your prayer, you may miss God's answer.

3. *Ask questions.* Ask the kind of probing questions that will reveal what is happening in people's lives. Don't merely chat about trivial matters with your friends and colleagues. Make inquiries of people who cross your path to find out what God is doing in their lives. Without being intrusive or aggressive, you can ask questions such as:

- What's been happening in your life lately?
- What's the greatest challenge in your life right now?
- What's the most significant thing happening in your life right now?
- You sound like you're carrying a heavy load. Is there any way I can help?
- How can I pray for you?

4. *Listen attentively.* Suppose the person responds, "I'm not much of a churchgoer, but lately with this problem with my teenager, I sure have been thinking about God." Or, "When I was a kid, I used to go to Sunday school. My parents made me go. I got away from it, but the financial problems I am facing have really caused me to think about God lately." Those statements reveal God at work in the person's life. He may be drawing the person to Himself, causing him or her to seek God or be convicted of sin.

5. *Be prepared to respond.* If someone confides a personal need, pray for that person and ask God how you might minister practically in response. Be ready to share clearly how Christ's presence has made a difference in your life and how Christ is ready to enter their life and change them as well.

To summarize: When you want to know what God is doing around you, pray. Watch to see what happens next. Make the connection between your prayer and ensuing events. Ask questions and listen attentively as people share their concerns. Be ready to make whatever adjustments are required to join God in what He is doing.

A Visitor Came by "Accident"

One Sunday, a visitor named Ben read a note at the bottom of our church bulletin: "Pray for our mission in Kyle; pray for our mission in Prince Albert; pray for our mission in Love; pray for our mission in Regina; pray for our mission in Blaine Lake," and others. He was intrigued.

I explained that our church had made a commitment that, if God ever shows us where someone desires a Bible study or a church, we will respond. Ben asked, "You mean to say that if I were to ask you to come and help us start a church in my town, you would come?" I told him we would, and he started to cry. Ben had a construction business in Leroy, a small town seventy-five miles east of our city. He said he had been pleading with people to start a church in his community for twenty-four years, but nobody had wanted to help. He asked us to come.

We purchased two lots on the main street and established a church in Leroy. Ben was so excited he bought a portable school building and moved it to the site. A few years later, he began acting as lay pastor in a mission church. Both of his sons responded to the call to the gospel ministry.

As a congregation, we were already conditioned to seeing things only God could do. When He revealed that He was working in Leroy through Ben, we immediately saw this as our invitation to join Him. Taking this approach meant we did not have to continually come up with new ministry or master plans for our church. Instead, we asked God to guide us to know each new church plant or outreach He wanted us to undertake. Frequently, the reason God's people miss His activity is that they are not committed to joining Him. They want God to bless their plans, not to adjust to His will.

Don't keep asking God to bless your plans and goals or those of your church. Rather, look for God's invitation to join Him in accomplishing His work. The presence and activity of God in your life will bring a blessing as a result of your obedience. When you identify where God is at work and respond in love to His invitation, you'll experience Him at work in and through your life. There is no more wonderful experience than being at the heart of God's activity.

Who can tell what a solitary visit by a stranger might mean in your church? Ask some questions about what God is presently doing in that person's life. Then you will know how to adjust your life to be an instrument of God so He will accomplish His purposes. In addition, the following two factors are important in responding to God's invitation.

When God Speaks

When God reveals to you what He is doing, that is the time for you to respond. He speaks when He is about to accomplish His purposes. That is true throughout Scripture. But keep in mind, the final completion of God's work may be a long time off. Abram's son was born twenty-five years after the promise from God. However, God began adjusting Abram's life as soon as He spoke to him.

The time God speaks to you is the moment for your response. You need to immediately begin adjusting your life to Him. You may need to prepare yourself for what He is going to do through you.

What God Initiates

God said through Isaiah, "Yes, I have spoken; so I will also bring it about. I have planned it; I will also do it" (Isa. 46:11). What God initiates, He completes. Earlier, Isaiah warned God's people, saying, "The LORD of Hosts has sworn: As I have planned, so it will be; as I have purposed it, so it will happen . . . The LORD of Hosts Himself has planned it; therefore, who can stand in its way? It is His hand that is outstretched, so who can turn it back?" (Isa. 14:24, 27). God says that if He ever lets His people know what He is about to do, it is as good as done—He Himself will bring it to pass (see also 1 Kings 8:56). Likewise in the New Testament, we read that "He who started a good work in you will carry it on to completion until the day of Christ Jesus" (Phil. 1:6). We must recognize when God is the One speaking. When He says something, we can be sure it will be so.

The implications of God's promises are enormous. Once we know we've heard from God, we can proceed with absolute confidence, even if we can't see how things will work out. God always stands by His word. He has never yet failed to fulfill His word, and He does not intend to fail in your life. So, when God shows you what He is about to do where you are, you can step out in obedience, assured that the Lord will accomplish His purposes.

Be sure you always base your understanding of God on Scripture, not on personal opinion or experience alone. Throughout history, people have claimed to have a word from the Lord, and then it did not come to pass. Just because people claim to have heard from God does not mean they have, indeed, received a divine message. The verification of God's message is that what a person hears becomes a reality.

Summary

God takes the initiative to involve His people with Him in His work. He does this on His timetable, not ours. He's the One who is already at work in our world. When He opens your spiritual eyes to see where He is at work, that revelation is your invitation to join Him. You will know where He is working when you see Him doing things only God can do. When God reveals His work to you, that is the time He wants you to begin adjusting to Him and His activity. What God purposes, He guarantees to complete.

The third reality concerning God's invitation is closely related to the fourth—God speaks. In fact, the two occur together. The next several chapters will describe more fully how to know when God is speaking to you. Read slowly, and allow God time to teach you to recognize His voice.

Experiencing God Today

Reflect on what is happening around you. Try to identify things God is presently initiating in your life. Pray over each one, and allow the Holy Spirit to give you further clarification regarding what He intends to do in and through your life.

QUESTIONS FOR REFLECTION

1. Are there times when God showed you His activity, and you missed it? If so, why do you think that happened?

2. Do you presently see God at work around your life? Are you willing to respond to His invitation to adjust your life and join Him? If not, what is holding you back?

10

GOD SPEAKS TO HIS PEOPLE

The one who is from God listens to God's words. This is why you don't listen, because you are not from God. (John 8:47)

GOD SPEAKS

If anything is clear from reading Scripture, this fact is apparent: God speaks to His people. At the beginning of the Bible, we find Him speaking to Adam and Eve in the garden of Eden. He conversed with Abraham and the other patriarchs. He spoke to the judges, kings, and prophets. God was in Christ Jesus speaking to the disciples. God communicated with the early church, and as the biblical record comes to a close, God spoke to John on the Isle of Patmos. God speaks to His people, and you can anticipate that He will communicate with you, too.

Years ago as I addressed a group of ministers, one pastor took me aside and said, "I vowed I would never, ever again listen to a man like you. You talk as though God is personal and talks to you. I just despise that." I asked him, "Are you having difficulty hearing God's voice?" He and I took time to talk, and before long, we were on our knees. He was weeping and grateful God had spoken to him.

Oh, there are people who argue that God no longer speaks to people, but don't let anyone intimidate you about hearing from God.

Deep within the heart of every believer is a desire and a need to commune with their God.

The crux of understanding and experiencing God is to know clearly when He is speaking. If a Christian doesn't know when God is speaking, that person is in trouble at the core of his or her Christian life! Read some of what the Bible says about God speaking to His people:

- Long ago God spoke to the fathers by the prophets at different times and in different ways. In these last days, He has spoken to us by His Son. (Heb. 1:1–2)
- "The one who is from God listens to God's words. This is why you don't listen, because you are not from God." (John 8:47)

The Old Testament

The Bible reveals that God spoke at many times and in a variety of ways. Some of the ways people heard God speak in the Old Testament were through:

- angels (see Gen. 16)
- visions (see Gen. 15)
- dreams (see Gen. 28:10–19)
- Urim and Thummim (see Exod. 28:30)
- symbolic actions (see Jer. 18:1–10)
- a gentle whisper (see 1 Kings 19:12)
- miraculous signs (see Exod. 8:20–25)
- prophets (see Deut. 18:18–22)
- burning bush (see Exod. 3:1-4)
- symbolic actions (see Isa. 20)

The fact *that* God spoke to people is far more important than *how* He spoke. When He spoke, people knew it was God, and they knew what God was saying. In studying the Old Testament Scriptures, I see four important factors present every time God spoke. The experience of Moses and the burning bush recorded in Exodus 3 provides a good example.

1. *When God spoke, the way He communicated was often unique to the individual.* For instance, Moses had no precedent for a burning bush experience. When he encountered one while herding sheep in the desert, he could not say, "At last! This is my burning bush experience. My fathers Abraham, Isaac, and Jacob had their encounters with burning bushes, and I guess this is mine." There are no other occurrences of God speaking that way. It was a singular event. There is no reference in Scripture that God ever again encountered someone in this way. And yet, that event with the shepherd Moses was perfectly suited to the moment as God revealed the amazing work He was about to accomplish.

God makes our experience with Him and His voice personal to us. He wants us to focus on our relationship with Him and not on the method by which He speaks. For example, if God chose always to communicate His will by having us roll a pair of dice, then every time we faced a confusing situation, we would immediately turn to the dice rather than to Him.

At times, I hear people say God speaks to them through certain preachers or conferences or activities, so they continually turn to those when they need to receive God's guidance. However, it is possible to trust more in a Christian conference or a preacher than in God. God will not tolerate any substitute for a relationship with Him. As with people in Scripture, the key in your life is not *how* God speaks but *that* He speaks.

2. *When God spoke, the person was sure it was God.* Moses did not have any reference point for hearing God speak from a burning bush. Yet the Scripture testifies that Moses had no question that his encounter was with God—the "I AM WHO I AM" (Exod. 3:14). He trusted God, obeyed what He told him to do, and experienced God acting just as He promised He would. Could Moses logically prove to someone else that he had heard from God through a burning bush? No, all Moses could do was testify to his encounter with God. Only God could cause His people to know that the word He gave Moses was a message from the God of their fathers, and the same truth applies today. Only God can verify a word He speaks to you.

When someone like Gideon lacked confidence, God graciously provided additional assurance. When Gideon first looked for a sign, he prepared a sacrifice. "The Angel of the LORD extended the tip of the staff that was in His hand and touched the meat and the unleavened bread. Fire came up from the rock and consumed the meat and the unleavened bread. Then the Angel of the Lord vanished from his sight. When Gideon realized that He was the Angel of the Lord, he said, 'Oh no, Lord God! I have seen the Angel of the Lord face to face!'" (Judg. 6:21–22). Gideon was sure God had spoken. Nevertheless, Gideon asked for an additional sign because he was frightened by what God had told him!

3. *When God spoke, the person knew what God said*. Moses knew what God was telling him to do. He knew how God wanted to work through him. That is why Moses raised so many objections. He knew God had high expectations. This was true for Moses, and it was true for Noah, Abraham, Sarah, Joseph, David, Daniel, and others. God didn't use riddles. He made His message clear.

4. *When God spoke, that* was *the encounter with God*. Moses would have been foolish to say, "This has been a wonderful experience with this burning bush. I hope it leads me to an encounter with God!" The bush *was* the encounter with God! When God reveals truth to you—by whatever means—that is an encounter with Him, an experience of His presence and work in your life. God is the only One who can cause you to experience His presence or hear His voice.

At times I'll hear someone tell me of a deeply moving worship service. Or talk about an awesome experience while mountain climbing or when reading the Bible. Often, it will become clear that this person has missed the most important aspect of what has happened. He or she did not merely experience a moving worship service or breathtaking scenery or a profound Scripture passage. This person just encountered God! It is all too easy for us to be distracted from God if we focus on the means through which God speaks.

This reality of God speaking is evident throughout the Old Testament. The methods He used to communicate differed from person to person. What's important is:

- God spoke uniquely to His people.
- Each person knew it was God.
- Each knew what He said.

The Gospels

The Gospels record God speaking through His Son, Jesus. The Gospel of John opens this way: "In the beginning was the Word, and the Word was with God, and the Word was God. . . . The Word became flesh and took up residence among us" (John 1:1, 14). God became flesh in the Person of Jesus Christ. (See also 1 John 1:1–4.)

Even though the twelve disciples knew Jesus personally, they did not immediately understand who Jesus was. On one occasion, Philip said, "Lord, show us the Father, and that's enough for us" (John 14:8). Jesus said to him, "Have I been among you all this time without your knowing Me, Philip? The one who has seen Me has seen the Father. How can you say, 'Show us the Father?' Don't you believe that I am in the Father and the Father is in Me? The words I speak to you I do not speak on My own. The Father who lives in Me does His works" (John 14:9–10).

When Jesus spoke, the Father was communicating through Him. When Jesus did a miracle, the Father was doing His work through Jesus.

The Gospels testify that God spoke through Christ Jesus. When the disciples heard Jesus, they heard God. Just as surely as Moses was face-to-face with God at the burning bush, the disciples were face-to-face with God in a personal relationship with Jesus. When Mary Magdalene or the rich young ruler or Zacchaeus spoke with Jesus, they were encountering God.

Acts to the Present

When we move from the Gospels to the book of Acts, which records that God sent His Holy Spirit, and then to the present, we often change our whole mind-set. We live as if God quit speaking personally to His people. As a result, we fail to realize that an encounter with the Holy Spirit is an encounter with God. God has spoken to His people throughout church history, and He speaks to us today. From the time of Pentecost to the present, God has been speaking to His people by the Holy Spirit.

At conversion, the Holy Spirit takes up residence in the life of every believer. "Don't you know that you are God's sanctuary and that the Spirit of God lives in you?" (1 Cor. 3:16). "Your body is a sanctuary of the Holy Spirit who is in you, whom you have from God" (1 Cor. 6:19). Because He is always present in every Christian, He can speak to you clearly at any time and in any way He chooses.

Jesus promised His disciples that the Spirit would help them in the same way Jesus had (see John 14:16). He said the Holy Spirit would guide them into all truth (see John 16:13); would convict them of sin, righteousness, and judgment (see John 16:7); prepare them for things to come (see John 16:13); glorify Christ; take what He heard from the heavenly Father and share it with them (see John 16:14–15); and bring to their remembrance what Jesus had said (see John 14:26). The Holy Spirit will also help believers to pray (see Romans 8:26). God intended for the Holy Spirit to be extremely active in believers' lives, communicating His will and purposes to them.

Spoken to at Church

My wife, Marilynn, and I attend a large church. Near the beginning of each worship service, the church has a prayer time where the pastor prays and people are invited to the front of the auditorium to meet with God. One Sunday as everyone bowed their heads, I looked around instead. Several people were kneeling at the front of the auditorium, and my attention was drawn to one young man who seemed to be praying fervently. I quickly sensed the Holy Spirit moving me to join the young man. I knelt beside him and, after a few moments, I prayed out loud that the young man would surrender himself to everything God was saying to him. Suddenly, he exclaimed, "It's you! It's you!" The man told me he had just completed law school, but God had been working powerfully in his life, leading him to go to seminary and become a minister. He feared telling his parents, knowing they'd be disappointed since they had put him through law school. So that morning he had come to pray. He asked God to send someone to help him know for certain whether he should pursue the ministry. He said, "Dr. Blackaby, you've written a book about doing the will of God. God sent you to help me."

How did I know at that moment a young life was at a pivotal moment? I didn't. But the Holy Spirit did. How could I have known that, of all those who were praying at the front that morning, this young man would be the most significantly impacted by my joining him? I didn't. But the Holy Spirit did. The Holy Spirit, on that Sunday morning at my church, knew the truth of that situation, and He guided me into action.

How Do I Know When God Speaks?

Sin has affected us so deeply (see Rom. 3:10–11) that you and I cannot understand the truth of God unless the Holy Spirit reveals it to us. He is our teacher. As you read your Bible, be open to the Spirit as He teaches you the Word of God. As you pray, watch how the Holy Spirit uses Scripture to confirm in your heart what God is saying. Observe what He is doing around you in the circumstances of life. The God who is speaking to you as you pray and the God who is speaking to you in the Scriptures is the same God who is at work around you daily.

The evidence of the Scriptures can encourage you at this point. The Bible illustrates that when God chose to speak to an individual, that person had no doubt it was God, and it was clear what God was saying. When God speaks to you, you can know He is the One speaking, and you, too, can understand clearly what He is saying. Jesus explained, "The one who enters by the door is the shepherd of the sheep . . . and the sheep hear his voice. He calls his own sheep by name and leads them out . . . I am the good shepherd. I know My own sheep, and they know Me" (John 10:2–4, 14).

Knowing God's voice is not a matter of honing a method or discovering a formula. Recognizing God's voice comes from an intimate love relationship with Him. Those who do not have the relationship do not hear what God is saying (see John 8:47). Since God will uniquely communicate with you in the intimacy of your walk with Him, your relationship with Him is of utmost importance.

The Key to Knowing God's Voice: A Love Relationship

You become familiar with God's voice as you experience Him. As God speaks and you respond, you will recognize His voice more and more readily. Some people try to bypass the love relationship. They look for a miraculous sign, or set out a "fleece" (see Judg. 6), or try a formula to discover God's will. But there is no substitute for an intimate relationship with God.

I've outlined below some of the ways well-meaning people try to discern God's voice. Yet, while these approaches may cite particular Scriptures, they misunderstand what the Bible is teaching.

1. *Asking for a miraculous sign.* When the scribes and Pharisees asked Jesus for a miraculous sign, He condemned them as "an evil and adulterous generation" (Matt. 12:38–39). They were so self-centered and sinful they could not recognize that God was present in their midst (see Luke 19:41–44). Don't be like them, seeking for miraculous signs to validate a word from God. Learn to know God's voice so you don't have to subject everything God says to a series of tests and proofs.

2. *Seeking a method.* A formula is not the way to hear God's voice, either. Moses heard from God through a burning bush. Balaam heard God speak through a donkey even though he had never heard God talk through a donkey before. If Balaam lived in our formula-driven day, perhaps he would have written a book, *Donkeys for Dummies*, so people could discern when God was speaking to them through a donkey, too!

How many other burning bush experiences were there? None, as I've said before. God does not want us to become experts at using a formula to hear Him speak. He wants an intimate love relationship with us, so we'll depend on Him alone.

3. *"Name it and claim it" method.* Some people like to open their Bibles, pick out a verse they want to use, and claim it as a word from God for their situation. This is a misguided and self-centered approach to determining God's will. You may ask, "Can't I get a word from God from the Bible?" Of course you can! But only the Holy Spirit can reveal to you which truth of Scripture is God's Word for your particular circumstance. You cannot force God to speak to you or to reveal truth by choosing a verse and declaring it to be God's word for you. God always takes the initiative in speaking to us and in revealing His will. He does it in His way and in His time.

You also need to be careful about publicly claiming you have received a word from God. Announcing that God spoke to you concerning a matter is serious business. If God did speak to you, you must continue in the direction He led you until what He promised comes to pass (even for twenty-five years, like Abram). If you have not been given a word from God, yet you say you have, you are perilously in danger of being a false prophet. Scripture warns: "You may say to yourself, 'How can we recognize a message the LORD has not spoken?' When a prophet speaks in the LORD's name, and the message does not come true or is not fulfilled, that is a message the LORD has not spoken, The prophet has spoken it presumptuously. Do not be afraid of him" (Deut. 18:21–22). The lesson is straightforward. If God has spoken, what He said will occur. God always vindicates His Word.

In Old Testament law, the penalty for a false prophet was death (Deut. 18:20). Do not take a word from God lightly. Likewise, people in the church ought to be held accountable if what they claim God told them doesn't come to pass.

4. *Open and closed doors.* Some folks try to hear God's voice and know His will only through circumstances. I hear people say things like: "Lord, I need to know if I should take this particular job. I'm going to tell them I will accept, but please stop the process if you don't want me to take that job." In each situation they pray: "Stop me if I am wrong, and bless me if I am right." Another version of this is: "Lord, I will proceed in this direction. Close the door if it is not Your will." The only problem is, this is not the pattern in Scripture for knowing God's will.

God does use circumstances to speak to us. But we will often be led astray if that is our only means of determining God's directions. Nowhere in the Bible does God promise to stop us from making mistakes! He does not assure us He will intervene if we proceed to take a job that will bring us heartache and frustration. He calls on us to seek Him and His will at the front end. It is foolish to walk carelessly through doors of opportunity without seeking God's guidance, blithely hoping God will work all things together for good.

THE WORD IS OUR GUIDE

The pattern I see in Scripture is that God always gives a direction on the front end of His assignments. He may not tell you all you want to know at the start, but He will reveal what you *need* to know to make the necessary adjustments and to take the first step of obedience. As long as you are doing all that God has already instructed, you don't have to fret about how every detail will work out.

You can't allow yourself to be guided by experience alone, and neither should you depend solely on tradition, a method, or a formula. Often people trust these ways because they seem easier than cultivating an intimate walk with God. People do as they please and put the burden of responsibility on God to rescue them from undesirable consequences of their actions. If they make a mistake in their haste to move forward, they assume God will intervene and stop them. If they end up in the wrong place, they blame Him for letting them go that way. If you want to know the will and voice of God, you must invest the time and effort to develop a love relationship with Him.

He wants you to recognize His voice and know His will. Your relationship to Him is the key to hearing when God speaks to you. If you do not already have that kind of relationship with God, start right now by praying. Ask God to guide you into such a relationship, and commit yourself to invest the time and effort to know Him better.

The Holy Spirit's Assignment

"What no eye has seen and no ear has heard, and what has never come into a man's heart, is what God has prepared for those who love Him. Now God has revealed them to us by the Spirit, for the Spirit searches everything, even the deep things of God.... No one knows the concerns of God except the Spirit of God. Now we have not received the spirit of the world, but the Spirit who is from God, in order to know what has been freely given to us by God" (1 Cor. 2:9–12). The Holy Spirit knows the thoughts and counsel of the heavenly Father. The Spirit understands the Father's purposes for your life, and the Spirit's exciting role is to help you understand and receive everything God wants to give you.

When God spoke to Abraham, Moses, Mary, and others, those events were encounters with God. An encounter with Jesus for the disciples was an encounter with God. In the same way, when you encounter the Holy Spirit, that is an encounter with God for you.

Now that the Holy Spirit has been given to believers, He is the One who guides you into all truth and teaches you all things. You understand spiritual truth because the Holy Spirit is working in your life. You could study the Bible at a great university and earn a

God Speaks to His People

doctor's degree in biblical studies, but unless the Holy Spirit opens your spiritual eyes to understand even the simplest spiritual truths contained in its pages, you will not recognize or understand them. When you come to the Word of God, the Author Himself is present to instruct you. You never *discover* truth; truth is *revealed*. When the Holy Spirit reveals truth to you, He is not leading you to an encounter with God. That *is* an encounter with God!

God's Voice in a Tornado

I was speaking at a conference one day when a retired couple approached me during a break. They told me that several years earlier, God had convicted them that they should take early retirement from their jobs and spend the next years of their lives doing international missions. They told God they would do that, but they were about to build a new home, and they had one child they were still helping through college. They assured God that, once all their children were out of school and they had built their home, they would go.

Their son eventually completed his studies, and their dream home was finished, but they didn't go. They enjoyed their comfortable home and the free time they now had to visit family and to golf at their club. Then recently, a violent tornado swept right over their house, tearing it to splinters and leaving only rubble.

"What do you think we should do?" they asked. "Obey immediately!" was my response. Receiving a word from God is always a serious matter. Never treat it casually or lightly. The Holy Spirit has any number of ways to speak to us. Some are louder than others.

Respond Immediately

When God spoke to Moses, Moses' next move was crucial. After Jesus spoke to the disciples, what they did next was pivotal. What you do after the Holy Spirit speaks will have enormous consequences for you and those around you. Too often when the Spirit of God speaks to us, we launch into a protracted discussion with Him, questioning the correctness of His directions. Moses tried it at the burning bush (see Exod. 3:11–4:13), and it limited him for the rest of his life. Because of Moses's objections, God assigned Aaron to be a spokesman for Moses. He had to speak to the people through his brother Aaron (see Exod. 4:14–16). Eventually, Aaron caused Moses considerable grief when he made a golden calf for the rebellious Hebrews (see Exod. 32:1–6). Aaron, together with Miriam, led a challenge to Moses' leadership. Moses paid a high price for arguing with God (see Num. 12:1–8).

I encourage you to review on a regular basis what you sense God has been saying to you. If God speaks and you hear but do not respond, a time could come when you will not hear His voice. Disobedience can lead to a "famine . . . of hearing the words of the LORD" (Amos 8:11).

When Samuel was a young boy, God began to speak to him. The Scriptures say, "Samuel grew, and the LORD was with him and let nothing he said prove false" (1 Sam. 3:19). Be like Samuel. Don't let a single word from the Lord fail to bear fruit in your life. Then God will do in you and through you everything He promises.

Luke 8:5–15 records Jesus' parable of the sower and the seeds. The seed that fell on the good soil represents those who hear the Word of God, respond positively, and produce fruit. Jesus said, "Therefore, take care how you listen. For whoever has, more will be given to him; and whoever does not have, even what he thinks he has will be taken away from him" (Luke 8:18). If you hear the Word of God and do not apply it to produce fruit in your life, your disobedience will cost you. Make up your mind now that when the Spirit of God speaks, you are going to do what He says.

BARREN DISOBEDIENCE

While I was a pastor, there was a man in my church who seemed to constantly struggle in every area of his life. He lost his job every few years. His marriage was in trouble. His children rebelled, and he was often at odds with other church members. It seemed that something was terribly wrong at the core of his walk with God. One day, I asked him to share with me about his life and spiritual pilgrimage. He told me that when he was a young man, God had profoundly encountered him and called him to prepare to serve in Christian ministry. The man applied to a Bible college and intended to attend that coming fall. But at that same time, he also met a young woman, and it appeared their relationship would lead to marriage. So he delayed going to Bible college.

They were married and sought to purchase a house. Children were soon on the way, and debts began mounting. At first, this man continued to plan how he could afford to go to Bible college and become a minister. But as the years rolled by, he eventually shelved those thoughts. The one thing the man had been vainly pursuing—financial security—was something God never granted him. Every time it seemed he was beginning to advance in his career and earn a comfortable salary, his company would go bankrupt, or it would be purchased by a competitor, and he would be let go. Now he was middle-aged, unhappy, and unfulfilled. It became obvious he had disobeyed a clear word from God, and his life had suffered spiritual barrenness ever since. How we respond to God's word to us contains profound, long-lasting consequences for us and for our families.

God Speaks with a Purpose

People often want God to give them some kind of nice devotional thought to help them feel good during the day, but if you want the God of the universe to communicate with you, you need to be ready for Him to reveal what He is doing where you are. In Scripture, God is not often seen speaking to people just for conversation's sake. He's always preparing to do something. When God speaks to you, He has a purpose in mind for your life.

When God spoke to Abram (see Gen. 12), what was He planning to do? He was about to begin building a nation through which He would bless all the nations of earth. Notice the timing. Why did God speak to Abram when He did? Because it was at that point God wanted to begin building a nation. The moment Abram learned what God was about to do, he had to adjust his life. He immediately had to begin living his life in accord with what God had said so he could be of service to God.

God Speaks at the Right Time

Some of us assume we have the next few months to think about what God said and to consider whether this is the best timing, to see when we can best fit His instructions into our crowded schedules. But God speaks in *His* timing. He communicates with His servant when He is ready to move. As God enters into the mainstream of your life, the promptness of your response is crucial. The moment God speaks to you, that is the time to respond.

God speaks when He has a purpose in mind for your life. Two things are crucial as you respond: First, you must immediately begin to adjust your life to what He says. Second, you must be prepared to remain obedient as long as it takes for God to fulfill His purposes. It took twenty-five years for Abraham to develop into a man suitable to raise Isaac, the child God had promised. God was concerned not just about Abram but about a nation. Abraham's quality as a father would affect his son and the generations that followed. Abram had to begin adjusting his life to God's ways immediately. He could not wait until Isaac was born and then try to become the man God wanted Isaac's father to be.

God Develops Character to Match the Assignment

When God speaks with the purpose of revealing an assignment to you, you need to trust what He says. He knows exactly what He is doing in and through your life. Don't rule out what God may be saying just because it doesn't match what you want to hear or what you think is possible.

When God called Abram, He said, "I will bless you, I will make your name great" (Gen. 12:2). That means: "I will develop your character to match your assignment." Nothing is more pathetic than a small character in a big assignment. Many of us don't want to give attention to our character. We just want the big assignment from God.

Serving Where God Places You

Suppose a seminary graduate is waiting for a big church to call him to be their pastor. Then a small congregation contacts him and says, "Will you be bivocational and help us out here in western Wyoming?"

"Well, no," the prospective pastor responds. He thinks, "I am waiting for God to give me a position that matches all my gifts and training. I have gained extensive education, and I can't waste my life serving in a small setting that doesn't utilize my experience and skills. It doesn't make sense."

Or suppose you want to serve in your church as an adult Bible teacher. However, the church's director of religious education tells you the only opening is with teaching youth. The director tells you of the difficulty she's had finding people who will invest their lives in the teenagers. But this is not what you were looking for. You taught married adults in your last church, and you enjoyed it so much you want to do the same in your new church. So you tell the director you will just bide your time until the right job comes along.

Do you see how self-centered that attitude is? Human reasoning will not give you God's perspective. If you can't be faithful in a little, God will not give you the larger assignment. He may want to adjust your character through small assignments in order to prepare you for larger ones. He may want to lead you into an entirely new experience so He can develop a particular dimension of your character. Moreover, God knows the needs of a smaller congregation or the youth at your church, and those needs are more important than you remaining in your comfort zone or relying on your expertise and perceived skills. God starts to work when you respond in obedience to what *He* wants, even if it isn't what you were seeking or anticipating. When you make the adjustments and obey, you come to know Him by experience. This is the goal of God's activity in your life—that you come to know Him.

Do you want to experience God working mightily in and through you? Then adjust your life to God in the kind of relationship where you follow Him wherever He leads you—even if the assignment seems small or insignificant. Wouldn't you love to hear: "Well done, good and faithful slave! You were faithful over a few things; I will put you in charge of many things. Share your master's joy" (Matt. 25:21)?

Do not misunderstand the point here. Don't assume an assignment must be from God just because it is small or unexpected. Whether the assignment is large or small in your eyes, you will still have to determine whether it is from God. God is the One who can tell you that. The important thing is not to rule out an assignment on the basis of your preconceived ideas. God may well give you an assignment that takes you outside your experience or comfort level. Remember—you will know what His will is through your relationship with God. *Don't bypass the relationship.*

I have known people who wouldn't interrupt a fishing trip or a football game for anything. They say they want to serve God, but they keep eliminating from their lives anything that might interfere with their own plans. They are so self-centered, they don't recognize when God comes to them. There are Christians who spend great time and energy to make their lives as comfortable as possible. They immediately reject any initiative God brings into their lives that could create discomfort.

God has a right to interrupt your life. He is Lord. When you surrendered to Him, you acknowledged His right to help Himself to your life at His prerogative. If you are God-centered, you will adjust your plans to what God wants to do.

Responsive Servants

Suppose that five times out of ten, when the master had something for his servant to do, the servant said, "I'm sorry. That's not on my agenda." What do you suppose the master would do? He would discipline the servant, of course. If the servant did not respond to the discipline, sooner or later the master would no longer come with assignments, and the servant would remain outside the activity and purpose of the master. This might suit a secular servant just fine, but it ought to break the heart of Christians to discover God is not working in or through their lives anymore.

You may be saying, "Oh, I wish I could experience God working through me the way John (or Beth) does." But every time God comes to John, John adjusts his life to God and is obedient regardless of the cost. When Beth has been faithful in little assignments, God has given her more important ones. Over the years, Beth has developed the character necessary so God can entrust her with major assignments.

Willing to Go

I've often wondered sort of what turn my life and Marilynn's would have taken if we had been unwilling to accept God's invitation to move to Saskatoon, Canada, to serve Him in that cold and distant place. That assignment called on us to start new churches, to build a college student ministry, and to establish a theological college—all by faith. These were things I had no experience doing and did not necessarily feel gifted to do. Yet now, almost forty years later, I realize that when God asked us to leave our familiar setting to go with Him to Saskatoon, He had far more in mind than we could have ever imagined! I am so glad I did not base the decisions for my life on what I considered to be my strengths and interests. There is no more rewarding or exciting way to live than in obedience to what the Lord asks you to do!

Once God has given you a sense of the direction He is leading and you have said "yes," give Him all the time He wants to develop you into the kind of person He can trust with the assignment. Don't assume that the moment God calls, you are ready for the role. Two important biblical characters demonstrate the need for a time to grow:

1. *David.* How long was it after God anointed David as king that David attained the throne? Perhaps ten or twelve years. What was God doing during that time? He was building David's relationship with Him so David could lead the nation according to God's purposes.

2. *Paul.* How long was it after the Lord called Paul on the Damascus Road that he went on his first missionary journey? Maybe ten or eleven years. God wanted to redeem a lost world, and He wanted to reach the Gentiles through Paul. God took time to prepare Paul for that critical assignment.

Is it for your sake alone that God takes time to prepare you? No, it is also for the good of those He wants to reach through your life. For their benefit, pursue the kind of relationship with God I am describing. Then, when He chooses to work mightily through your life, He will achieve what He wants in the lives of those you touch.

God Gives Specific Directions

Several years ago, I attended a conference where the speaker challenged participants to obey whatever God was asking us to do. Then he told us to take a moment in prayer and think of anything God had asked us to do that we had not yet completed. The only thing I sensed I had not responded to was to write. I had not seen myself as a writer and had been far too busy, I thought, to have time to be an author. I sensed God was asking me to be open to writing, but I really had not been. So during the conference, I surrendered that area of my life to the Lord and told Him that if He wanted me to write anything, I would do so.

To be honest, this did not seem like a major decision. No one had ever asked me to write a book before, so I felt pretty safe with that new commitment. But soon afterward, a man approached to ask if I would write a small book about how God had led our church to be on mission with Him! Immediately, the Holy Spirit reminded me of the commitment I had just made, and I knew I had to agree to this request. I could not have known then that God would provide opportunities for me to write dozens of books. What seemed a task beyond my ability was something God intended to make into a major part of my life and ministry.

God Guides Specifically

A popular teaching says God does not give people specific directives. It claims He gave us brains and the Bible, and these two are sufficient to guide us in all decision making. This position implies that a Christian always thinks correctly, according to God's will. It doesn't take into account that the old nature is constantly at odds with the spiritual nature (see Rom. 7), and it neglects the important fact that our ways are not God's ways (see Isa. 55:8).

After God spoke to Noah about building an ark, Noah knew the size, the type of materials, and how to put it together. When God spoke to Moses about constructing the tabernacle, He was extremely specific about the details. When God became flesh, He gave specific directions to His disciples—where to go, what to do, how to respond to people who accepted or rejected their message, and what to preach.

God called Abraham and said, "Go out from your land, your relatives, and your father's house to the land that I will show you" (Gen. 12:1). Since He was not very specific at first, God's instructions required faith on Abraham's part. But God did promise to reveal His plans as Abraham obeyed. God always provides enough specific directions so you can do what He wants you to do at the moment. When you need to know more, He will guide you. As time went on, God revealed to Abraham that a son would be born to him.

He also spoke to Abraham about the number of his descendants, the territory his people would inhabit, and He revealed that Abraham's descendants would go into bondage, eventually to be delivered.

The Holy Spirit continues to give clear directives today. He will give you unmistakable guidance for your life. You may say, "That has not been my experience." But be careful not to let your personal experience become the measure of what the Christian life is supposed to be like. Rather than dismissing anything you read in the Bible that does not match what you have experienced, ask the Lord to raise the level of your experience to the standard presented in Scripture.

If you have not received instructions from God on a matter, pray and wait. Learn patience. Depend on God's timing, for His agenda is always best. Don't be in a hurry. Don't try to skip over the relationship to get on with the activity.

Satanic Deception?

Frequently, I'm asked, "How can I know whether the word I receive is from God, or if it is actually my own selfish desires, or even Satan?" At times, people are immobilized when they have a sense they should do something because they're afraid Satan may be trying to mislead them. Some Christians go to great trouble studying Satan's ways so they can identify his deceptions, but I don't do that. I'm determined not to focus on Satan—he is defeated. Christ, who guides me and implements His will through me, is the victor. The only way Satan can affect God's work through me is when I believe Satan and doubt God. Satan will try to deceive you, but he cannot ultimately thwart God's purposes.

Counterfeits

When the Royal Canadian Mounted Police train their people in anti-counterfeiting work, the trainees don't focus on counterfeit bills. It is impossible to know all the ways to make fake money. However, only one genuine type of ten-dollar bill exists. So, they thoroughly study the legitimate bill. That way, anything which doesn't measure up can be readily identified as counterfeit. The more intimately aware you are of a genuine article, the easier it is to recognize a fake.

When you sense a leading in your spirit, you may ask, "Is this impulse coming from God, from my own desires, or from Satan?" How can you prepare to know if God is the One guiding you? You need to understand the ways of God thoroughly, and if something doesn't measure up to God's ways, turn away from it immediately. That's what Jesus did when He was tempted in the wilderness (see Matt. 4; Luke 4).

Satan tempted Jesus to take shortcuts: "You want people to follow you? Well, turn these stones into bread, and people will follow you in droves. Or jump from the highest point in the city. When the crowds below witness angels miraculously save you, they'll certainly follow you. Or bow down and worship me. Do that, and you won't have to endure the pain of crucifixion. I'll give you all the nations to serve you." Each time, Satan sounded like he was trying to help Jesus accomplish His work.

Satan was too subtle to try convincing Jesus to abandon His mission. He simply attempted to get Jesus to do God's work in the world's way. But Jesus refused (see Matt. 4:1–11). He never discussed the options with Satan. He never argued. He measured everything against the Scriptures and discarded anything that did not line up with what God had said and done.

Like Jesus' encounter with Satan, your spiritual warfare may involve being tempted to do something that sounds good but is not God's way. Jesus clearly knew His mission and how the Father wanted Him to accomplish it. When Satan tried to get Jesus to go a different route—for "instant success"—Jesus recalled the assignment His Father had given and rejected the false counsel.

Summary

God has always spoken to His people. Today He communicates by the Holy Spirit. The Holy Spirit will use the Bible, prayer, circumstances, and other believers to speak to you. The method, however, is not the key to knowing God's voice. You learn to know the voice of God through an intimate love relationship. God may choose to speak in ways that are unique to you. But be assured that He will be able to convince you that you have heard a word from Him.

When God speaks to you, He will do so with a purpose. The time God speaks is the occasion for you to begin adjusting your life and orienting your thinking to Him. He will work to develop your character for the assignment He has in mind. Let God take all the time He wants to prepare you.

Experiencing God Today

Take some time with God in prayer and think about experiences when you clearly knew God was speaking to you. Ask God to help you recognize His voice. If you do not currently keep a spiritual journal, you may want to begin recording the things God has said to you in the past and what He is saying to you now. Anything Almighty God says to you is important enough to write down!

QUESTIONS FOR REFLECTION

1. What are some ways God has spoken to you? How did you know it was God?

2. How might God be building your character and trust in Him right now in preparation for a new assignment?

3. Have you been willing to accept small assignments from God? How do you think God would evaluate your willingness to be faithful in a little?

4. Do you need God to guide you specifically in a situation in your life? If so, how might you prepare to receive the next guidance He gives you?

11

GOD REVEALS HIMSELF, HIS PURPOSES, AND HIS WAYS

For My thoughts are not your thoughts, and your ways are not My ways. (Isaiah 55:8)

Come, let us go up to the mountain of the Lord . . . He will teach us about His ways so we may walk in His paths. (Micah 4:2)

GOD REVEALED

In a conference I was leading, I explained how Scripture reveals God as a loving Father. At a sharing time that afternoon, a woman rose and, through tears, told the group her story. As she grew up, her father never seemed satisfied with her. She could not earn high enough grades in school to please him. She could not play the piano well enough or achieve anything that satisfied him. Then when she was a teenager, her father abandoned his family and moved in with another woman. She never saw him again. Devastated, this woman constantly wondered whether he might not have turned his back on her if she had been a better daughter or had made him happier at home.

Now, as a married woman with teenage children of her own, she lived in constant fear that she would lose her husband and children, too. Surely when they discovered what she was really like—someone even her own father couldn't love—they would reject her just like he did. She had lived her entire life under this fear. She kept her family and friends at arm's length so they could never get too close. Her painful upbringing tainted her view of God as she had concluded God was just as judgmental, unloving, and hard to please as her earthly father had been. As I had been sharing from Scripture what God was like, however, the Holy Spirit opened her eyes to see that her heavenly Father loved her dearly. This woman had grown up going to church every Sunday and had heard countless sermons about God's love, but not until that day—when the Spirit helped her understand what God was truly like—did she grasp all she'd been missing.

That is one of the roles of the Holy Spirit—to help us know God's nature. The Spirit also helps us understand the ways of God, for God does not act the same way people do. Finally, the Spirit helps believers understand the purposes of God. On our own, we will never discover what God intends to do. God must reveal that to us through His Holy Spirit.

God Reveals His Character

When God speaks by the Holy Spirit to you, He often reveals something about Himself. Notice in the following Scriptures what God reveals about Himself:

- When Abram was 99 years old, the Lord appeared to him, saying, "I am God Almighty." (Gen. 17:1)
- The Lord spoke to Moses: "Speak to the entire Israelite community and tell them: Be holy because I, the Lord your God, am holy." (Lev. 19:1–2)
- "I, Yahweh, have not changed . . . Since the days of your fathers, you have turned from My statutes; you have not kept them. Return to Me, and I will return to you," says the Lord of Hosts. (Mal. 3:6–7)
- [Jesus said to the Jews,] "I am the living bread that came down from heaven. If anyone eats of this bread he will live forever." (John 6:51)

God Reveals Himself, His Purposes, and His Ways

God speaks when He wants to involve people in His work. He unveils His character to help them respond in faith. People can better respond to God's instructions when they believe God is who He says He is and that God can do what He indicates He will do.

God identified Himself to Abram by the name God Almighty. Ninety-nine-year-old Abram needed to know God was all powerful so he could believe God could give him a son in his old age.

To Moses, God revealed His holy nature. Then through Moses, God told His people He was holy. God's people had to believe He was holy so they would respond by being holy themselves. Their lives depended on it.

God spoke through Malachi to Israel and reiterated that He is unchanging and forgiving. God revealed His forgiving nature so the people could believe they would be forgiven if they returned to God.

Jesus called Himself "living bread" and the source of eternal life. Jesus declared He was the way to eternal life so people could believe and respond to Him and receive life.

God makes Himself known to increase our faith so we will obey Him. We must pay close attention to what God reveals about Himself. When God discloses something to you about Himself:

- You will have to believe God is who He says He is;
- You will have to believe God can do what He says He will do;
- You will have to adjust your thinking in light of this belief;
- You will be called upon to obey God, demonstrating your trust in Him;
- When you obey, God will do His work through you and demonstrate that He is who He says He is;
- You will know God by experience;
- You will know He is who He says He is.

For example, when did Abram know God as almighty? Well, perhaps he knew it in his mind as soon as God said it. But he grew to know the Lord by experience as God Almighty when God did something in his life that only God could do. When God gave Abraham (one hundred years old) and Sarah (ninety years old) a son, Abraham knew God to be almighty.

God Reveals His Purposes

A World Missions Strategy Center

Gary Hillyard was the pastor of Beverly Park Church in Seattle, Washington, when attendance averaged around one hundred on Sunday mornings. Forty church members took training to learn to pray, and eight of them subsequently committed themselves to pray daily for God to show them how He wanted to grow their church. Nineteen members began a study of *Experiencing God*.

When immigrants from the Ukraine began attending Beverly Park, the members paid attention and asked God to reveal why He was bringing these international people to their church. One day, one of the new Ukrainian families asked Gary if the church would like to have his father's house in Lugansk, a city of 650,000 in the Ukraine. Gary called me to ask how I thought his church should respond to such an unusual offer. I responded that this sounded like God's invitation for the church to become involved in missions.

Though behind in its budget, Beverly Park voted to accept the house, and the members continued praying. Within weeks, Don English, a friend of Gary's, called. "Do you remember our prayer time seven years ago [before the fall of communism] when I sensed God would one day call me as a missionary to the former Soviet Union? Well, God has told me that now is the time to go."

Gary replied, "I have good news for you. We have your house, and it's in Lugansk, Ukraine." Beverly Park voted to sponsor Don and his family as its missionaries. Gary called me again and said the church only had $21.00 in the bank. "Now what do we do?" he asked.

I suggested they clarify that this was indeed the Lord's leading. Then they needed to trust the Lord to provide for what He called them to do. They spent their Sunday evening service in prayer for God's provision. By the end of the week, they had $4,000 to send to Don and his family in Lugansk.

Once there, Don received invitations to lead Bible studies in homes, in the elementary and high schools, for university faculty, and even for five hundred people at a medical center. When the government heard about Don, they invited him to participate in a ceremony to thank America for their city library, which had been partially funded by the Marshall Plan following World War II. Don agreed. The national television station that broadcast the ceremony asked Don to say a few words. Less than two months into his work, Don was on national television telling the Ukraine about Jesus! Later, he was also invited to speak to the parliament.

Don worked with the local churches to hold evangelistic meetings, and almost five hundred people were converted in a week. They wanted to distribute Bibles in the Lugansk region, so Don called Beverly Park to request prayer. One hour after Beverly Park's prayer meeting, a church in Texas called and said they wanted to buy Bibles for the Ukraine. The Ukrainian government asked for food and medical supplies for the elderly, handicapped, and children in the city. Again, Don called Beverly Park. The next day, Bob Dixon called from a Christian men's organization in Texas. They had been asked by the state department to oversee the distribution of food in the former Soviet republics. He had three forty-foot shipping containers of food that could be sent immediately.

Workers also started a Bible college, provided medical equipment, planted churches, and cared for orphans. Gary wept as he shared with me how his church, which once struggled to pay its electric bill, was now being used by God to touch the world.

God always has far more on His heart to accomplish through our lives and churches than we could possibly imagine. How tragic for us to become so preoccupied with our plans and strategies that we do not even take time to hear what God intends to do.

The Bible is full of examples of people who willingly set aside their plans to follow God's. Mary and Paul are two of the most fascinating.

When God came to Mary, He did not ask her to tell Him her life goals or how she intended to glorify God. The angel of the Lord exclaimed, "Rejoice, favored woman! The Lord is with you!" (Luke 1:28). Then the angel told Mary the incredible news of how God was going to use her to give birth to the Savior of the world. Truly, God's plans dwarfed anything Mary might have planned for herself.

Saul of Tarsus had specific plans he intended to accomplish for God. He was going to hunt down and arrest any Jewish people who had embraced Christianity. But then the risen Christ intercepted him and revealed what God's plans were. God was going to use his life to carry the good news of the gospel to the Gentiles around the known world. Saul would share the gospel before some of the most powerful people in the Roman Empire. To this day, the world feels the impact of what God did through Saul. God's plans were far superior to anything Saul could have set out to accomplish.

This sequence is seen throughout the Bible: patriarchs, judges, David, prophets, and the disciples. When God was about to do something, He took the initiative to involve His servants: "Indeed, the Lord GOD does nothing without revealing His counsel to His servants the prophets" (Amos 3:7). He spoke in order to reveal His purposes and plans. Then God invited those people to become involved so He could carry out His eternal purposes through them.

God's Purposes Versus Our Plans

We often dream our dreams of what we want to do for God. We formulate plans based on our priorities. Then we pray and ask God to bless our efforts and to help us accomplish our goals. (After all, we're doing it for Him!) We mobilize fellow believers to make our schemes successful. What is really important, however, is what God plans to do where we are and how He wants to accomplish His purposes through us. Here is what the Scriptures say about our plans and purposes: "The LORD frustrates the counsel of the nations; He thwarts the plans of the peoples. The counsel of the LORD stands forever, the plans of His heart from generation to generation" (Ps. 33:10–11). "Many plans are in a man's heart, but the LORD's decree will prevail" (Prov. 19:21).

If your agenda is not the same as God's, you will not experience God working through you. God reveals His purposes so you will know what He plans to do. Then you can join Him. His plans and purposes will not be thwarted. They will succeed. The Lord foils the worldly plans of the nations, but His plans come to pass.

Planning is a valuable exercise, but it can never become a substitute for hearing from God. Your plans only have merit when they are based on what God has told you He intends to do. Your relationship with God is far more important to Him than any scheming you can do. The biggest problem with planning is when we try to carry out in our own wisdom what only God has a right to determine. We cannot know the when or where or how of God's will until He tells us.

God intends that we follow Him. He expects us to get our directives from Him, and He wants to equip us to do the assignment he gives. If we try to spell out all the details of His will in a planning session, we'll have a tendency to forget the need for a daily, intimate relationship with God. We may accomplish our objectives but forgo the relationship. It is possible to achieve all of our goals and yet be outside God's will. God created us for an eternal love relationship. Life is our opportunity to experience Him at work in us and in our world.

Planning is not wrong. Just be careful not to plan more than God intends for you to. Let God interrupt or redirect your plans anytime He wants to. Remain in a close relationship with Him so you can always hear His voice when He speaks to you. I have found that the best planning meetings are prayer meetings where we spend time with our Father finding out what He is up to. If churches are really serious about doing God's will, they will spend more time seeking God's will and less time arguing and debating about what each member thinks the church ought to be doing.

Which Method?

My son, Richard, and I were speaking at a conference based on our book *Spiritual Leadership*. I talked about how people and churches must seek to be on God's agenda in all they do. During a break, a pastor hurried up to me to say that he was seeking to move his church forward and that he had been looking at two different church growth models. He mentioned both models and then asked me which one I thought he should use. I told him I thought he should pray and ask God to tell him how to grow his church. The man paused, and then as if he had not even heard me, he went on to explain the merits and drawbacks of each model and then again asked me which model I thought he should follow. Again, I told him he should have his whole congregation cry out to God and ask how He wanted to grow His church in their community.

The pastor never did understand what I was saying. He had been trained that, as a leader, it was up to him to grow his church through the vision he cast and the leadership principles he practiced. Yet Scripture repeatedly tells us that God is always at work to accomplish His purposes among His people. Christ said He would build His church (see Matt. 16:18). The reason there are so many divided and splintered churches today is that church leaders have sought to impose their plans on God's people rather than seeking what God intends to do through them by His amazing power.

God Reveals His Ways

Even the casual or uninformed reader of the Bible can see that God's ways and plans are different from those of people. God uses kingdom principles to accomplish kingdom purposes.

God's ways are redemptive, loving, and compassionate. His ways bring cleansing and forgiveness and build people up. His ways bring humility. His way is the way of service and love. God does not simply wait to help us achieve our goals for Him. He desires to accomplish His own purposes through us—and in His own way.

God said, "For My thoughts are not your thoughts, and your ways are not My ways" (Isa. 55:8). We will not carry out God's plan with our methods. This is one of the basic sin problems people face: "We all went astray like sheep; we all have turned to our own way" (Isa. 53:6). It is foolish to think we can accomplish God's work by using the world's methodology and values.

Our ways may seem good to us. We may even enjoy some moderate successes. If we measure our success strictly by whether our numbers are growing or if we have built an impressive building, we can easily assume we have been successful. But of course, many secular organizations and non-Christian religions are growing in numbers, buildings, and wealth, though they are not pleasing to God.

The world says you should never commit to do anything you cannot afford. Yet God says without faith, it is impossible to please Him (Heb. 11:6). The world values hierarchy and a chain of command. God seeks to give His people one heart and mind. The world upholds the powerful; God said, "Blessed are the meek." The world claims results are important; God values people.

When we do the work of God in our own strength and wisdom, we will never see the power of God in what we do. We will only see what we can do through our own creativity and hard work. God reveals His way to us because that is the only means to accomplish His purposes. When God achieves His purposes in His ways through us, people will come to know God, and God will be greatly glorified. People will recognize that what has happened can be explained only by God. He alone will receive the glory!

Jesus asked His disciples to feed the multitude. Their response was, "Send them home!" (Luke 9:10–17). But Jesus, using kingdom principles, sat the people down, fed them, and had twelve baskets full of leftovers. The people witnessed the Father work a miracle. What a contrast! The disciples would have sent the people home empty and hungry whereas God displayed to a watching world His love, His nature, and His power.

The disciples witnessed this kind of mighty work many times while they walked with Jesus. They had to learn to function according to kingdom principles to accomplish kingdom work. If the disciples had ministered to the multitude in their way and with their plans, the people would have gone away wanting. Every time we minister to people in our strength rather than in God's power, people lose out.

When I was first learning to walk with God, I depended too much on other people. Every time God began leading me in a direction, I would run to other people and ask, "Do you think this is really God? Here is what I think. What do you think?" I would unconsciously—or consciously—depend on them rather than on my relationship with God.

Finally, I had to say, "I'm going to go to the Lord and clarify what I think He is saying to me. Then I am going to proceed and watch God confirm His word to me." I began that process over a period of time in many areas of my life. My love relationship with God became all-important. I began to discover a clear, personal way in which God made His ways known to me.

In the next chapter, we'll look at how God speaks through His Word. In later chapters, we'll look at how God speaks through prayer, circumstances, and the church to confirm His will to us.

Summary

God wants us to know Him and follow Him. As He speaks to us, He reveals His nature so we can have faith to trust Him in the assignment He calls us to do. He reveals His purposes so we will become involved in His work and not just dream up plans of what we will do for Him. God reveals His ways so He will accomplish His work through us in a manner that gives Him glory and shows that He is God.

Experiencing God Today

Prayerfully read through the list of names at the end of chapter 1 by which God has already identified Himself in Scripture. Mark the ones that you have come to know through personal experience.

QUESTIONS FOR REFLECTION

1. What aspect of God's character have you experienced recently that has been particularly meaningful to you?

2. What has God shown you about what He is currently seeking to accomplish in your life, someone else's life, or in your church? How did God make His activity evident? How have you responded?

3. What is one of the ways of God you have learned recently? (For example, God's ways are that the first will be last; the least is the greatest; by saving your life you will lose it.) How have you been applying what you learned?

4. Has God's revealing of Himself to you increased your faith to trust Him in other areas of your life as well?

12

GOD SPEAKS THROUGH THE BIBLE

All Scripture is inspired by God and is profitable for teaching, for rebuking, for correction, for training in righteousness, so that the man of God may be complete, equipped for every good work. (2 Timothy 3:16–17)

CRITICISM AND GOD'S WORD

There came a time while I was a pastor in Canada that I faced an unusual onslaught of criticism from other pastors and denominational leaders. Some who were critical of the way we were seeking to walk by faith and plant new churches even went so far as to write letters to those who were financially supporting our mission work. They misrepresented what we were doing and how we used our funds. As a result, some who had been undergirding our work stopped sending support.

I realized I wasn't a perfect pastor, but I also knew that in my heart I was trying to honor the Lord in all I did. Friends who alerted me to what was happening urged me to refute the criticism and rebuke those who slandered my church and me. But during that time, I had been reading through 1 and 2 Samuel. I came across 1 Samuel 2:30: "I will honor those who honor Me, but those who despise Me will be disgraced." As I read that verse, the Lord confirmed that this was the way He wanted me to serve Him. In essence, God said, "Henry, when you began serving Me, you entrusted your reputation to Me. It belongs to Me now, and I can do with it whatever I wish. If you want to spend all your time defending your reputation and seeking honor for yourself, then you can do that on your own. But if you will seek to honor Me with all your heart and life, then I will honor you in My own way and in My own time."

I decided I would never go out of my way to defend myself before my detractors—and there have been many! Rather, I would invest my effort in bringing honor to my Lord and leave my reputation in His hands. That decision has freed me immensely! To this day, I don't spend time disputing critics. God gave me some extremely practical counsel through His word at a vulnerable time in my life. Over and over, God has given me clear instruction as I read the Bible. As I have obeyed, God has honored His word in my life a thousandfold.

As we have seen, God speaks to us by the Holy Spirit to reveal Himself, His purposes, and His ways. Perhaps the questions people ask most about God's speaking are:

- How does God speak to me?
- How can I know when God is speaking?
- How can God be more real and personal to me?

Knowing God's Voice

Jesus likened His relationship with His followers to that of a shepherd and his sheep. He said, "The one who enters by the door is the shepherd of the sheep . . . The sheep hear his voice . . . The sheep follow him because they recognize his voice" (John 10:2–4). When God speaks, you will recognize His voice and follow Him.

God is sovereign. He will do whatever He chooses. Therefore, with Scripture as our guide, God speaks to individuals in unique ways so His people hear and recognize His voice.

The Bible: God's Word

"For the word of God is living and effective and sharper than any two-edged sword, penetrating as far as to divide soul, spirit, joints, and marrow; it is a judge of the ideas and thoughts of the heart" (Heb. 4:12). The Bible chronicles God's revelation of Himself to humanity.

It is not a history book, although it certainly contains history. Nor is it simply a book of moral teachings, although it provides helpful guidelines for godly living. It is not merely a record of God's encounters with people in times past, though we can learn much about how God relates to people by studying those encounters. No, the Bible is much more than these things. Through the pages of your Bible, you can hear the dynamic, convicting, living voice of God Himself.

Have you ever been reading the Bible when suddenly you were gripped by a fresh new understanding of God? That was God speaking! A person cannot understand spiritual truth unless the Spirit of God reveals it. In fact, the Holy Spirit is "the Spirit of truth" (John 14:17). When you understand the spiritual meaning and application of a Scripture passage, God's Holy Spirit has been at work. Remember: this understanding does not *lead* you to an encounter with God; it *is* the encounter with God. When God speaks to you through the Bible, He is relating to you in a personal and real way.

When the Holy Spirit reveals a truth from the Word of God, He is personally relating to you. The sequence is this:

1. You read God's Word.

2. The Spirit of truth takes the Word of God and reveals truth to you.

3. You adjust your life to God through the truth of God.

4. You obey Him.

5. God works in and through you to accomplish His purposes.

6. You come to know God in a more personal and real way as a result of this experience.

The Spirit uses the Word of God (the sword of the Spirit—Eph. 6:17) to reveal God and His purposes and to instruct us in the ways of God. On our own, we cannot understand the truths of God: "But the natural man does not welcome what comes from God's Spirit, because it is foolishness to him; he is not able to know it since it is evaluated spiritually. The spiritual person, however, can evaluate everything, yet he himself cannot be evaluated by anyone" (1 Cor. 2:14–15).

Unaided by the Holy Spirit, the ways of God will appear foolish to us. Aided by the Spirit, we can understand all things. When God reveals spiritual truth to you through a passage of Scripture, you are experiencing God Himself working in your life!

Responding to Truth

Opening my Bible is an exciting time of anticipation for me. The Spirit of God knows the mind of God (see 1 Cor. 2:9–12), and He knows what God is preparing to do in my life. The Spirit of God then opens my understanding about God's purposes and His ways. I take that process extremely seriously. Here is how I respond when God reveals truth to me in His Word:

> I write down the passage of Scripture. Then I meditate on it. I try to immerse myself in the meaning of that verse or passage. I adjust my life to the truth and, thus, to God. That means I agree with God, and I commit to take any actions necessary for Him to work in the way He has just revealed to me. As I leave the place of Bible study, I begin looking for ways God will use that truth in my life during the day.

You may want to follow this same process as God reveals truth to you. When God leads you to a fresh understanding of Himself or His ways through Scripture, do this:

- Write down the specific verse or verses in a notebook, spiritual journal, or diary.
- Meditate on the passage.
- Study the passage to immerse yourself in its meaning. What is God revealing about Himself, His purposes, or His ways?
- Identify the adjustments you need to make in your personal life, your family, your church, and your work life in response to God's revelation.
- Write a prayer response to God.
- Begin immediately to make the necessary adjustments in your life to God.

- Watch to see how God uses that truth in your life during the coming days.
- Take action! Obey what God told you to do. Enjoy a fresh experience as He works in and through you.

God's Word and Borrowing

Claude King had a practical experience with God in His Word. One morning while reading Psalm 37, the Holy Spirit called his attention to verse 21: "The wicked borrows and does not repay." The Holy Spirit drew him back to that verse, and he read it again. At that moment, he remembered borrowing money from his parents with a promise to repay them when he received his next paycheck. Now, months later, he had forgotten about the loan. God used Psalm 37:21 to remind him of the unpaid debt. More importantly, God alerted Claude to the fact that He views those who borrow and don't repay as wicked. Claude said, "I prayed and asked the Lord to forgive me. Then I wrote a check and immediately delivered it to my parents."

Although Claude had read Psalm 37 many times, the Holy Spirit spoke in a special way to Claude that day. Claude encountered truth. Suddenly, he understood that those who borrow but don't repay are sinful. The Holy Spirit called his attention to a specific instance where this verse applied to him. This was the Holy Spirit convicting him of sin (see John 16:8) to which Claude responded in a prayer of confession. Then he adjusted his life to that truth, paid the debt, and was reconciled to his parents and to the Lord. Claude's relationship with God proved real, personal, specific, and life-changing—just as God intends it to be.

Adjust, Obey, and Experience

God wants no hindrances to His love relationship with you. Once God has spoken through His Word, how you respond is crucial. You must adjust your life to the truth. In Claude's case, the adjustment looked like this:

- He agreed with the truth—those who borrow and do not repay are wicked in God's sight;
- He agreed that the truth applied to him in the particular instance that was brought to his memory.

This agreement with God is confession of sin. But agreeing with God is not enough. Claude knew he would continue to sin until he took action. To obey what God had told him through the Bible, Claude had to repay the debt.

Adjusting your beliefs to the truth God has revealed to you is the first step, but you also must respond to that truth in obedience. Then you will experience a closer relationship with God. Always connect a revealed truth to your understanding of God and your relationship with Him.

God's Call to Missions

Robert was a dentist in Rusk, Texas, who sensed God calling him into some form of mission service, perhaps as a pastor. For more than a year, the sense of God's call grew stronger. However, his wife, Gail, didn't sense God's call to be a pastor's wife, so they continued to pray and seek God's directions.

During that time, their pastor, James Goforth, announced he was resigning from their church and moving to New York state to work as a missions director. Before Goforth moved, he enlisted Robert and two other men to lead a men's prayer retreat in New York. During the retreat, several people approached Robert and said things like: "We don't have a dentist in our town. Why don't you move up here and become our dentist?" And, "We don't have a pastor. Why don't you move up here and become our pastor?" Robert assumed they were saying similar things to the other two retreat leaders as well.

Before Goforth left his church for his new missions assignment, his church in Rusk held an "Experiencing God Weekend" where the congregation studied the Seven Realities of Experiencing God. On Saturday morning at 2:30 a.m., Gail woke up. The Scripture reference Luke 4 kept running through her mind. She didn't know what Luke 4 was about, but she promised the Lord she would read it when she got up later that morning. Unable to sleep, however, she decided that she had better read Luke 4 at that moment instead of waiting any longer.

The Lord spoke powerfully through the passage. Gail realized that even Jesus had to leave His hometown in order to "proclaim the good news about the kingdom of God to the other towns also" (Luke 4:43). She sensed the Holy Spirit saying she would have to

God Speaks through the Bible

leave the comforts and security of home to go with her husband as they served the Lord together. Later that morning, in the *Experiencing God* seminar, she gave her testimony of what God had said.

The leader asked: "Why did God speak to you today instead of six months ago or six months from now? Since God speaks when it is His timing, is it possible that God wants you two involved in missions in New York?"

During the morning break, Robert asked the two other men who led the prayer retreat with him, "When we were in New York, did anyone ask you to move up there and work or pastor a church?" When both men responded, "No," Robert and Gail sensed God's leadership even more profoundly. Then a small church in Chataguay, New York, called Robert to be their part-time pastor.

Robert and Gail sold their new home at a loss and moved a long way from their Texas hometown. When Robert arrived in New York, the association of churches was praying about starting a ministry to thousands of Native Americans on a nearby reservation. Guess who became the dentist on the reservation? And God has continued to unfold His plans and purposes to reach the people of the Adirondacks for Himself.

Can you see how Robert and Gail learned by experience the Seven Realities of Experiencing God? They had a love relationship with the Lord. God invited them to join in His work. He spoke clearly through the Bible, prayer, circumstances, and other believers (I will explain these three in more detail in the coming chapters). Robert and Gail had to make major adjustments to join the Lord, but when they obeyed, they experienced God working through them to touch people with the gospel of Jesus Christ. The way God spoke to Gail through the Bible was a major turning point in their knowing and doing God's will.

SUMMARY

As you spend time in a love relationship with God, you'll come to know His voice. God has already given many messages and commands in the Bible. As you read Scripture, the Holy Spirit will be working to reveal truth about God, His purposes, and His ways. When He speaks, you must adjust yourself to the truth revealed and obey God. When you obey, you will experience Him working in and through you to accomplish His work.

Experiencing God Today

Spend time with God in prayer. Ask Him to bring to your memory the times and ways He has already spoken to you through the Bible. If you have a spiritual journal, you may want to review some of the ways God previously spoke to you through His Word. As He brings experiences to your mind, list them and describe what God has said through them.

QUESTIONS FOR REFLECTION

1. What has God been saying to you through His Word? How have you been responding?

2. Are you spending time regularly reading your Bible so you can hear God speak?

3. If you keep a journal as you read Scripture, take time to review it and see if there's a pattern to what God has been saying lately.

4. If you haven't been hearing God speak to you through His Word, why do you think that is? What might you need to do to change that?

13

God Speaks through Prayer

The Spirit also joins to help in our weakness, because we do not know what to pray for as we should, but the Spirit Himself intercedes for us with unspoken groanings. And He who searches the hearts knows the Spirit's mind-set, because He intercedes for the saints according to the will of God. (Romans 8:26–27)

The Answer Was in the Garage

For his sixth birthday, we gave my oldest son, Richard, a bicycle. I had searched for the perfect one and found a beautiful blue Schwinn. I bought it and hid it in the garage. Then I had a task—to convince Richard that he needed a blue Schwinn bike!

Richard had become enamored with some popular toys that would have quickly broken or been discarded, so I wanted to raise his aspirations for something I knew was of quality and from which he would derive countless hours of joy in the years to come. After his mother and I influenced his thinking, Richard eventually decided that what he really wanted for his birthday was a blue Schwinn bike. What did Richard receive? The bike, of course, was already in the garage. I just had to convince him to ask for it. Eventually, he did ask for it, and he got it!

What happens when you pray? The Holy Spirit knows what God already has waiting for you. His task is to get you to want it—to get you to ask for it. And what happens when you request things God already wants to give? You will always receive it. Why? Because you have asked according to the will of God.

When God answers your prayer, He receives the glory, your faith is increased, and you have a fresh experience of His love. And, as with Richard's bike, what you get far exceeds what you would have sought on your own (Eph. 3:20).

Hearing from God in Prayer

As I've explained, it's crucial to know when the Holy Spirit is speaking. But how do you know what the Holy Spirit is saying? While I can't give you a formula, I can say that you will know His voice when He speaks (see John 10:4). You must decide that you only want His will. You must dismiss any selfish or fleshly desires of your own. Then, as you start to pray, the Spirit of God will touch your heart and cause you to ask in the direction of God's will. "For it is God who is working in you, enabling you both to will and to act for his good purpose" (Phil. 2:13). Our prayers tend to request far less than what God wants to give us, so the Holy Spirit often has to raise our thoughts and desires to a higher level. We become too easily enamored with the things of this world and the values and thinking of those around us, but God wants to relate to us on a much higher plane.

If you are not keeping a spiritual journal or diary, you should start one. When the God of the universe tells you something, it is important enough to write down. When God speaks to you in your quiet times with Him, immediately record what He says, before you forget. Then add your prayer response.

I write down the Scripture verse God uses and what He says to me about Himself from that passage as well as my prayer response so I have a record of my encounter. I also write out how I need to adjust my life to experience God relating to me in the way He has shown me.

Here is a summary of how I have tried to live out my relationship with God:

- God creates in me the desire to participate in His mission to reconcile a lost world to Himself.
- I respond, seeking to know God's will.
- When God reveals a truth to me, I know He is alerting me to what He is doing around me.
- I know that the revelation is His invitation for me to adjust my life and to respond in obedience to what He has shown me.

Prayer Is a Relationship

Prayer is not a one-way conversation where you simply recite everything you want God to do for you. It is two-way fellowship and communication. You speak to God, and He speaks to you. Prayer also includes listening. In fact, what God says to you in prayer is far more important than what you say to Him. After all, God already knows what you're going to tell Him, but He has amazing things to revel that you don't know (see Jer. 33:3).

Prayer is a relationship, not a religious activity. Through prayer, you adjust to God; God doesn't adjust to you. He *wants* you to pray, but He doesn't *need* you to. You, however, need to pray because of what God wants to do in your life during your prayer time.

When the Holy Spirit reveals a truth to you in prayer, He is present and actively working in your life. This kind of prayer is a divine encounter. Here's what happens as you seek God's will in prayer:

1. God takes the initiative by causing you to want to pray.

2. The Holy Spirit, through the Word of God, reveals God's will to you.

3. You pray in agreement with the will of God.

4. You adjust your thinking and attitudes to God's truth.

5. You look and listen for confirmation or further direction from the Bible, circumstances, and the church (other believers).

6. You obey.

7. God works in and through you to accomplish His purposes.

8. You experience Him as the Spirit revealed when you prayed.

Praying and reading your Bible are inextricably connected. The Spirit of God often uses the Word of God when you pray. When I pray about something, Scripture often comes to mind, and I immediately open my Bible to the passage I believe the Spirit of God brought to my attention. I see this as God guiding me by His Word. As I pray about a particular matter, the Spirit of God takes the Word of God and applies it to my heart and mind to reveal the truth of the situation for which I am praying.

Praying in the Spirit

God's Word tells us that we have a divine intercessor—the Holy Spirit (Rom. 8:26–27). The Spirit has an advantage over us—He already knows God's will—and when He intercedes for us, He is in absolute agreement with God's will and helps us know the will of God as we pray.

The Holy Spirit "will not speak on His own, but He will speak whatever He hears. He will also declare to you what is to come" (John 16:13). When you pray, anticipate that the Holy Spirit already knows what God has prepared for you. The Spirit does not guide you on His own initiative. He tells you what He hears from the Father and guides you to pray for what He knows the Father wants to do in your life.

When I review what I've journaled that God is saying to me when I pray and read His Word, I begin to see what God is telling me about Himself, His purposes, and His ways. I often see a pattern develop. As I watch the direction the Spirit is leading me to pray, I get an indication of what God is saying to me.

You may be asking: But how do I know that the requests I'm praying are the Spirit's leading and not my own selfish desires? Do you remember what George Mueller said he does first when seeking God's directions? He said he tries to reach the point where he has no will of his own. That is easier to say than to do, of course. But it is possible, and the Spirit is eager to help you in that regard.

Denying Self

The first thing to do as you seek God's will is to deny yourself. Examine your heart for any selfish or worldly motives. In all honesty—with yourself and before God—come to the point where you are certain your only desire is to know and to do God's will. Then ask yourself:

- What is the Holy Spirit saying to me through God's Word?
- What is He saying to me in prayer?
- Is He confirming through circumstances what He said?
- Is the Holy Spirit verifying what He said through the counsel of other believers?

God will never lead you to do something that contradicts His written Word. If what you sense in prayer runs contrary to Scripture, it is wrong. For instance, God will never lead you to commit adultery, to steal, or do anything that goes against His biblical precepts. Watch for God to use the written Word to confirm what you are sensing in prayer. Don't play games with God. Don't look for a Scripture that seems to say what you selfishly want to do and then claim it is God's will. That is dangerous. Don't do it.

Praying for One Thing and Getting Another

Have you ever prayed for one thing and received another? I have. Then some dear soul would advise, "God is trying to get you to persist in your request. Keep on praying until you get what you ask for!"

During a time when I was asking God for one thing but receiving something else, I started reading from the second chapter of Mark. That passage recounts the story of four men who brought a crippled friend to Jesus for healing. Because of the crowd, they opened a hole in the roof of the house where Jesus was, and then lowered the man down to the Lord. These four enterprising men were doggedly determined to get their friend to Jesus so he could be healed, but when Jesus looked at the crippled man, He declared, "Son, your sins are forgiven" (Mark 2:5).

As I read that verse, I sensed the Holy Spirit saying, "Henry, did you see that?" I went back and meditated on that Scripture. Under the guiding, teaching ministry of the Holy Spirit, I began to understand a wonderful truth. The four men asked Jesus to heal the man, but Jesus forgave the man's sins. They asked for one thing, and Jesus gave another. While this man and his friends asked for one particular gift, Jesus wanted to make the man a child of the King so he could inherit everything!

I found myself weeping before God and saying: "Oh God, if I ever give You a request and You have more to give me than I am asking, please cancel my request!"

What Is Happening When You Pray?

If I ask God for one thing and something different happens, I ask God to help me understand what He is doing in my life. It could be that God is refusing to grant my small request and is instead desiring to do something much greater. I have found that God always has far more to give me than I could even ask or think. Paul said, "Now to Him who is able to do above and beyond all that we ask or think—according to the power that works in you—to Him be glory in the church and in Christ Jesus to all generations, forever and ever!" (Eph. 3:20–21).

Here's the reality: You can't even imagine a prayer that comes close to what God wants to give you. If God wants to grant you more than you are asking, would you rather have what you are requesting or what God wants to give? Only the Spirit of God knows what God purposes in your life. So let God give you all He wants to give. "For the Spirit searches everything, even the deep things of God. For who among men knows the concerns of a man except the spirit of the man that is in him? In the same way, no one knows the concerns of God except the Spirit of God. Now we have not received the spirit of the world, but the Spirit who is from God, in order to know what has been freely given to us by God" (1 Cor. 2:10–12). Just realize that what God intends to give you might not look like anything you had imagined or desired to that point. Yet He always knows what is best. Likewise, if God wants you to persist in your current praying, He will confirm that too.

A Mission Church

Suppose your congregation wanted to start a mission church in a particular area of your city. You have taken a survey to identify the needs of that community. You have carefully developed long-range plans. You have asked God to bless and guide your work. Then God begins to bring to your church a group of ethnic people who don't live in the target area. What would you do? You have these options:

- I would "keep on keeping on" in prayer until God helps us start the mission church we have planned.
- I would get frustrated at the delay and quit the process until a more opportune time.
- I would start asking questions to see if we should start an ethnic mission church instead of—or in addition to—the original one.

You should, of course, immediately go before God and clarify what He is saying. If you have been working and praying in one direction and you see God moving in a different way, adjust your life to what God is doing. In this sort of situation, you must decide whether you're going to do what you want and ask God to bless it, or go to work where He is working.

While I served as a denominational leader in Vancouver, we started a special emphasis to reach university students. We began with thirty students in the fall, and by the end of the spring semester, we had about two hundred and fifty attending, two-thirds of whom were international students. We could have said to them, "We didn't plan for a ministry to internationals, so please go to a ministry that is prepared to meet your needs, and may God bless you." We didn't, of course. Rather, we adjusted our plans to what God was doing and an entirely new and exciting ministry developed that we hadn't anticipated.

Spiritual Concentration

For many of us, the problem is that we pray and then never relate what happens next to our prayers. After you pray, the greatest single thing you need to do is to pay close attention to God's response. When you pray, anticipate the activity of God in answer to your prayer. I see this truth all the way through the Scripture. When God's people pray, God responds.

Here's what happens if you pray and then forget about what you asked. Unusual things may occur throughout the day, but you view them as distractions and try to ignore or get rid of them. You fail to connect them with what you just prayed.

When I pray, I watch closely for what happens next. I prepare to make adjustments to what God is doing. Expect God to answer your prayers, but stick around for the answer. His timing is always right and best. Because of that, His answer may arrive sooner than you expected!

The Silences of God

I went through a lengthy time when God was silent. You probably have had that experience, too. I had been praying for many days, and there seemed to be complete silence from God. I sensed heaven was closed, and I didn't understand what was happening. Some people told me that if God was not responding to my prayers, there must be unconfessed sin my life. Someone even gave me a "sin checklist" to work through. Wanting to make sure I was right with God, I prayed through the list, but the silence persisted.

My problem was much like Job's. You'll recall that his counselors said his problems were due to sin. But Job felt he and God were on right terms. Job did not know all God was doing during that time, but for sure, his advisors were wrong. There was another reason for what was happening.

The only thing I knew to do was go back to God. I believe God, who loves me, will let me know what is going on in my life when and if I need to know. So I prayed, "Heavenly Father, I don't understand this silence. You are going to have to tell me what You're doing in my life." And in time, He did—from His Word! This became one of the most meaningful experiences in my life.

I did not go searching frantically throughout the Bible for an answer. I continued my daily reading of the Word. I believed that as I read the Bible, the Spirit of God would help me understand what God was doing in my life.

In God's Time

One morning, I was reading the story of the death of Lazarus (see John 11:1–45). Keep in mind that John says Jesus loved Lazarus, Mary, and Martha. But having received word that Lazarus was mortally ill, Jesus delayed going to him. In the meantime, Lazarus died.

Mary and Martha had asked Jesus to come help their brother, but all the way through the final sickness and death of Lazarus, Jesus did not come. They received no response from the One who claimed to love Lazarus!

Mary and Martha went through the entire funeral process for their beloved brother. They prepared his body and sealed him in a tomb. Still, they experienced silence from God. Only then did Jesus tell His disciples it was time to go to Lazarus.

When Jesus arrived, Lazarus had been dead four days. Mary said to Jesus, "Lord, if You had been here, my brother would not have died" (John 11:32). As I read her words during my "silent period," the Spirit of God began to help me understand something. It seemed as if Jesus said to Mary and Martha:

> You are exactly right. If I had come when you asked, your brother would not have died. You know that I could have healed him because you have seen Me heal people many times. If I had come when you asked Me to, I would have healed him. But you would have never experienced any more about Me than you already know. I knew you were ready for a greater revelation of Me than you have yet known. I wanted you to see that I am the resurrection and the life. My refusal and My silence were not rejection. They were an opportunity for Me to disclose to you more of Me than you have ever known.

When that began to dawn on me, I almost jumped out of my chair. I said, "That's what's happening in my life! That's what's happening! The silence of God means He is ready to bring into my life a greater revelation of Himself than I have ever known." I immediately changed my attitude. With great anticipation, I began to watch for what new revelation God would teach me about Himself. I then had some incredible opportunities happen in my life that I might have missed without that kind of readiness and anticipation.

When there is silence from God now, I still pray through my sin checklist. If there is unconfessed sin, I confess and make it right. If, after that, there is still silence, I prepare for a new experience with God. Sometimes God is silent as He prepares you for a deeper understanding of Himself. Whenever silence comes, continue doing the last thing God told you and watch and wait for a fresh encounter with Him.

When you do not hear from God, you can respond in one of two ways. You can become discouraged and suffer guilt and self-condemnation. Or you can expect that God is about to bring you into a deeper knowledge of Him. The response you choose will make all the difference in how you experience God.

Summary

Prayer is not a religious activity. It is a relationship to a Person, a two-way communication with holy, Almighty God. When you pray, you enter the throne room of heaven—the nerve center of the universe. You do not have to enter prayer alone. Christ and the Holy Spirit are intercessors with you. The Holy Spirit helps you know *what* to pray and *how* to pray. He guides your praying according to the will of God because He already knows what God wants to give you or to do in your life. His job is to guide your praying in that direction.

Often the Holy Spirit will use Scripture to reveal truth, but truth is not a concept. Truth is a Person. When the Holy Spirit reveals truth, you adjust your life to God and obey Him. Your prayer life is one of the best indications of the health of your love relationship with the Father.

Experiencing God Today

Spend some prayer time asking the Holy Spirit to direct your praying according to the Father's will. Have your notebook ready to record what He says.

QUESTIONS FOR REFLECTION

1. What has God been saying to you in your prayer times?
2. Could it be that God is seeking to elevate your praying to a level He would be pleased to answer? How might God be leading you to pray?
3. Have you been experiencing a period of silence from God? Why might God be withholding His Word?

14

God Speaks through Circumstances

Trust in the LORD with all your heart, and do not rely on your own understanding; think about Him in all your ways, and He will guide you on the right paths. (Proverbs 3:5–6)

Prevented by Circumstances

While Marilynn and I were serving in our second church, we attended a missions conference. We both felt God calling us to surrender our lives to international missions. We went home and applied to our denomination's mission board. After the extensive application process was complete, our oldest son experienced some perplexing health problems. The mission board cautioned us against moving forward until our son's condition improved. We had sensed God asking us to prepare for missions, and yet when we attempted to move forward in that direction, Richard's illness occurred.

This could have been a confusing circumstance in our lives, so we continued to pray and watched to see why God had told us to prepare for a missions assignment. Before long, we were contacted by a small church in Saskatoon, Canada. This church had gone through a bitterly discouraging time and had been reduced to a remnant of only ten disheartened members. Although this church was much smaller than the one where we were serving, we sensed the spiritual need in Canada was enormous and that God wanted to use us to start churches all over the western portion of the country. This small church was unable to pay the full salary the mission agency would have, but the opportunity to serve in my home country—which so desperately needed more ministers and churches—excited us. Because God had prepared us to serve on the mission field, we were ready to accept the call to Canada.

Interestingly, after we moved to Canada, we took our son to a local doctor to continue treatments for his mysterious condition. After running several tests, the Canadian medical experts announced there was nothing wrong with our son, and there never had been! But now we were in Canada. Why had God allowed this unusual medical ailment to afflict our son at the very time we were preparing for missions? We began to serve the Lord as faithfully as we knew how, and if we had gone to Africa where our hearts were leaning, our denomination's mission board would have provided a full salary, with medical and retirement benefits. Although the lifestyle change would have been drastic, there would have been an extensive missions network to assist in our efforts. In Canada, by contrast, there was not enough money to pay much of a salary, no retirement, and no denominational funds to assist us. All we had was God and His provision. Yet, to our delight, we repeatedly experienced that this was more than enough. God consistently provided for all our needs.

Ultimately, God led our small church and its missions to begin thirty-eight new churches. We experienced God working so powerfully that I was eventually asked to write a study describing how I had learned to walk with God in such a practical and powerful way. That study, of course, is *Experiencing God*.

Experiencing God was so widely used by churches around the world and by missionaries in our international missions agency that I was asked if I would travel internationally to teach missionaries the truths we learned in Canada. To date, I have been privileged to minister in one hundred fourteen countries. I was recently in India and, to my surprise, I discovered that churches all across that great country had been studying *Experiencing God*. One pastor had used the material to lead his church to start more than one hundred churches.

It might have appeared that our son's illness closed the door to our involvement in world missions. However, from God's perspective it was just another step in His guidance that enabled us to have the maximum impact for His kingdom. We never know the truth of our circumstances until we have heard from God.

Experience Alone Is Unreliable

At times as I'm leading a seminar, someone will get upset with me and say, "Well, I don't care what you say; I've experienced such and such." I respond as kindly as I know how by saying, "I do not deny your experience. I do question your interpretation of what you experienced because it is contrary to what I see in the Word of God."

Your experience alone cannot be your guide. Every experience must be held up against the Scriptures. Throughout your life, there will be times when you want to respond based on your experiences or your wisdom. However, we can't see all that God sees in our situation. We don't know the long-term results of our present circumstances. We don't know how God intends to use good or difficult life events to build our character, to influence other people, or to further His kingdom. Trying to discover God's will based on our understanding of circumstances alone can be misleading. Always rely on the Holy Spirit to reveal the truth of your situation through God's Word.

Also, see how God works by looking through the entire Bible. Don't rely on one or two isolated passages. When you learn how God has worked historically, you'll better recognize Him at work in your life. Your experience is valid only when it is confirmed in the Scriptures.

The Bible Is Our Guide

The Word of God is the infallible guide to what we should be doing (see 2 Tim. 3:16). Some people argue, "That's not practical." They want to move beyond the Bible and rely on the world's ways, on personal experience, or on popular thinking. As a Christian disciple, I cannot abandon the guidance I find in Scripture. The Bible is my guide for faith and practice, and it is remarkably practical.

Jesus Watched the Father's Activity

Jesus knew the Father's will for His life daily by watching the Father's activity. He describes the process in John 5:17, 19–20: "My Father is still working, and I am working also . . . I assure you: The Son is not able to do anything on His own, but only what He sees the Father doing. For whatever the Father does, the Son also does these things in the same way. For the Father loves the Son and shows Him everything He is doing."

Jesus did not take the initiative in what He did for the Father (see John 5:19). Only the Father is the initiator. The Father had been working throughout history and was carrying out His purposes in Jesus' time on earth (see John 5:17). The Father let the Son know what He was doing (see John 5:20). When Jesus saw the Father's activity, that was Jesus' invitation to join His Father.

Jesus did not ever have to guess what He should do. Nor did He have to dream up what He could do for the Father. Rather, He simply watched to see what the Father was doing around Him, and He immediately aligned His life that way. Then the Father accomplished His purposes through Jesus.

This is how Jesus wants us to respond to His lordship in our lives. He reveals what He is doing, and then we adjust our lives, our plans, and our goals to Him. We are to place our lives at His disposal—where He is working—so He can accomplish His purposes through us.

Sometimes circumstances appear to be "bad." Maybe you're in the middle of a difficult situation, and you're asking God, "Why is this happening to me?" If so, you're not alone.

God's Perspective Is Vital

Joseph needed God's perspective to understand his circumstances. He had visions of greatness when he was a youth (see Gen. 37:1–11). Yet his older brothers maliciously turned against him and sold him as a slave.

Joseph was taken to a foreign country where it appeared he would spend the rest of his life in bondage, never to see his family again. Then things got worse. He was falsely accused of a heinous crime and thrown in jail. Later, when a fellow prisoner Joseph had helped was released, he hoped the man might help him in return.

Instead, the man forgot about Joseph. For someone who had committed no offense, Joseph's life appeared to be undeservedly harsh and unfair.

Then the pharaoh had a dream, and all of Joseph's life experiences began to fall into place (see Gen. 41:1–8). His fellow prisoner remembered and mentioned Joseph to Pharaoh. Joseph interpreted the pharaoh's dream, which was a warning from God of impending disaster. Joseph was appointed the second in command in all of Egypt, and ultimately he saved his father, brothers, and their families from a devastating famine.

Reviewing all God had allowed in his life, Joseph declared to his brothers, "You planned evil against me; God planned it for good (Gen. 50:20). When Joseph's life was placed in the context of God's eternal purposes, every major experience in his life—both good and bad—could be seen to have a purpose and to result in good.

When you face difficult or confusing circumstances, they can overwhelm you. If you bury yourself in the circumstances, you will always have a distorted understanding of God. For instance, you might say, "God doesn't love me" or "God is not fair," but both of those statements are false. Have you ever been in the middle of a tragic or fearful situation where, in your prayers, you began to accuse God of some things that you know are not true? Perhaps you began to question God's love or His wisdom. Maybe you were afraid to say that He was wrong, but you sort of said, "God, you deceived me in letting me believe that this was the right thing to do. Why didn't you stop me?" A whole lot of wrong conclusions can result if you try to look at God from the middle of a painful situation.

What should you do instead? First, ask God to show you His perspective on what's happening. Look back at your situation from what you already know about God. When you face a troublesome time, the Holy Spirit will take the Word of God and help you understand the event from God's perspective. He will reveal to you the truth of your circumstances. Then you can adjust your life and thinking to what God is doing.

Our Daughter's Cancer

Earlier in the book, I told you about our daughter Carrie's bout with cancer, an extraordinarily difficult circumstance for our family.

Her condition had gone undetected for two years, which meant she was in an advanced stage of Hodgkin's Disease. The doctors prepared us for six to eight months of chemotherapy, to be followed by aggressive radiation treatments. We knew God loved us, but everything looked grim. We prayed, "What are You doing in this experience, and what adjustments do we need to make?"

As we prayed, a Scripture promise came that we believed was from God. The promise was accompanied by letters and calls from many people who quoted the same Scripture. The verse reads, "This sickness will not end in death but is for the glory of God, so that the Son of God may be glorified through it" (John 11:4). While it would not have been unexpected for us to gravitate to this encouraging verse, we were inundated with people who sensed this was God's word for our particular situation.

Our sense that God was speaking to us grew stronger as the Bible, prayer, and the testimony of other believers began to line up and say the same thing. We adjusted our lives to that truth and began to watch for ways God would use the situation for His glory.

During this time, people from many places in Canada, Europe, and the United States prayed for Carrie. Individuals, college student groups, and churches called to tell us of their prayers. Many said something like this: "Our prayer life had become dry and cold. We haven't seen any special answers to prayer in a long time. But when we heard about Carrie, we put her on our prayer list and felt unusually burdened to pray for her."

After only three months of treatments, the doctors ran more tests and to their surprise, all tests were negative. They could not find any trace of cancer. I immediately began to contact those who had prayed for Carrie and shared with them this answer to their intercession. Person after person indicated that seeing God's answer totally renewed their prayer lives. Church prayer ministries were revitalized. Student prayer groups found new life.

For God's Glory

Then I began to see what God had in mind for this circumstance. Through this experience, God was glorified in the eyes of His people. Many people sensed a fresh call to prayer. They personally experienced anew the presence of truth—as a Person. Carrie's closest friends began to pray fervently, and some students came to know the Lord after observing what God had done in Carrie. God brought glory to Himself through this sickness, and many people's lives were changed forever. We faced a trying situation and could have looked at God from the middle of it only to gain a distorted understanding of Him. Instead, we sought His perspective.

God walked with my family and me through that experience so closely and lovingly—and He spoke to us through His Word so clearly, directly, and powerfully—that we came to understand at a fresh, new level God's love for us and our daughter. Even if the Lord had chosen not to heal Carrie, I believe we would have been assured that He loved us. I also believe He would have shown us, through His Word and through subsequent circumstances, that He had a purpose for what He did. The key was not that God healed our daughter. The important thing was that God walked with us through that experience and gave us His perspective.

I have known other Christian parents who lost a child to terminal illness. Many of these experienced God walking just as closely with them, and they came to see that God could take the most devastating circumstances and bring good out of what happened.

In our case, the Holy Spirit took the Word of God and revealed to us God's view on the end result of that circumstance. We believed God and adjusted our lives to Him and to what He was doing. Then we went through the circumstance, looking to see how His purposes would be accomplished in ways that would bring Him glory. When the answer to prayer came, I knew immediately that my job was to declare the wonderful works of the Lord to His people. In the process, we came to know God in a new way because of the compassion He showed us.

Let me summarize how you can respond when circumstances seem bewildering:

1. Settle in your mind that God forever demonstrated His absolute love for you on the cross. His love will never change.

2. Do not try to understand what God is like from the middle of your circumstances.

3. Go to God, and ask Him to help you see His perspective on your situation.

4. Wait on the Holy Spirit. He will take the Word of God and help you understand your circumstances.

5. Adjust your life to God and what you see Him doing in your situation.

6. Do all He tells you to do.

7. Experience God working in and through you to accomplish His purposes.

God is sovereign. You may face a situation like Joseph's in which God does not tell you what He is doing—at first. If so, acknowledge His love and sovereignty, and depend on His sustaining grace to see you through the situation. There are some things that happen in our lives we may never understand until they are revealed in heaven. Then we will celebrate with people like Joseph and Job that God was indeed faithful and loving—even when we didn't understand all He was doing or allowing in our lives.

Truth and Your Circumstance

You can't understand the truth of your circumstance until you have heard from God. Exodus 5–6 records that Moses did what God told him to do and asked Pharaoh to release the Israelites. Pharaoh refused, instead multiplying the Israelites' hardship. The Israelites turned against Moses and criticized him for causing so much trouble. What would you have done if you had been in Moses' place?

The human tendency would be to assume you'd missed God's will. You might get mad at Israel for treating your good intentions so ungratefully, or you might become angry at God for asking you to do something that only magnified your problems.

Moses blamed God and accused Him of failing to do what He promised, and I suppose most of us would have responded the same way. Moses said, "Lord, why have You caused trouble for this people? And why did You ever send me? Ever since I went in to Pharaoh to speak in Your name he has caused trouble for this people, and You haven't delivered Your people at all" (Exod. 5:22–23). Moses was discouraged and ready to quit (see Exod. 6:12).

I'm glad God is patient with us! He took time to explain His perspective to Moses. God wanted Pharaoh to resist so the people could witness God's mighty hand of deliverance. He wanted His people to come to know Him by experience as the great "I AM." God was allowing His people's problems to increase so they could witness a greater measure of God's power when He delivered them!

Learn from Moses' example. When you face confusing circumstances, don't start blaming God. Don't quit following Him. Ask Him to reveal the truth of your circumstances, to show you His perspective. Then wait on the Lord (see Ps. 25:3–5).

You need to have your life firmly anchored in God. The most difficult thing you'll ever have to do is deny self, embrace the will of God, and follow Him (see Matt. 16:24). The hardest part of your relationship to God is remaining God-centered. If you were to record a whole day in your life, you might find that your prayers, your attitudes, your thoughts—everything about that day—was radically self-centered. You may not be seeing things from God's perspective. You may try to explain to God what your perspective is, but the key is God's will. As your Father, He has every right to be:

- the Initiator in your life;
- the Focus of your life;
- the Director of your life.

That is what it means for Him to be Lord.

Hearing from Truth

When the Holy Spirit talks to you, He will reveal truth to you. He is going to talk to you about a Person, Jesus Christ. Yes, truth is a Person! Jesus said, "I am . . . the truth" (John 14:6).

Truth in a Storm

The disciples were in a boat when a terrifying storm struck (see Mark 4:35–41), but Jesus was asleep in the back of the boat. If you had asked those disciples in the middle of the storm, "What is the truth of this situation?" they would have said, "We perish!" But was that the truth? No. Truth was asleep at the back of the boat. In a moment, Truth Himself would stand up and calm the storm. Once that happened, they knew the truth of their circumstances. The Person of Truth is always present in your life. You cannot know the truth of your circumstance until you have heard from God.

Truth at a Funeral

Notice the difference truth made in this circumstance:

> [Jesus] went into a town called Nain. His disciples and a large crowd were traveling with Him. Just as He neared the gate of the town, a dead man was being carried out. He was his mother's only son, and she was a widow. A large crowd from the city was also with her. When the Lord saw her, He had compassion on her and said, "Don't cry." Then He came up and touched the open coffin, and the pallbearers stopped. And He said, "Young man, I tell you, get up!" The dead man sat up and began to speak, and Jesus gave him to his mother. Then fear came over everyone, and they glorified God, saying, "A great prophet has risen among us," and "God has visited His people," This report about Him went throughout Judea and all the vicinity. (Luke 7:11–17)

If you had asked the grieving mother, "What is the truth of this situation?" she might have replied, "My husband died several years ago. We only had one son, and I hoped that we would enjoy wonderful times together and that he would take care of me in my old age. Now my son is dead and I have no one to care for me." But was that the truth? No. Truth was standing in front of her! When He reached out and touched her son, everything changed. When Jesus demonstrated His power, the people marvelled at what they witnessed, and they proclaimed all over the countryside that a great prophet had come (Luke 7:16–17).

Never determine the truth of a situation by looking at the circumstances. Don't evaluate your situation until you have heard from Jesus. He is the Truth of every circumstance.

Truth with Hungry People

Jesus was surrounded by more than five thousand hungry people (see John 6:1–15), and He wanted to feed them. In a test of Philip's faith, Jesus asked where they could buy enough bread to feed the multitude. If you had asked the disciples at that moment about the truth of the situation, they would have told you, "We can't do it. Feeding this multitude is impossible." But was that true? No. We know the rest of the story. So wouldn't we be better off if we trusted God with the other half of the story in *our* lives? Truth Himself fed five thousand men, plus their families, and had twelve baskets full of leftovers!

I wonder if God ever tests our faith as He did Philip's. Does He say, "Feed the multitudes," and the church responds, "We don't have that much money in our budget"? Truth stands in the middle of the church, and the Head of the church says, "Believe Me. I will never give you a command for which I will not release the power to enable it to happen. Trust Me, obey Me, and it will happen."

Yes, Lord

In making a decision, the greatest difficulty may not be in choosing between good and bad but in choosing between good and best. You may have several options that all appear good. The place to start is to say with all of your heart: "Lord, whatever I know to be Your will, I will do. Regardless of the cost and regardless of the adjustment, I commit myself to follow Your will. No matter what that looks like, Lord, I will do it!"

You need to commit to that before you seek God's will. Otherwise, you do not mean "Thy will be done." Instead, you are saying, "Thy will be done as long as it does not conflict with my will." Two words in the Christian's language cannot go together: "No, Lord." If you say "no," He is not your Lord. If He is your Lord, your answer must always be "yes." In decision making, do not proceed until you can honestly say, "Whatever you want of me, Lord, I will do it."

Physical Markers of Spiritual Encounters

When Israel crossed the Jordan River into the Promised Land, God gave Joshua the following instructions: "Choose 12 men from the people, one man for each tribe, and command them, 'Take 12 stones from this place in the middle of the Jordan where the priests' feet are standing, carry them with you, and set them down at the place where you spend the night'" (Josh. 4:2–3).

These stones were to serve as a monument to the Israelites. Joshua explained: "This will be a sign among you. In the future, when your children ask you, 'What do these stones mean to you?' you should tell them, 'The waters of the Jordan were cut off in front of the ark of the LORD's covenant. When it crossed the Jordan, the Jordan's waters were cut off.' Therefore, these stones will always be a memorial for the Israelites" (Josh. 4:6–7).

The stones were to be a visible reminder of God's mighty act in providing for His people. In Old Testament times, others also built altars or set up stones as reminders of significant encounters with God (Noah: Gen. 6–8; Abram: Gen. 12:1–8 and 13:1–18; Isaac: Gen. 26:17–25; Jacob: Gen. 28:10–22 and 35:1–7; Moses: Exod. 17:8–16 and 24:1–11; Joshua: Josh. 3:5–4:9; Gideon: Judg. 6:11–24; and Samuel: 1 Sam. 7:1–13). Places like Bethel ("house of God") and Rehoboth ("room") became reminders of God's activity in the midst of His people. Moses named an altar "The Lord is my Banner," and Samuel named a stone "Ebenezer," saying, "Thus far the LORD has helped us" (1 Sam. 7:12). These altars and stones were physical markers of great spiritual encounters with God. They provided opportunities for parents to teach their children about God's activity on behalf of His people.

A Spiritual Marker

I have found it helpful to identify spiritual markers in my life. Each time I encounter God's call or directions, I mentally build a marker. A spiritual marker identifies a time of transition, decision, or direction when I clearly know that God has guided me. Over time, I can look back at these spiritual markers and see how God has faithfully directed my life according to His divine purpose. When I review my markers, I see more clearly the directions God has been moving my life and ministry. Sometimes, it is unclear as we look forward to where God is leading us. But when we look back, we can more readily discern the purposeful guidance of God at key times in our lives.

At times, I may face several options by which I could serve God, and I need to know which of these good things is what God desires of me. When I face a decision about God's direction, I review my spiritual markers. I don't take the next step without the context of God's full activity in my life. This helps me see God's perspective for my past and present. Then I look at the options before me to see which one is most consistent with what God has been doing in my life up to that point. Often, one of the potential directions follows on what God has already been doing. If that is not the case, I continue to pray and wait for the Lord's guidance and timing.

My Own Spiritual Markers

Several years ago, I was approached about taking on a new ministry with my denomination's home missions agency. The organization asked me to direct its emphasis on prayer and spiritual awakening, but I had never had such a job in my life. If I accepted, it meant leaving Vancouver, where we were settled and happy, and moving to Atlanta, Georgia. Only God could reveal whether this was part of His divine purpose, and the spiritual markers in my life helped me view this decision from God's perspective.

My own spiritual markers start before I was born. My heritage goes back to England, where a number of my family members were graduates of Spurgeon's College when Charles Spurgeon was trying to win England for Christ. Revival and awakening were "in my blood," you might say.

I grew up in a Canadian town where there was no evangelical church. There, my father served as a lay pastor and helped start a mission church. Way back in my teen years, I sensed a deep burden for communities all across Canada that did not have an evangelical church. While I was in seminary, God assured me that He loved my nation enough to bring a great movement of His Spirit across the land. When I accepted God's call to Saskatoon, He used the prospect of a spiritual awakening there to affirm my call. A revival and spiritual awakening did occur and spread across many parts of Canada in the early 1970s. Now I was part of exciting events in British Columbia where God was obviously at work.

Then one day someone from Atlanta, Georgia, called me. He said, "Henry, we have prayed much about filling a position in prayer for spiritual awakening. We have been seeking a person for over two years. Would you consider coming and directing our denomination in this emphasis?"

The spiritual markers in my life showed that spiritual awakening was an important element throughout my ministry. Although I had assumed I would spend the rest of my life serving the Lord in Canada, when I heard this invitation was in the area of spiritual awakening, I sensed the Holy Spirit's involvement in the opportunity. After prayer and confirmation in the Word and by other believers, I accepted the position. God didn't lead me into something in which I had never been interested. Rather, this job brought together things God had been building into my life for decades.

Summary

God used circumstances to reveal to Jesus what He was to do. Jesus paid attention to know where the Father wanted to involve Him in His work. God also will use circumstances to reveal His directions to you. However, you must check these against what God says through the Scriptures, prayer, and other Christians. Reviewing your spiritual markers is one way in which God may give you a sense of direction through your circumstances. When God is ready for you to take a new step or direction, it will be in agreement with what He has already been doing in your life.

Sometimes, you may find yourself in difficult or confusing circumstances. To understand these events, God's perspective is vital. Never determine the truth of your situation by focusing on the circumstances. You cannot know the reality of any situation until you have heard from God.

Experiencing God Today

Ask God to help you identify your own spiritual markers. These may begin with your heritage, your salvation experience, times you made significant decisions regarding your future, and so forth. What are some of the times of transition, decision, or direction in your life when you knew for sure that God guided you? Start developing a list of your own spiritual markers, but don't feel like it has to be comprehensive. Add to it as you reflect and pray about God's activity in your life.

QUESTIONS FOR REFLECTION

1. Are you in the midst of a confusing situation? How are you seeking God's perspective on it?

2. Is God speaking to you through a circumstance in your life? What is He saying? How is that being confirmed by God's word, your times of prayer, and other believers?

3. As you review your spiritual markers, do you see a clear direction God has been leading? What might that suggest about a current decision you are facing?

15

GOD SPEAKS THROUGH THE CHURCH

Speaking the truth in love, let us grow in every way into Him who is the head—Christ. From Him the whole body, fitted and knit together by every supporting ligament, promotes the growth of the body for building up itself in love by the proper working of each individual part. (Ephesians 4:15–16)

GOD SPEAKS THROUGH A REFUGEE

When I lived in Vancouver, I served as the interim pastor of a church with less than fifty in attendance. A Laotian refugee family had joined the church the week before I came, and I knew God never adds members to a church body by accident (see 1 Cor. 12:18). Those God adds are my ministry, so my responsibility as pastor was to see what God was doing when He brought them to our congregation. I (and others) had the opportunity to witness God's activity in this family.

Thomas, the father of the Laotian family, had been converted in a refugee camp in Thailand. When he became a Christian, His life was so gloriously transformed that he immediately sought to help Laotian people know Jesus. He went all through the community trying to lead his fellow Laotians to Christ. In the first week, Thomas led fifteen adults to the Lord. The next week, he led eleven more, and he wept because he felt he had been unfaithful to his Lord.

The Lord led Thomas to immigrate to Canada, where he became a member of our church. We asked the Lord why He had added this fine family to our congregation. As our small congregation talked with Thomas and observed his life, it became clear God was at work among the transplanted Laotian refugees in our city. We prayed with Thomas and discovered that God had given him a pastor's heart. He had a burden for evangelism, and he had just enrolled in a local theological college to obtain ministerial training in order to do whatever God wanted. Our church voted to call Thomas as the pastor of a mission to the Laotian community, and Thomas accepted.

Two months after becoming the pastor, Thomas was invited to a meeting for ethnic pastors being held in the United States, several days' drive away. He asked if our denomination had funds that would allow him to take some of his church members to the conference. I thought that was an excellent idea but had no idea he was thinking of taking eighteen people with him! Thomas told me he had Laotian relatives and friends in all the major cities across Canada. On his way home from the conference, he wanted to drive through several of those cities and share Christ with them. God had already given Thomas a heart to establish Laotian churches in every major city. Later that year—at Christmas—Laotian people came from all over Canada to Vancouver to celebrate with Thomas their new life in Christ.

Years later, I visited Vancouver and asked about Thomas. By then, the Laotian government had granted permission to start churches in his home country. Thomas returned to Laos, preached the gospel, and one hundred thirty-three friends and family members came to know the Lord! He started four mission churches and linked the church in Vancouver with the Laotian churches, sharing his heart's desire to see all Laotian people come to know Christ.

All of this began when one Laotian refugee joined our church. But what did God see? He saw a whole nation being drawn to Himself. When God honors your church by placing a new member in the body, ask God to show you what He is up to. Then share what you sense of God's activity. God speaks through the members of the body to help others know and understand God's assignment.

THE PARABLE OF THE TRAIN TRACKS

Suppose the eye could say to the body, "Let's walk down these train tracks. The way is clear. Not a train is in sight." So the body starts down the tracks.

Then the ear says, "I hear a whistle coming from behind us." The eye argues, "But nothing is on the track as far as I can see. Let's keep on walking." The body listens only to the eye and keeps on walking. Soon the ear says, "That whistle is getting louder and closer!" Then the feet say, "I feel the vibration of a train coming. We'd better get our body off these tracks!" If this were your body, what would you do?

- Would you try to ignore the conflict between the body parts and hope it passed?
- Would you take a vote of all your body members, and let the majority rule?
- Would you trust your eyes and keep on walking since sight is an extremely important sense?

No—you would get off the train tracks. God gave our bodies many different senses and parts. When each part does its job and when each part pays proper attention to the others, the whole body works the way it should.

A church is the body of Christ. It functions best when all of its members are able to share what they sense God is doing and saying. Members of a congregation can't fully know God's will for their lives apart from the testimony of other members. A church needs to hear the whole counsel of God through its members. Then it can proceed in confidence and unity to do God's will.

THE BODY OF CHRIST

Many Christians today feel that their walk with God is private and independent. They see no need for joining a church or making themselves accountable to other believers. Some view the church in terms of how it can help them accomplish the ministry God has given them personally, rather than seeking how their lives fit into the larger work the Lord is doing in the congregation. The Bible teaches that our walk with God is personal, but it is not private. Sin makes people independent. Salvation makes us interdependent on one another. Scripture teaches that the church is a body in which each member is vitally important to the others.

While Christians have personal access to God through Christ as their one Mediator (see 1 Tim. 2:5), God created the church as His redemptive agent in the world. He is at work accomplishing His purposes, and He places every member in a church to accomplish His purposes through each congregation.

Jesus Christ is present as Head of every local church (see Eph. 4:15), and every member is placed in the body as it pleases God (see 1 Cor. 12:18). The Holy Spirit manifests Himself to every person for the common good (see 1 Cor. 12:7), and the whole body is fitted together by the Father. Members are enabled and equipped by the Holy Spirit to function where the Father has placed them in the body. Then the body functions as Christ leads, until every member becomes spiritually mature (see Eph. 4:13). Believers need each other. What one member lacks, others can supply.

What God is doing in and through the body is essential to my knowing how to respond to Him. Where I see Him working in the body, I make the necessary adjustments and put my life there too. In the church, I let God use me in any way He chooses to complete His work. This was Paul's goal when he said, "We proclaim Him, warning and teaching everyone with all wisdom, so that we may present everyone mature in Christ" (Col. 1:28). Paul constantly urged believers to become vitally involved with his life and ministry. The effectiveness of Paul's ministry rested on them (see Col. 4:3; 2 Thess. 3:1–2; Eph. 6:19).

The Church Helped Me Know God's Will

While in seminary, I was involved in a local church. In the first year, I was asked to teach teenage boys, which I did with a willing heart. The next year, the church asked me to be the music and education director, something I had never done before. I had sung in a choir but had never led congregational music, and I knew nothing about directing the educational program of a church.

Here's how I approached the decision. The people of God at this church needed a leader. As they prayed, they sensed that God had put me in their congregation on purpose so I could meet that need.

I, too, saw the need and realized God was leading me to serve in that position. As a servant of Jesus Christ, I did not have an option to say no. I believed that the Head—Jesus Christ—could speak through the rest of the body to guide me to know how I should function in His body. So, I said I would do the best I could, and for two years I served as music and education director.

Then the church voted to call me as their pastor. I hadn't preached three sermons in my life and hadn't gone to seminary with a calling to be a pastor. I had, however, felt called by God to maintain a relationship with Him so I would do whatever He asked me to do. To that end, I sensed I needed to get seminary training so I would be better equipped to serve God. I didn't say, "I am going into foreign missions." I didn't say I would pursue a music ministry or do youth work or preach. I said, "Lord, whatever You direct me to do in relation to Your body, I will do. I am Your servant for Your purposes." And God responded by leading me in ways I had never anticipated. I agreed to be the pastor and thoroughly enjoyed serving as a pastor in various churches for the next thirty years.

Apart from hearing from other members of the body, you can't know how you are to function in the church. Every member needs to listen to what other members say. If the members are not sharing what they sense God is doing, the whole body is in trouble. I depend on others in the church to help me understand God's will. Likewise, I take seriously my role to help other believers in the same way.

Depending on God to Speak through the Church

It is important to note that a need does not constitute a call. Without proper guidance, many well-meaning Christians see every need in their church as a divine call for them to respond. Don't ever be afraid to let the body of believers assist you in knowing God's will.

Sometimes God may speak through one person. Keep in mind, however, that one individual is not the church. Usually, you need to take all the counsel of people for clear direction. What you will find is that a number of things begin to line up. What you are hearing from the Bible, prayer, circumstances, and the church will all point to the same thing. Then you can proceed with confidence.

You may say, "Henry, you don't know my church. I can't depend on them to help me know God's will." Be careful. When you say that, you have said more about your opinion of God than about your church. You are saying, "Not even God can work through these people." But I don't think you really believe that. You place yourself in danger when you isolate yourself from the counsel of God's people. Trust God to give direction through other believers. Turn to them for advice on major decisions. Listen to anything the church has to say to you. Then let God confirm what His message is for you.

Sharing in the Body

As a pastor in Saskatoon, whenever God moved and expressed His will to church members, I guided them to share with other members what God had said to them. We could not adjust our lives to God if we did not know what He was saying. When the Head spoke to any member, all of us listened and heard what He said to our church. All were given an opportunity and encouraged to share. Each member was welcome to respond as God guided him or her.

This happened not only in worship (usually at the close of a service) but also in prayer meetings, committee meetings, business meetings, Sunday school classes, home Bible studies, and personal conversations. Many called the church office and shared what God was saying to them in their quiet times. Still others shared what they experienced at work or at school. The entire church became experientially and practically aware of Christ's presence and guidance in our midst.

Often, relating what God is doing in your life may help someone else encounter God in a meaningful way. For instance, when someone made a significant commitment to the Lord in one of our services, I gave that person an opportunity to share with the body. Sometimes that testimony prompted others to respond in a similar way. This is how God spoke through the church to other believers.

Summary

God speaks to His people by the Holy Spirit. He can speak in any way He chooses, but the most common ways through which God speaks today include the Bible, prayer, circumstances, and the church. He speaks to reveal Himself, His purposes, and His ways.

When what God says through the Bible, prayer, circumstances, and the church line up to say the same thing, you can proceed with confidence to follow God's directions.

Each believer is interdependent with all the others to function correctly in that body. You cannot fully know God's will for your involvement in the body of Christ apart from the counsel God provides through other members. All members of the body belong to each other, and they need each other. You can and should depend on God to speak through other believers and the church to help you know what assignment you are to carry out in the ministry of the kingdom.

Experiencing God Today

Pray for your church and the way God works in and through its members to help believers understand God's call. Reflect on times and ways God has spoken to you through other believers, and thank God for using them to speak to you. Sometime soon, get together with two or three other believers from your church to pray for each other and your church.

QUESTIONS FOR REFLECTION

1. Are you interconnected in a church body so God can speak to you through other church members? If so, what is something God has said to you through fellow Christians?

2. How do you respond when you become aware of a need in your church that you might meet? How do you know if you are the person God wants to use to meet that need?

3. How is God presently using you to minister to other members of your church body? Are you actively seeking His will in this regard?

16

God's Invitation Leads to a Crisis of Belief

Now without faith it is impossible to please God, for the one who draws near to Him must believe that He exists and rewards those who seek Him. (Hebrews 11:6)

A Faith Budget for Our Church

One year when I was a pastor, the people on our church finance committee said, "Pastor, you have taught our congregation to walk by faith in every area except in the budget." I asked them to explain. They said, "Well, when we set the budget, we establish it on the basis of what we believe we can afford to do. It does not reflect that we expect God to do anything."

"Hmmm," I reflected. "Then how do you feel we ought to set the budget?" They said, "First, we should determine all that God wants to do through us. Second, we need to estimate what the cost will be. Finally, we need to divide the budget goal into three categories: (1) what we plan to raise through our tithes and giving, (2) what others have promised to do to help us, and (3) what we must depend on God to provide."

As a church, we prayed and decided that God did want us to take this approach to budgeting, but we did not try to dream our own dreams for God. We had to be absolutely sure God was leading us to do the things we put in the budget. Then we estimated what God's plans would cost. We listed what we thought our people would give and what others (denominational agencies, partnership churches, and donors) had promised to give. The difference between what we could reasonably expect to receive and the total needed was what we would ask God to provide.

The big question was: What is our operating budget? Do we actively proceed on everything covered in the first two columns and hold off on the faith column until we see the funds come in? Or do we proceed with all God has said to do, trusting God to provide as we go? At this point, we reached a crisis of belief. Did we really believe that the God who led us to do these things would also provide the resources to bring them to pass? By faith, we adopted the grand total as our operating budget.

Anytime God leads you to do something that has God-sized dimensions, you'll face a crisis of belief. When you face a crisis of belief, what you do next reveals what you really believe about God. That year, based on all we sensed God leading us to do, we established a budget that was more than twice what we would have set, given our own resources. God poured out His blessing and taught us a radical lesson in faith—we received more funds than even our expanded faith budget had anticipated.

Did you notice our turning point—our crisis of belief? It came when we decided to operate on the greater total—the faith budget—rather than merely setting out to do what we thought we could afford and waiting to see if God supplemented our income. We could have settled on the lesser budget and never known anything more about God, but people in the community watching our church would have seen only what people can do. They would not have seen God and what He can do.

A Crisis of Belief

This chapter focuses on a turning point necessary in your following God's will. When God invites you to join Him in His work, He presents a God-sized assignment He wants to accomplish. It will be obvious you can't do it on your own. If God doesn't help, you will fail. This is the crisis point at which many people decide not to follow what they sense God is leading them to do. Then they wonder why they do not experience God's presence, power, and activity the way some Christians do.

The word *crisis* comes from a Greek word that means "decision." The same word is often translated "judgment." We aren't talking about a calamity in your life such as an accident or death. This crisis is not a disaster or a bad thing. *It is a turning point or a fork in the road that calls for a decision. You must decide what you believe about God.* How you respond when you reach this turning point will determine whether or not you proceed with God in something only He can do or whether you continue on your own way and miss what God has purposed for your life. This is not a one-time experience. How you live your life daily is a testimony of what you believe about God.

THE CRISIS OF BELIEF

These are the characteristics of every crisis of belief:

- An encounter with God requires faith.
- Encounters with God are God-sized.
- What you do in response to God's invitation reveals what you believe about God.
- True faith requires action.

THE FAITH REQUIREMENT

All through Scripture when God revealed Himself, His purposes, and His ways, the response required faith. Read what God says about faith:

- Now faith is the reality of what is hoped for, the proof of what is not seen. (Heb. 11:1)
- For we walk by faith, not by sight. (2 Cor. 5:7)
- [Jesus said,] "The one who believes in Me will also do the works that I do. And he will do even greater works than these, because I am going to the Father." (John 14:12)
- "For I assure you: If you have faith the size of a mustard seed, you will tell this mountain, 'Move from

- here to there,' and it will move. Nothing will be impossible for you." (Matt. 17:20)
- [Paul said,] "My speech and my proclamation were not with persuasive words of wisdom, but with a demonstration of the Spirit and power, so that your faith might not be based on men's wisdom but on God's power." (1 Cor. 2:4–5)
- If you do not stand firm in your faith, then you will not stand at all. (Isa. 7:9)

Faith is confidence that what God promised will come to pass. Sight is the opposite of faith. If you can see clearly how something can be accomplished, faith is more than likely not required. If our church had chosen to operate on a budget based on what we knew we could accomplish, faith would not have been necessary.

Christians (as well as everyone else) have a natural tendency to try building a life in which faith is unnecessary. We establish a comfort zone where everything is in our control, but this is not pleasing to God. God will allow things into our lives that drive us to utter dependence upon Him. Then we see His power and His glory.

Your faith does not rest on a concept or an idea. Faith must be centered on a Person—God Himself. Our generation promotes a dangerous concept that encourages people to "have faith." In this abstract doctrine, faith itself is the pursuit. It matters little what the faith is based on—it is the act of believing that is important—but this teaching is unbiblical. Faith is only valid if it is focused on God and what He says He is purposing to do. Before you call yourself, your family, or your church to exercise faith, be sure you have heard a word from God.

Jesus said if His followers have faith in God, they will do even greater things than He has done. Our faith in the Lord must be based on God's power, not on human wisdom. Without a firm faith in the Lord, we will stumble and fall.

In his own power, Moses could never have delivered the Israelites from Pharaoh's army, crossed the Red Sea on dry land, provided water from a rock, or furnished bread and meat to his people. Moses had to believe that God, who called him, would do the things He said He would do.

Joshua could not take the Israelites across the Jordan River on dry land, bring down city walls, and defeat heavily armed enemies. Only God could do those things. Joshua had to have faith in God.

On their own, the disciples could not feed the multitudes, heal the sick, or raise the dead. But God could and did do these very things through them.

When God lets you know what He wants to do through you, it will be something only He can do. What you believe about Him will determine your response. If you have faith in the God who called you, you will obey, and He will bring to pass what He purposes to do. If you lack faith, you will not do what He wants, and that is disobedience.

Jesus questioned those around Him, "Why do you call me, 'Lord, Lord,' and don't do the things I say?" (Luke 6:46). Jesus frequently rebuked His disciples for their lack of faith. Their unbelief revealed that they really had not come to know who He was. Thus, they did not know what He could do.

Obedience Shows Faith

Faith was required of Moses and the disciples. When God calls a person to join Him in a God-sized task, faith is always necessary. Obedience indicates faith in God. Disobedience reveals a lack of faith. Without faith, a person cannot please God (Heb. 11:6). Without faith, a church cannot please God.

We face the same crisis of belief the people in the Bible experienced. When God speaks, what He asks of us requires faith. Our major hindrance to obedience is our self-centeredness. We think we have to accomplish the assignment in our own power and with our current resources. We think, "I can't do that. That's not possible." In other words, we lack faith.

We forget that when God speaks, He always reveals what He is going to do—not what He wants us to do for Him. We join Him so He works through us. We are not called upon to accomplish the task by our ingenuity, ability, or limited resources. With faith, we can proceed confidently because we know He is going to bring to pass what He purposes. "Looking at them, Jesus said, 'With men it is impossible, but not with God, because all things are possible with God'" (Mark 10:27).

Len Koster and Mission Churches

In the Saskatoon church where I was the pastor, we sensed God wanting to use us as His instruments to reach people for Christ throughout the many cities, towns, and villages scattered across our 588,276 square-mile province. Since there were numerous communities without any evangelical church, we would have to start many new churches. To do that, we felt God leading us to call a man named Len Koster to equip our congregation to start other churches.

Len lived in British Columbia, in a town more than one thousand miles from Saskatoon. Over the previous fourteen years, Len and Ruth had served in small churches. Len, in fact, was so committed to the Lord that he worked as a service station attendant in order to supplement his meager income. Without a part-time pastor, these churches would have had no pastor at all. In that time, Len and Ruth had saved $7,000 toward the goal of buying their own home. When we contacted him, Len was absolutely convinced he ought to help us start churches.

I said, "Len, we have no money to move you and no money to pay you." To which he replied, "Henry, God has called me. He will provide for me. We will use the money from our savings to move." And so they did.

One day, Len came to me and said, "Henry, my wife and I prayed and talked all night. I have worked bivocationally for fourteen years, and I have no problem with working to provide for my family. But the need is so great, and the direction of God is such that I feel I need to serve the Lord here full-time. I am going to devote all my energy to starting mission churches. Don't worry about our financial support. God will show us how to live."

When Len left my office, I fell on my face and wept before the Lord. I said, "Father, I don't understand why such a faithful couple should have to make this kind of a sacrifice." I saw in Len and Ruth—the parents of five children—a great faith demonstrated by their actions.

Two days later, I received a brief letter from a Presbyterian layman in Kamloops, British Columbia. It said simply, "I understand a man by the name of Len Koster has come to work with you. God has laid it on my heart that I am to help support his ministry. Enclosed find a check for $7,000 to be used for his support." When I opened that letter, I went back on my knees and wept before the Father. This time, I asked Him to forgive me for not trusting Him.

I called Len and said, "Len, you placed your life savings on the altar of sacrifice, but God had something else in the bushes. The God who says, 'I am your Provider' has just provided!" Then I told him what had happened.

Do you know what that did in Len's life? Do you know what it did for our church's faith? We all grew to believe God to a greater degree than we had before. After that, we stepped out in faith to obey God time and time again. We watched God accomplish astounding things through our ordinary congregation. We never could have experienced God that way if Len and his family had not responded in faith to God's call. Len has now gone to be with the Lord, but his legacy of faith remains in the dozens of churches he helped start. Len's youngest son is currently in seminary.

GOD-SIZED ASSIGNMENTS

God wants the world to know Him. That way, people will come to understand what God is like when they see Him at work. They will know His nature when they see it expressed in His activity.

Some people believe God will never ask them to undertake anything that seems impossible. They believe God will never lead a church to attempt something they cannot afford, ask someone to do something outside their giftedness, or lead someone to do something they are afraid of doing. Yet if people are going to see God at work, they must witness more than just sincere Christians doing the best they can. People must see God at work in Christians' lives.

At times, people ask if they will experience a crisis every time God asks them to do something. God will often tell His people to do mundane things. Holding a church potluck dinner, for example, is not miraculous. Yet when God is involved in an activity, traces of God's character are always evident. At times, we do things with the love of Christ such as forgiving someone who has wronged us, and when we do things God's way, we always exalt Christ.

Scripture indicates that God will ask us to attempt things that are impossible apart from divine intervention. While some church leaders believe this is irresponsible, the fact is that when we accomplish things that can only be explained by God, we provide a powerful witness to God's presence and guidance. The God-sized assignments in the Bible are how He demonstrated His nature, strength, provision, and love to His people—and to a watching world. Those who witnessed God powerfully at work through His people saw what God is truly like.

Consider a few of these God-sized assignments. God told Abraham to father a nation when Abraham had no son, and Sarah was long past the age to bear children. He told Moses to deliver the children of Israel, to cross the Red Sea, and to provide water from a rock. He told Gideon to defeat a Midianite army of a hundred and twenty thousand with three hundred men. God told a virgin that she would give birth to the Messiah. Jesus told the disciples to feed the multitudes and to make disciples of all the nations. Not one of these things was humanly possible. But when God's people and the world see something happen that only God can do, they come to know God.

People Come to Know God

Moses

God directed Moses to lead the Israelites to camp beside the Red Sea. From a military perspective, this encampment was utterly foolish because it allowed no escape route from the pursuing Egyptian army. But God knew He was going to deliver them by dividing the sea and letting them cross on dry ground. God said, "I will receive glory by means of Pharaoh and all his army, and the Egyptians will know that I am the Lord" (Exod. 14:4). What was the result? "When Israel saw the great power that the Lord used against the Egyptians, the people feared the Lord and believed in Him and in His servant Moses" (Exod. 14:31).

Joshua

God commanded Joshua to lead the Israelites across the Jordan River at flood stage. Why? "This is so that all the people of the earth may know that the Lord's hand is mighty, and so that you may always fear the Lord your God" (Josh. 4:24).

King Jehoshaphat

A vast army came to war against Israel. King Jehoshaphat proclaimed a fast and led the people to seek God's counsel. He prayed, "Our God . . . we are powerless before this vast multitude that comes to fight against us. We do not know what to do, but we look to You" (2 Chron. 20:12). God responded, "Do not be afraid or discouraged because of this vast multitude, for the battle is not yours, but God's . . . You do not have to fight in this battle. Position yourselves, stand still, and see the salvation of the LORD. He is with you" (2 Chron. 20:15, 17). Jehoshaphat sent a choir in front of the army, singing praise to God for His enduring love. Again, as a military strategy this would have appeared suicidal. But God destroyed the invading army before Jehoshaphat and Israel even arrived at the battlefield. Then, "The terror of God was on all the kingdoms of the lands when they heard that the LORD had fought against the enemies of Israel" (2 Chron. 20:29).

Shadrach, Meshach, and Abednego

Shadrach, Meshach, and Abednego obeyed God rather than the pagan king Nebuchadnezzar. Before being thrown into a blazing furnace for their alleged insolence, they proclaimed, "If the God we serve exists, then He can rescue us from the furnace of blazing fire, and He can rescue us from the power of you, the king" (Dan. 3:17). Although nearby soldiers were killed by the fierce blaze, God delivered these three faithful men.

King Nebuchadnezzar said, "Praise to the God of Shadrach, Meshach, and Abednego! He sent His angel and rescued His servants who trusted in Him. Therefore I issue a decree that anyone of any people, nation, or language who says anything offensive against the God of Shadrach, Meshach, and Abednego will be torn limb from limb and his house made a garbage dump. For there is no other god who is able to deliver like this" (Dan. 3:28–29). The king then announced to the whole nation, "I am pleased to tell you about the miracles and wonders the Most High God has done for me. How great are His miracles, and how mighty His wonders!" (Dan. 4:2–3).

The Early Church

Christians in the early church followed the directions of the Holy Spirit, and here is the testimony of the impact God had on their world:

- The disciples were filled with the Holy Spirit and spoke in foreign languages they had not learned. Peter preached and "those who accepted his message were baptized, and that day about 3,000 people were added to them." (Acts 2:41)
- Peter and John healed a crippled beggar in the name of Jesus. They preached, and "many of those who heard the message believed, and the number of men came to about 5,000." (Acts 4:4)
- God used Peter to raise Dorcas from the dead. "This became known throughout all Joppa, and many believed in the Lord." (Acts 9:42)

What our world often sees are devoted, committed Christians serving God to the best of their ability. But they are not seeing God. They comment, "Well, there's a dedicated, faithful group of people." But they don't witness anything happening that can only be explained in terms of God's activity. Why? Because we aren't attempting anything that only God can do!

The World Comes to Know God

Our world is not attracted to Christ because we don't allow them to see Him at work. They don't hesitate to attack the Christian position on morality because they have no fear of the God we serve. They see us doing good things for God and say, "That's fine, but that's not my thing." The world passes us by, not wanting to become involved because they are merely seeing *people* at work, not God.

Let the world see God at work, and He will attract them. Let Christ be lifted up—not in words, but in life. Let them see the difference the living Christ makes in a life, a family, or a church, and this will affect how they respond. When the world sees things happening through God's people that cannot be explained except that God Himself has done them, then people will be drawn to

God. Let world leaders see the miraculous signs of an all-powerful God, and they, like Nebuchadnezzar, will declare that He is the one true God.

The world comes to know God when they see God's nature expressed through His activity. When God starts to work, He accomplishes something only He can do, and both God's people and the world come to experience Him in ways they have never known Him before. *That* is why God gives God-sized assignments to His people.

A Dangerous Church Field

I know of a church that was established in a country where the official religion is Islam. At times, there were violent riots against Christians, and the government regularly passed laws that discriminated against Christians, making it difficult for churches to own property.

A small group of believers were meeting as a church and praying for God to use this little congregation to impact their large city. They eventually studied *Experiencing God* and were reminded that God is working all around them. They decided to see where God was at work and join Him.

This congregation began to witness God doing amazing things in their midst. A Christian professional in their city felt God lead him to resign his lucrative career and become the pastor of this flock. People noticed the dynamic faith and love of these people, and their numbers grew. When they needed a larger facility, a businessman sold them space in a major office building, even though this was frowned upon by local government and religious officials. When my son Richard visited this church, it was teeming with enthusiastic worshipers and ministering to other communities in the name of Christ.

As long as this congregation remained intimidated by the forces opposing them and as long as they focused on their small size and lack of resources, not much happened and not many people were drawn to them. But when they allowed God to work through them to do what could only be explained by His presence, suddenly the church overflowed with excited, exuberant Christians impacting their nation for Christ.

The reason much of the world is not attracted to Christ and His church is that God's people lack the faith to attempt things only God can do. If you or your church are not responding to God and pursuing things only He can accomplish, then you are not exercising faith. "Without faith it is impossible to please God" (Heb. 11:6). If people in your community are not responding to the gospel as they did in New Testament times, one possible reason is that they do not see God in what you are doing as a church.

Joining God Requires Faith and Action

Our growing Saskatoon church needed more space. We sensed God leading us to start a building program, even though we had only $749 in our building fund. The building was going to cost $220,000, and we didn't have the foggiest notion how to pay for it. Our congregation consisted primarily of college students, along with several families of modest income. God also had brought a number of people to our congregation with physical, mental, and emotional needs. We certainly did not have the resources within our membership to fund a building project.

Although we did much of the work ourselves to save on labor costs, halfway through that project we were still $100,000 short. Those dear, faithful people looked to their pastor to see if I believed God would do what He had called us to do. God put a confidence in my heart that the God who was leading us would show us how to do it.

God began providing the necessary funds. Near the end of the project, we were about $60,000 short. We had been expecting some money from a Texas foundation, but delay after delay came along that we could not understand. Then one day, for two hours, the currency exchange rate for the Canadian dollar hit one of the lowest points in its history—at exactly the time the Texas foundation wired the money to Canada. You know what that did? It gave us $60,000 *more* than we would have received otherwise.

God's timing, as always, had been perfect. When that happened, I magnified what the Lord had done in the eyes of the people and made sure we gave the credit to Him. God revealed Himself to us, and we came to know Him in a new way through that experience.

God Leads into Politics

Several years ago, I was speaking at a conference in Arkansas while Mike Huckabee was governor. He extended an invitation for me to come to the governor's mansion for dinner one evening and, during the meal, Governor Huckabee explained why he had invited me. He said that while he was the pastor of a church, the Lord had begun to impress on him that He wanted to use Mike in new ways. Huckabee had trained to be a church minister, and that is what he had been doing. But as he and his wife began to study *Experiencing God*, it became clear that God was leading him to resign from the great church he was leading and to run for governor of his state.

The state government at that time had been rocked with scandal, and the political system appeared rife with corruption. It did not seem like a world that would welcome a Christian minister into its leadership. Yet as he followed what he sensed God leading him to do, he won a surprising victory and became governor.

Huckabee served well and returned integrity to the governor's office. After completing the maximum terms of service, Huckabee felt led by God to run for president of the United States. As a result, he has had many opportunities to represent his faith on national television and has become a prominent national figure. Mike Huckabee could never have imagined what his life would become. But God knew and has been guiding him to accomplish things far beyond what would have seemed possible to this Arkansas pastor.

David's Faith Demonstrated

First Samuel 16:12–13 tells us God chose David—and had Samuel anoint him—to become the next king over Israel. Then God brought David into the middle of His activity. David did not gain the throne immediately, however. Saul was still king and the Israelites were at war with the Philistines. Though still a young man, David was sent by his father to visit his older brothers in the army. He arrived while Goliath, a huge soldier nine feet tall, was taunting the Israelites and challenging them to send a man to fight him. The losing nation would become the slaves of the winner. Israel's army was terrified, yet David asked in amazement, "Who is this uncircumcised Philistine, that he should defy the armies of the living God?" (1 Sam. 17:26). David faced a crisis of belief. He had to recognize that God had brought him to the battlefield and had prepared him for this assignment.

David offered to fight the giant. He stated his belief, "The LORD, who delivered me from the paw of the lion and from the paw of the bear will rescue me from the hand of this Philistine" (1 Sam. 17:37). David refused to take the normal weapons of war. Instead he took a sling and five smooth stones. He said to Goliath, "You come against me with a dagger, spear, and sword, but I come against you in the name of the LORD of Hosts, the God of Israel's armies—you have defied Him. Today, the LORD will hand you over to me . . . then all the world will know that Israel has a God, and this whole assembly will know that it is not by sword or by spear that the LORD saves, for the battle is the LORD's. He will hand you over to us" (1 Sam. 17:45–47). David killed Goliath, and Israel won a victory.

David's bold statements indicate his belief that God was his deliverer. He acknowledged God is almighty and that He would defend Israel's armies. But it was David's actions that confirmed his belief. Many thought David was a foolish young boy, and even Goliath scoffed at him. But God gave a mighty victory through David so the world would know Israel's God was powerful and able to deliver His people from whatever they faced.

SARAI'S LACK OF FAITH

God promised to make Abram's offspring as numerous as the stars. Abram questioned God about this promise since he remained childless into his old age, but God reaffirmed, "One who will come from your own body will be your heir. . . . Abram believed the LORD, and He credited it to him as righteousness" (Gen. 15:4, 6).

Abram's wife, Sarai, was in her mid-seventies when God promised her a son. She knew she was past childbearing years, so she decided she would have to build a family in a different way. She gave her maid to Abram as a wife and asked for a child through her. Abram consented, and Ishmael was born to Hagar a year later. Sarai's actions indicated what she believed about God. In this experience, Abraham joined Sarai in trying to achieve God's purpose in human ways.

Do you see how Sarai's actions reveal what she really believed about God? She lacked the faith to believe God could do the impossible. Her faith in God was limited by her human reasoning, and this act of unbelief was extremely costly. Ishmael caused Abram and Sarai much grief in their old age. What's more, Ishmael and his Arab descendants have lived in hostility toward Isaac and his descendants from that time until today.

Actions Speak

When God invites you to join Him and you face a crisis of belief, what you do next reveals what you believe about God. When two blind men demonstrated that they believed Jesus was merciful and that He was the Messiah, Jesus healed them according to their faith (see Matt. 9:27–31). A woman who had been hemorrhaging for years believed that just a touch of Jesus' garment would allow His healing power to flow to her. She risked public ridicule in order to experience Jesus' healing power. She acted in faith, and Jesus healed her (see Matt. 9:20–22).

The disciples were caught in a storm at sea. Jesus rebuked them, not for their human tendency to fear but for their failure to recognize His presence, protection, and power (Matt. 8:23–27). Their actions revealed their unbelief rather than their faith. When the storms of life overtake us, we often respond as if God does not exist or does not care.

When a centurion sought Jesus' help to heal his servant, he said, "Only say the word, and my servant will be cured" (Matt. 8:8). Jesus commended the centurion's faith in His authority and power, and He healed the servant because of the faith of his master (see Matt. 8:5–13).

In each of these biblical examples, what people did indicated to Jesus their faith—or lack of it. What you do—not what you *say* you believe—reveals what you really believe about God. "For just as the body without the spirit is dead, so also faith without works is dead" (James 2:26).

True Faith Requires Action

Hebrews 11 is sometimes referred to as "the roll call of faith." The individuals listed there took action that demonstrated faith. While studying Hebrews 11, however, you may notice that a faithful life does not always bring rewards in human terms. While verses 33–35a describe the victory and deliverance some people of faith experienced, verses 35b–38 describe the torture, mockery, and death other faithful people endured. Were some of them more faithful than the others? No. They all "obtained a good testimony through faith" (Heb. 11:39). Verse 40 explains that God has planned something far better for people of faith than the world has to offer, and the next chapter encourages us to follow in their footsteps:

> Therefore since we also have such a large cloud of witnesses surrounding us, let us lay aside every weight and the sin that so easily ensnares us, and run with endurance that race that lies before us, keeping our eyes on Jesus, the source and perfecter of our faith, who for the joy that lay before Him endured a cross and despised the shame, and has sat down at the right hand of God's throne. For consider Him who endured such hostility from sinners against Himself, so that you won't grow weary and lose heart. (Heb. 12:1–3)

A Leper Pays the Price

I heard the remarkable story of an Indonesian pastor on the east coast of Java. He knew English and had studied *Experiencing God*. His life was changed dramatically by the truths he encountered, and he wanted all of his people who didn't know English to be able to read the material for themselves. So he began the arduous task of translating the course into his native language. Missionaries saw him sitting at his manual typewriter every day for three or four hours, translating—even though this man had leprosy. His hands were severely marred by the disease, and sitting still for very long caused him great discomfort. Nevertheless, he kept at his ancient typewriter every day until his people finally had the material for themselves.

When I heard this, I wept and asked the missionary who told me the story if she could get a picture of the man at his typewriter, showing his hands. She said he was very humble and might not let her. Several years later at a large meeting in Salt Lake City, I saw the missionary running toward me holding a picture. "I've got the picture for you!" I have it hanging in my prayer room at home, where I pray

God's Invitation Leads to a Crisis of Belief

for this dear pastor and his people and am reminded how costly it is for some of God's precious people to join His activity.

The outward appearance of success does not always represent faith, and the outward appearance of failure does not always indicate that faith is lacking. A faithful servant is one who does what the Master says, no matter what the outcome. As our model, we need only to consider Jesus who endured the cross but who is now seated at the Father's side. What a reward for His faithfulness! Do not grow weary—a great reward awaits faithful servants.

I pray you are trying to please God by earnestly seeking Him (see Jer. 29:11–13). In the next chapters, we'll look more carefully at the adjustments required to follow God's will. Obeying the Lord will require adjustments that are costly to you and to those around you.

Summary

When God invites you to be involved in His activity, He wants to reveal Himself to you and to a watching world. Therefore, He will give you a God-sized assignment. When you are confronted with such a task, you'll face a crisis of belief. You'll have to decide what you really believe about the God who called you, and the way you respond to God will reveal what you believe, regardless of what you say. Following God requires faith and action. Without faith you cannot please God. And without action, your faith is dead (see James 2:26).

Experiencing God Today

Read Hebrews 11, and think about the biblical heroes of the faith. Ask the Lord to increase your faith to believe Him in all things. Pray that He will enable you to walk by faith, even if the outcome matches the last half of the chapter rather than the first half.

QUESTIONS FOR REFLECTION

1. Are you presently experiencing a crisis of belief? If so, what is God asking you to do? What is it that keeps you from obeying?

2. What does your present walk with God reveal about what you believe about Him? What is the evidence of God at work in and through your life?

3. What in your life or the life of your church can only be explained by the presence of Almighty God?

4. Is there something in your life you struggle to turn over to God? How is God presently seeking to increase your faith in Him?

17

JOINING GOD REQUIRES ADJUSTMENTS

If anyone wants to come with Me, he must deny himself, take up his cross daily, and follow Me. For whoever wants to save his life will lose it, but whoever loses his life because of Me will save it. (Luke 9:23–24)

Many of us want God to speak and lead us in His will. We want the excitement of God working through us, but we are loath to make any major adjustments so He will. The Bible reveals that every time God speaks to people about something He wants to do, they have to realign their lives in some way. When God's people are willing to take the necessary actions, God accomplishes His purposes through those He calls.

A SECOND CRITICAL TURNING POINT

As we discussed in the last chapter, the first turning point in knowing and doing the will of God is the crisis of belief—you must believe God is who He says He is and that He will do what He says He will do. Without faith in God, you will make the wrong decision at this critical point.

The second critical turning point is adjusting your life to God. If you choose to make the necessary adjustments, you can go on to obedience. If you refuse, you could miss what God has in store for your life.

Obedience begins in the heart as a willingness to do whatever God says. Obedience is expressed through action, by words and deeds. Our obedience can be costly—to you and to those around you. Let me give you an example.

Making Adjustments for Missions

In Saskatoon, a need arose in one of our missions forty miles away. I asked the church to pray God would call someone to move to that community to be a lay pastor of the mission. A young couple responded and said they were willing to move there. Yet the husband was attending the university, and they had very limited finances.

If they took up residence in the mission community, he would have to commute eighty miles a day to and from school. I knew they couldn't afford that. Moreover, winter road conditions in our area could be extremely hazardous, so I said, "No, I can't let you do that." I went through all the reasons why they should not consider such a venture.

In response, the young man looked at me and said, "Pastor, don't deny me the opportunity to sacrifice for my Lord." His statement crushed me. How could I refuse? Yet I knew that this couple would have to pay a high price for our church's obedience in starting new missions.

We had prayed for God to call a lay pastor, and I should have been open to God's answering in an unexpected way. When this couple responded with such a deep commitment and willingness to sacrifice, the body (our church) affirmed their sense of call—and God provided for their needs!

You Can't Stay Where You Are and Go with God

When God speaks, revealing what He is about to do, that revelation is your invitation to adjust your life to Him. As you adjust your heart and mind to Him, His purposes, and His ways, you are in a position to obey. You can't continue business as usual or stay where you are and go with God at the same time. This truth is clearly evident in the Scriptures.

- Noah could not continue life as usual and build an ark at the same time. (see Gen. 6)
- Abram could not stay in Ur or Haran and father a nation in Canaan. (see Gen. 12:1–8)
- Moses could not stay on the back side of the desert herding sheep and stand before Pharaoh at the same time. (see Exod. 3)
- Rahab could not obey the king and save the lives of the Israelite spies (see Josh. 2:1–24).
- Ruth could not remain with her relatives and join the people of God in Israel (see Ruth 1:16–18).
- David had to leave his sheep to become king. (see 1 Sam. 16:1–13)
- Amos had to leave his sycamore orchard to preach in Israel. (see Amos 7:14–15)
- Jonah had to leave his home and go against what he had been taught in order to preach in Nineveh. (see Jonah 1:1–2; 3:1–2; 4:1–11)
- Esther could not remain silent before the king and save her people (see Esther 4:14)
- Peter, Andrew, James, and John had to leave their fishing businesses in order to follow Jesus. (see Matt. 4:18–22)
- Matthew had to leave his lucrative tax collecting job to follow Jesus. (see Matt. 9:9)
- Saul had to completely change direction in order for God to use him to preach the gospel to the Gentiles. (see Acts 9:1–19)

Enormous changes and adjustments were required whenever God's people determined to obey His calling. Some had to leave family and country. Others had to abandon long held prejudices and reorient their thinking. Men and women were willing to leave behind life goals, ideals, and desires. Everything had to be yielded to God and their entire life adjusted to Him. The moment the necessary adjustments were made, however, God began to accomplish His purposes through them. Each one learned that adjusting one's life to God is always well worth the cost.

You may be thinking: But God will not ask me to make major adjustments. If you look to Scripture for your understanding of God, you will see that God most certainly does require changes of His people. His own Son gave up more than anyone: "For you know the grace of our Lord Jesus Christ: although He was rich, for your sake He became poor, so that by His poverty you might become rich" (2 Cor. 8:9). Jesus emptied Himself of position and glory in heaven to join the Father in providing salvation through His death on the cross. Jesus couldn't stay where He was in heaven and be a part of the Father's plan to redeem humanity on earth.

If you want to be a disciple of Jesus, you have no choice. You will have to make significant alterations in your life. Following your Master means going where He goes. Until you are ready to make *any* change necessary to follow and obey what God has said, you will be of little use to God. Your greatest difficulty in following God may come at this point.

Our tendency is to want God to adjust to us and our plans. We want to obey God but only on our terms! His ways are different from ours, though. God says, "For as heaven is higher than earth, so My ways are higher than your ways, and My thoughts than your thoughts" (Isa. 55:9). The only way to follow Him is to align our thinking and our actions with His ways. Before we can follow Jesus, we must be willing to make whatever adjustment is necessary.

The Rich Young Ruler Refused to Adjust

The rich ruler wanted eternal life, but he could not bring himself to pay the price Jesus asked (see Luke 18:18–27). Wealth stood in the way of his following the Lord, but Jesus knew this man could not wholly serve God and cling to his money at the same time (see Matt. 6:24). So He asked the young aristocrat to put away the thing that had become god to him—his wealth. The man refused to do as Jesus asked, and he went no further with God.

The Lord knows what it is in each of our hearts that hinders us from fully giving ourselves over to following Him. Ephesians 5:5 says greed is a form of idolatry. Prosperity and the love of worldly things may tempt some of us away from following God. Jesus said, "You cannot be slaves of God and of money" (Matt. 6:24). Ephesians 5:5 also cites immorality as a stumbling block to eternal life.

Doubt and fear of the future are behind the reluctance of many to wholeheartedly accept and follow God's invitation to join Him. For many Christians, the thought of moving from home and leaving extended family keeps them from following Christ. Adjusting our lives to God means dealing with financial, physical, emotional, spiritual, and relational barriers that prevent us from absolute obedience to Him.

Elisha's Adjustments

Read 1 Kings 19:15–21. God told Elijah to select Elisha to be his successor as a prophet to God's people. Elijah found Elisha in a field plowing with twelve yoke of oxen. When Elisha heard God's call through Elijah, he immediately made major adjustments. He left his family and farming career to follow God's call. Elisha burned his farm equipment and killed his twenty-four oxen. Then he cooked the meat and fed the people of the community. He was giving tangible evidence of the permanence of his decision!

When Elisha made the necessary adjustments, he was in a position to obey God and serve Him as a prophet. As a result, God worked through Elisha to perform some of the greatest signs and miracles recorded in the Old Testament (see 2 Kings 2–13). Elisha proved from the outset that he was serious about obeying God. But not until he had made the adjustments did God accomplish miracles through him.

No one can sum up all God is able to accomplish through one life, completely yielded, adjusted, and obedient to Him. Do you want to be that person? You can't go on to obedience without first making the adjustments in your heart and life that God requires.

Jesus told His disciples, "If anyone desires to come after Me, let him deny himself (adjustment), and take up his cross (adjustment), and follow Me (obedience)." Those who attempt to follow Jesus without making the adjustments will always find it impossible.

The Necessary Adjustments

What kind of adjustments does God require? Trying to answer that question is like attempting to list all the things God might ask you to do. The list could be endless. Here are a few examples of general categories where adjustments may be required of you:

- your circumstances (job, home, finances),
- your relationships (family, friends, business associates),
- your thinking (prejudices, methodology, planning),
- your commitments (to family, church, job, plans, tradition),
- your actions (how you pray, give, serve),
- your beliefs (about God, His purposes, His ways, your relationship to Him).

A major adjustment will come at the point of acting on your faith. Your intellectual decision may be the easy part. The hard part is adjusting your life to God and acting in a manner that demonstrates your faith. You may be called upon to attempt things only God can do, whereas formerly you may have done only that which you knew you could accomplish.

Sometimes an adjustment involves several of the above areas at once. For instance, Peter was a faithful Jewish man who ate only kosher food. He had no dealings with "unclean" Gentiles, but one day while Peter was praying, God gave him a life-changing vision. He wanted to convince Peter that anything He had created was not unclean. He told Peter to go with some Gentiles to preach to Cornelius and his household.

The experience with Cornelius required adjustments in Peter's thinking and beliefs about what is clean and unclean, his commitments to traditions of the Jewish people, and his habits about associating with Gentiles (see Acts 10:1–20). Peter made the necessary changes and obeyed God. When he did, God worked through him to bring Cornelius's whole household to faith in Christ.

Being able to identify an adjustment is not as important as making it. Once you understand what change God wants you to make, He will help you know how to do it. Your part is to obey.

Adjusted in Russia

One of the great privileges Marilynn and I have had is to travel around the world encouraging some of God's finest missionaries. On one trip to Russia, a few years after the Cold War had ended, we spent an afternoon with a delightful couple. After the husband had retired from his job in the United States, they felt the Lord placing His heart for the world on them. As they looked to see where God was working, they were drawn to the former Soviet Union where evangelism and preaching the gospel had long been prohibited.

They ultimately sensed God leading them to serve in a bitterly cold region of northern Russia. But they had to count the cost. They had retired and now were in a position to enjoy their sunset years traveling and attending events at their church. They had a lovely home and grandchildren to think of. Russia was on the other side of the world. Yet God was clearly leading. So they left everything and took up residence in a Russian city where they did not speak the language.

As the two began ministering, they found themselves in the midst of a bitter conflict among the churches in the area. When the couple refused to take sides in the dispute, both groups took offense and ostracized them. Both sides discouraged their people from having anything to do with the missionaries.

At the time we met them, they were extremely discouraged. They had sacrificed all the comforts of their former lifestyle. They were living in a small apartment a fraction of the size of their beautiful home in America. Worst of all, the people they had traveled so far to help would have nothing to do with them! They were planning to return home shortly.

We empathized with their pain, but I sensed they had not made all the adjustments necessary for God to use them in this extremely difficult assignment. They had changed their lifestyle, their living conditions, and their geographical location. But they still were holding the belief that they deserved to be treated in a certain way. They felt their sacrifice and effort ought to be appreciated by those they had come to serve, and because they were not being shown gratitude and acceptance, they were going home.

Now, that is a very human response when we are misunderstood or mistreated, but I challenged them with some tough questions. I asked them to describe how Jesus was treated when He left the comforts of heaven and came to people who desperately needed Him. I asked how many people truly appreciated His sacrifice. Finally, I asked, "If Jesus had taken the same approach you're taking, what would that have cost others?" Jesus—who was despised, rejected, and murdered by the very people He came to save—had come wanting sweet fellowship with them.

Having shared tangibly in Christ's sufferings, these missionaries could glimpse the love of Christ in a way many could not. I reminded them that Christianity is not about serving where we are appreciated or where we enjoy success but about enjoying a relationship with our Savior who gave up everything so we could experience salvation.

Their response was genuine humility. The Lord enveloped this dear couple in His loving arms at that moment. They smiled through their tears and said they would continue to serve their Lord right where He had placed them. God had given them an arduous assignment, and it required them to make extensive and deep adjustments in their actions and attitudes. Without those adjustments, they could not serve the Lord as He had invited them to.

Absolute Surrender

God frequently requires adjustments in areas you have never considered before. Peter couldn't have dreamed God would ask him to enter the home of a Gentile, but that was exactly what the Lord did. Just because you have never seen yourself as a Bible teacher, author, or missionary does not mean God will never ask you to teach or write or go on a mission trip. God is looking for absolute surrender. We must have a willing heart to do whatever He asks, and then trust Him to enable us to do it. God does not delight in making us do things we don't like. But He does love us enough to involve us in His work, and He refuses to leave us where we are when He knows we could be experiencing much more of Him. Any adjustment God expects you to make is for your good and for the welfare of those He intends to bless through your life.

The adjustments required are in direct response to God's leadership. Sometimes we make decisions to please our church or our friends or our parents, and these may or may not be good decisions. To truly follow and experience God, we must reorient our lives to Him. We change our viewpoints to align with His. We amend our ways to be like His. After we make the necessary alterations, He tells us what to do next. Pleasing God is more important than satisfying friends, pastors, or even our families.

Some have questioned whether major adjustments are always necessary in order to follow God. Anytime you go from where you are to where God is working, or from your way of thinking to God's way of thinking, or from your ways to God's ways, or from your purposes to His purposes, a major adjustment will be involved. That is because God's ways and His plans are much better than our own best plans and thinking.

Total Dependence on God

Absolute surrender involves giving up our desires, goals, and preferences to God and accepting God's will, regardless of how difficult it may be. Another adjustment we must make to do God's will is reaching a place of total dependence on God. Jesus said, "You can do nothing without Me" (John 15:5). As God's servants, we must be in that intimate relationship so He will complete His work through us. We must depend on God alone. When we surrender our lives completely, we become totally dependent on Him. Then we understand that, apart from Him, we can do nothing. We must learn to live in constant awareness of our absolute reliance on God if He is to accomplish His purposes through us.

This adjustment requires a shift from doing work for God according to our abilities, gifts, goals, likes, and dislikes to being totally dependent on God, His working, and His resources. It requires courage and faith.

Read the following Scriptures, and notice why we must depend on God to carry out His purposes:

- "I am the vine; you are the branches. The one who remains in Me and I in him produces much fruit, because you can do nothing without Me." (John 15:5)
- By God's grace I am what I am, and His grace toward me was not ineffective. However, I worked more than any of them, yet not I, but God's grace that was with me. (1 Cor. 15:10)
- I have been crucified with Christ; and I no longer live, but Christ lives in me. The life I now live in the flesh, I live by faith in the Son of God, who loved me and gave Himself for me. (Gal. 2:20)
- The Lord of hosts has sworn, saying, "As I have planned, so it will be; as I have purposed it, so it will happen." (Isa. 14:24)

- "Do not fear, for I am with you; do not be afraid, for I am your God. I will strengthen you; I will help you; I will hold on to you with my righteous right hand." (Isa. 41:10)
- "I am God, and there is no other. . . . My plan will take place, and I will do all My will. . . . Yes, I have spoken; so I will also bring it about. I have planned it; I will also do it." (Isa. 46:9–11)

If God is not at work in you, you can do nothing to bear spiritual fruit. As you are crucified with Christ, He lives through you to accomplish His purposes by His grace. When God sets out to do something, He guarantees that it will come to pass. He is the One who will accomplish what He intends to do. If you depend on anything other than God, you are asking for failure.

Waiting on the Lord

Sometimes as you adjust your life to God, He requires that you wait on Him. Learning to wait on God is one of the hardest but most important aspects of the Christian life. God seeks a love relationship with you, and waiting develops your absolute dependence on Him. It assures that you will act in His timing, not your own. The Scriptures frequently commend waiting on the Lord:

- "Stop your fighting—and know that I am God." (Ps. 46:10)
- We wait for the Lord; He is our help and shield. (Ps. 33:20)
- Wait for the Lord and keep His way, and He will exalt you to inherit the land. (Ps. 37:34)
- I put my hope in You, Lord; You will answer, Lord my God. (Ps. 38:15)
- Those who trust in the Lord will renew their strength; they will soar on wings like eagles; they will run and not grow weary; they will walk and not faint. (Isa. 40:31)

You may think of waiting as passive, but waiting on the Lord is anything but inactive. While you wait on Him, you will be praying with a passion to know Him, His purposes, and His ways. You will be evaluating your circumstances and asking God to reveal His perspective on them. You will share with other believers to find out what God is saying to them. As you wait on the Lord, you will actively ask, seek, and knock: "Keep asking, and it will be given to you. Keep searching, and you will find. Keep knocking, and the door will be opened to you. For everyone who asks receives, and the one who searches finds, and to the one who knocks, the door will be opened" (Matt. 7:7–8).

While you wait, continue doing the last thing God told you to do. In waiting, you are shifting the responsibility of the outcome to God—where it belongs. Then, when God gives you specific guidance, He will do more through you in days and weeks than you could ever accomplish in years of labor. Waiting on Him is always worth it. His timing and His ways are always right. You must depend on Him to guide you to accomplish His will.

Summary

You can't stay where you are and go with God in obedience to His will. To go from your ways, thoughts, and purposes to God's will always require adjustments. These may call for changes in your circumstances, relationships, attitudes, commitments, behavior, and beliefs. Once you have made the necessary changes, you can follow God obediently. Keep in mind: the God who calls you is also the One who will enable you to do His will (1 Thess. 5:24).

When you surrender everything in your life to Christ's lordship, you, like Elisha, will find the adjustments well worth the reward of experiencing God. If you have not reached a point where you have surrendered everything, decide today to deny yourself, take up your cross, and follow Him (Luke 9:23).

Experiencing God Today

People who have been mightily used by God have always had to make major adjustments in their lives. Read the statements on the following page made by some choice servants of God. Think about the significant level of commitment reflected in each:

David Livingstone. David Livingstone considered his work as a medical missionary in Africa to be a high honor, not a sacrifice. He said: "Forbid that we should ever consider the holding of a commission from the King of Kings a sacrifice, so long as other men esteem the service of an earthly government as an honor. I am a missionary, heart and soul. God Himself had an only Son, and He was a missionary and a physician. A poor, poor imitation I am, or wish to be, but in this service I hope to live. In it I wish to die. I still prefer poverty and missions service to riches and ease. This is my choice."[1]

Jim Elliot. Jim Elliot was a missionary to the Quichua Indians in South America. He was willing to give up earthly things for heavenly reward. Jim wisely noted: "He is no fool who gives what he cannot keep to gain what he cannot lose."[2] Jim was killed by South American natives as he sought to spread the gospel to those who had never heard about Jesus. Later, his wife and others were able to share the gospel message with Jim's murderers, and as a result, many came to a saving knowledge of Christ.

Bob Pierce. Bob Pierce was used by God to establish World Vision and Samaritan's Purse, both ministries to impoverished people around the world.

This was Bob's prayer: "Let my heart be broken by the things that break the heart of God."[3] He allowed God to adjust his thinking so he cared deeply for needy people and devoted himself to caring for them.

Oswald Smith. He said, "I want Thy plan, O God, for my life. May I be happy and contented whether in the homeland or on the foreign field; whether married or alone, in happiness or sorrow, health or sickness, prosperity or adversity—I want Thy plan, O God, for my life. I want it; oh, I want it!"[4] He was a missionary statesman who served as a pastor in Toronto, Canada.

C. T. Studd. He said, "If Jesus Christ be God and died for me, then no sacrifice is too great for me to give for Him."[5] Studd served as a missionary to China, India, and Africa.

Which of these quotes was most meaningful or moving to you? If you are willing to make a similar commitment to the lordship of Christ, spend a few moments in prayer expressing your willingness to adjust your life to Him, His purposes, and His ways.

QUESTIONS FOR REFLECTION

1. What adjustment is God presently asking of you? Do these include values? Attitudes? Actions? Relationships?

2. Is there an adjustment God has been asking you to make which you have found difficult? Is there something God is asking you to do right now that you are resisting?

---

1. David and Naomi Shibley, *The Smoke of a Thousand Villages* (Nashville: Thomas Nelson Publishers, 1989), 11.
2. Elisabeth Elliot, *Shadow of the Almighty: The Life and Testament of Jim Elliot* (New York: Harper and Brothers Publishers, 1958), 247.
3. Franklin Graham with Jeanette Lockerbie, *Bob Pierce: This One Thing I Do* (Waco, TX: Word Books, 1983), 220.
4. Shibley, 11.
5. Shibley, 98.

18

JOINING GOD REQUIRES OBEDIENCE

Jesus replied, "If anyone loves Me, he will keep My word. My Father will love him, and We will come to him and make Our home with him." (John 14:23)

Every one of you who does not say good-bye to all of his possessions cannot be My disciple. (Luke 14:33)

OBEDIENT AT ALL COSTS

As a pastor, I watched people develop a love relationship with God and come to the place where they would do whatever He instructed. One college student sensed God leading her to be baptized, but her father was an atheist and was adamantly opposed to her baptism. He threatened dire consequences if she followed through. However, she declared that she must do what God was telling her to do, and at the service in which I baptized her, she trembled with fear. When friends took her home, she found her suitcase packed and sitting on the front step. She was no longer welcome in her own home.

Others in my congregation sold their homes and left to serve in missions. Some donated cars to people in need. Many made large financial sacrifices. It was heartwarming to watch people, out of their devotion to Christ, do anything He asked of them. This was not because they were afraid or felt guilty but because they had come to experience God's love in a life-transforming way, and now there was nothing they would not do for Him.

In chapter 7, we studied the relationship between love and obedience. Jesus said, "If you love Me, keep My commandments. The one who doesn't love Me will not keep My words" (John 14:15, 24). To review, here are some important ideas from that chapter:

- Obedience is the outward expression of your love for God.
- The reward for obedience is that God will make Himself known to you.
- If you have an obedience problem, you have a love problem.
- If you love Him, you will obey Him!

Jesus said, "For whoever does the will of My Father in heaven, that person is My brother and sister and mother" (Matt. 12:50). Jesus made it clear that obedience is the outflow of our love relationship with God (see John 14:15–21).

James, in his letter to believers, emphasized that faith without active obedience is dead—useless. When the disciples obeyed Jesus, they saw and experienced God's mighty power working in and around them. When they did not act in faith, they did not experience His mighty work.

What Is Obedience?

Servants of God do what He directs. They obey. The servant doesn't have the option of deciding whether or not to obey. Choosing not to do what God commands is rebellion, and such disobedience has consequences.

People are naturally self-centered; we want to please ourselves. We don't like others to tell us what to do! Jesus told a parable about obedience: "But what do you think? A man had two sons. He went to the first and said, 'My son, go, work in the vineyard today.' He answered, 'I don't want to!' Yet later he changed his mind and went. Then the man went to the other and said the same thing. 'I will, sir,' he answered. But he didn't go" (Matt. 21:28–30).

Which son did the will of his father? Was it the one who said "no" but later repented, or the one who said "yes" but never went? The first son, of course, is the one who obeyed the father. Obedience means doing what is commanded. How much better to be a child who immediately says "yes" and then promptly goes and obeys!

Obey What You Already Know to Be God's Will

When my two oldest grandsons were teenagers, the older one, Mike, got a part-time job serving fast food. It was hectic, tiring work for minimum pay. Before long, his younger brother Daniel was offered a similar job at a burger place. Having observed Mike's experience, Daniel responded, "No thanks. I think I'll just skip the menial stuff and go straight into upper management!"

We Christians can be like that. We long for an important assignment from God, yet we are unwilling to prove ourselves faithful in the smaller, seemingly less important tasks. Have you ever wondered why a major assignment from God has not come your way? Consider your obedience in what God has already shown you. God gave the Ten Commandments. Are you obeying? Jesus commanded us to love our enemies. Are you doing that? Are you doing all you know to spread the gospel to all nations as Christ directed (see Matt. 28:18-20)? The Scriptures command us to live in unity with our Christian brothers and sisters. Do love and harmony characterize your relationships?

God's commands are not given so we can pick and choose the ones we want to obey. He expects us to do everything He tells us. When we are faithful and obedient in a little, He trusts us with more.

Obedience and God's Assignments

As I've said already, God has always been at work in our world, and He is now active where you are. When God is ready to involve you in an assignment, He will take the initiative to reveal what He is doing or what He is about to do. When He does, this will be His invitation for you to join Him.

Joining God may require major adjustments of your life to Him so He will accomplish His will through you. When you understand what God has said, when you know what He is about to do, and when you have made the necessary adjustments in your life, there is one remaining response to God. To experience Him at work in and through you, you must obey Him.

This chapter focuses on the last of the seven realities: You come to know God by experience as you obey Him, and He accomplishes His work through you. The entire process outlined above may happen quickly, or it may be extended over a long period of time.

Moment of Truth

In the process of experiencing God, obedience is your moment of truth. Your obedience (or lack of it) will:

1. Reveal what you believe about God;

2. Determine whether you will experience His mighty work in and through you;

3. Determine whether you will come to know Him more intimately.

You obey because you trust God. You trust Him because you love Him. As you grow in your faith and obey God at every step, you'll move from a head knowledge of God to a personal, experiential, dynamic relationship with the Person of Jesus Christ.

The Lord initiates the relationship by revealing His character and activity to you. The Holy Spirit is your teacher and guide, helping you trust God and obey Him. But you are the one who must respond in obedience. No one else can do this for you. When you trust God and take action to obey Him, you grow in Him. As 1 John 2:3–6 says: "This is how we are sure that we have come to know Him: by keeping His commands. The one who says, 'I have come to know Him,' without keeping His commands, is a liar, and the truth is not in him. But whoever keeps His word, truly in him the love of God is perfected. This is how we know we are in Him: the one who says he remains in Him should walk just as He walked."

Likewise, Jesus said:

> "Not everyone who says to Me, 'Lord, Lord!' will enter the kingdom of heaven, but only the one who does the will of My Father in heaven. On that day many will say to Me, 'Lord, Lord, didn't we prophesy in Your name?' Then I will

announce to them, 'I never knew you! Depart from Me, you lawbreakers!'" (Matt. 7:21–23)

The Importance of Obedience

Because you know God loves you, you should never question a directive from Him. It will always be right and best. When He expresses His will, you are not just to observe, discuss, or debate it. You are not called to "wrestle with it" as many do. You are to obey it. This is what the Scriptures say about obedience:

> Now if you faithfully obey the Lord your God and are careful to follow all His commands I am giving you today, the Lord your God will put you far above all the nations of the earth. . . . The Lord will grant you a blessing on your storehouses and on everything you do. (Deut. 28:1, 8)

> But if you do not obey the Lord your God by carefully following all His commands and statutes I am giving you today . . . the Lord will send against you curses, confusion, and rebuke in everything you do until you are destroyed and quickly perish, because of the wickedness of your actions in abandoning Me. (Deut. 28:15, 20)

> Obey Me, and then I will be your God, and you will be My people. You must walk in every way I command you so that it may go well with you. (Jer. 7:23)

> Why do you call Me 'Lord, Lord,' and don't do the things I say? I will show you what someone is like who comes to Me, hears My words, and acts on them: He is like a man building a house, who dug deep and laid the foundation on the rock. When the flood came, the river crashed against that house and couldn't shake it, because it was well built. But the one who hears and does not act is like a man who built a house on the ground without a foundation. The river crashed against it, and immediately it collapsed. And the destruction of that house was great! (Luke 6:46–49)

> Jesus answered them and said, "My teaching isn't Mine but is from the One who sent Me. If anyone wants to do His will, he will understand whether the teaching is from God or if I am speaking on My own." (John 7:16–17)

God blesses those who are obedient to Him (see Deut. 28:1–14). The benefits of obedience are beyond our imagination, but they include being God's people (see Jer. 7:23), having a solid foundation when the storms of life rage against you (see Luke 6:46–49), and knowing spiritual truth (see John 7:16–17).

Rebellion against God—disobedience—is a serious rejection of God's will. Deuteronomy 28:15–68 speaks of the costs of disobedience. (For further study on the results of obedience and disobedience, see Deut. 30 and 32).

The Cost of Obedience

Obedience, likewise, has its costs. You cannot know and do the will of God without paying the price of adjustment. Counting the cost to follow God's will is one of the major adjustments you'll have to make. It is at the point of counting the cost that many cease following Jesus. In fact, at this point "many of His disciples turned back and no longer accompanied Him" (John 6:66). Churches, too, must understand that obedience often requires sacrifice. A congregation will not know and experience the fulfilling of God's purposes if its members are unwilling to pay the price of obedience. Church leaders do a disservice to their congregation if they do not help their people understand this reality.

In the first century, Saul, a Pharisee, was firmly established in the religious power structure of Jerusalem. He ruthlessly searched out Christians for imprisonment or execution. Then, on his way to Damascus, Saul encountered the living Christ. The resurrected Savior told Saul he had been chosen to preach the gospel to the Gentiles, and Saul had to make an about-face in his life. His name was even changed to Paul. He went from persecuting Christians to proclaiming that Jesus is the Christ.

For Paul, the decision to obey Christ was costly. The persecutor became the persecuted. He was beaten and imprisoned many times, and his life was constantly at risk with the religious establishment he had once helped to lead.

Following God frequently leads to criticism and misunderstanding. Jesus told His followers to expect persecution if they followed Him (John 15:18–21). Paul concluded one letter by saying, "I carry the marks of Jesus on my body" (Gal. 6:17). Paul didn't have these experiences before he began doing the will of his Lord. Even so, Paul maintained that the one consuming passion of his life was "to know Him and the power of His resurrection and the fellowship of His sufferings, being conformed to His death, assuming that I will somehow reach the resurrection from among the dead. Not that I have already reached the goal, or am already fully mature, but I make every effort to take hold of it because I also have been taken hold of by Christ Jesus" (Phil. 3:10–12).

The apostle described his adjustments this way: "I have become all things to all people, so that I may by all means save some" (1 Cor. 9:22). The Scriptures are replete with examples of costly adjustments and obedience.

Moses and the Israelites

When Moses did as the Lord instructed and told Pharaoh to set Israel free, what did it cost the Israelites? Their workload was increased and the Israelite foremen were beaten. Ultimately they were delivered, but the Israelites paid a high price for their leader to do God's will (see Exod. 5:1–21).

Jesus and Mary

When Jesus went to the cross, what was the cost to His mother as she watched Him suffer and die? Is there a more agonizing experience than to watch your son be cruelly killed? (see John 19:17–37). Jesus' obedience put His mother through a heartbreaking experience, and His obedience brought fear and pain to the lives of His disciples. For Jesus to do the will of God, others endured a high cost.

Paul and Jason

When Paul obediently preached to the Gentiles at Thessalonica, many people responded to the gospel message. However, others who opposed God's work reacted violently, and they took out their anger on some of the local Christians. Jason, a supporter of Paul, along with some other Christians were arrested by a rioting mob and accused of treason because of their association with the itinerant preacher. Frequently, Paul's obedience endangered the lives of those who were with Him (see Acts 17:1–9).

You must not overlook this real element in knowing and doing God's will. God will reveal His plans and purposes to you, but your obedience will cost you and those around you.

Cost to My Family

I have five children, and when they were still young, God directed our family to leave a strong, secure pastorate in California to go to a tiny, struggling congregation in Saskatoon, Canada, that could not adequately support our family. Over the years, God often called me away from home to speak in other churches and in conferences. As a result of my travel and responsibilities with the church and Bible college, Marilynn often had to care for our five children on her own. At times, she paid a high price for me to do what we sensed God asking me to do.

I have heard many people say, "I really think God is calling me, but my children need me. I can't put my family through that." Or "I sense God wants me to serve on the mission field, but my children deserve the opportunity to live near their grandparents." It's true, your children do need your care, and it is great when they can live near relatives. But don't you think that if you were to respond obediently to the activity of God, He would care for your children?

What do you suppose the cost would be to your family if you chose *not* to obey Him? We believed God would honor our obedience to Him and that the God who called us would help us raise our children. We came to believe that the heavenly Father could take better care of our children than we could. We believed God would show us how to relate to our children in a way that would make up for the lost time with them. Now, I could not let that become an excuse for neglecting my family, but when I was obeying the Father, I could trust Him to care for my family.

We baptized only three persons the first year we were in Saskatoon, and after more than two years of hard work, we averaged forty in our worship services. One day Marilynn said to me, "Henry, Richard came to me today and said he really feels sorry for you. He said, 'Dad preaches such good sermons. He gives an invitation week after week, and nobody comes forward.'"

I went to Richard and said, "Richard, don't ever feel sorry for your father. Even if God lets me labor for ten years and I see very little results, I will gladly wait for the day when He brings the harvest." I had to help Richard understand what was taking place. I explained God's promise: "Though one goes along weeping, carrying the bag of seed, he will surely come back with shouts of joy, carrying his sheaves" (Ps. 126:6). God worked through that situation to teach my son a deeply meaningful spiritual truth.

God Took Care of Marilynn

I remember when Marilynn hit a low point of discouragement. Although our church was growing and God was obviously at work, she began to wonder if her sacrifices and effort were making any difference. The next Sunday after I preached, Richard came down the aisle to share a decision with the church. He said, "God is calling me into Christian ministry."

Right behind him came another young fellow Marilynn had spent many hours ministering to. He said, "I also feel God has called me to the ministry." Then he turned and said, "And a lot of the credit goes to Mom Blackaby."

Then another young adult stood up and said, "I want you to know that God is calling me to the ministry also, and I'd like to thank Mrs. Blackaby for encouraging me." At a crisis time in this boy's life, our family had ministered to him and encouraged him to seek God's will. That day, God showed Marilynn some of the fruit of her obedience to Him. Yes, it had come at a cost, but the rewards were worth it.

All five of our children are now in vocational ministry or mission work. During those years when I was often away from home, God promised to help Marilynn in the practical aspects of rearing our children. He never promised it would be easy, and often it wasn't, but only God could have done such a powerful work with our four sons and our daughter. As of today, our two oldest grandsons who are in their early twenties both feel called into full-time Christian ministry, and all fourteen of our grandchildren love the Lord.

I want you to know you can trust God with your family! I would rather entrust my family to God's care than to anyone else in the world.

Adjustments in Prayer and the Cost

When our church encountered a directive from God, I often experienced a turning point in my own prayer life. Often God waits to act until we ask in prayer. The crisis was this: Was I willing to pray until God brought an answer? Mark 11:24 holds a prayer promise that has challenged me regarding the relationship of faith and prayer: "All the things you pray and ask for—believe that you have received them, and you will have them."

This verse is sometimes used to promote a name-it-and-claim-it theology. You decide what you want. You name that in your prayer, claim it, and it's yours. But that's a misguided and self-centered notion. Remember that only God takes the initiative. He gives you the desire to do His will (see Phil. 2:13) and His Holy Spirit guides you to pray according to God's will (see Rom. 8:26–28). In the God-centered approach, God leads you to pray according to His will and to believe that He will bring to pass what He has led you to pray. Then, continue praying in faith and watching for Him to keep His word.

Because an encounter with God entails a crisis of belief that may require major adjustments in your life, you need to learn how to pray. Even the prayer may be costly. You may need to let God wake you up in the middle of the night to pray. You may need to spend much time in prayer. Times may come when you pray late into the night or even all night. Becoming a person of prayer requires a major adjustment of your life to God. Prayer will always be a part of your obedience because it is in a prayer relationship that God gives you direction.

Another cost will come as you try to guide the people around you to pray. Most of our churches have not learned how to pray together. The greatest untapped resource I know of is the united prayer of God's people. Jesus, quoting from Isaiah 56:7, said, "My house will be called a house of prayer" (Luke 19:46). To help your church become a praying church will be a rewarding experience.

Second Chances

People frequently ask me, "When a person disobeys God's will, does God give him or her a second chance?" The answer is yes—sometimes. He does not always give second chances, and He is not obligated to.

When God planned to call Nineveh to repentance, He asked Jonah to join Him. Jonah refused because he was prejudiced against these "pagan enemies." Jonah would rather have seen God destroy the city. Disobedience to God is extremely serious. Jonah went through the trauma of being thrown into a raging sea and spending three days inside a big fish. Jonah confessed and repented of his disobedience, and God gave him a second chance.

The second time Jonah did obey, though reluctantly. On the first day, Jonah preached a one-sentence message, and God used it to bring one hundred twenty thousand people to repentance! Jonah said, "I know that You are a merciful and compassionate God, slow to become angry, rich in faithful love, and One who relents from sending disaster" (Jon. 4:2). God's response to Jonah and to the inhabitants of Nineveh speaks volumes about how deeply God cares for all people and wants them to come to repentance.

Some of God's most faithful servants were once broken by sin and disobedience, yet God did not give up on them. If God allowed people only one mistake, Moses would never have become the person he became. He erred several times (see Exod. 2:11–15). Abraham started out with a great walk of faith, but He went into Egypt and blew it—more than once (see Gen. 12:10–20). David failed miserably (see 2 Sam. 11), and so did Peter (see Matt. 26:69–75). Paul even began his "service for God" by persecuting Christians (see Acts 9:1–2).

Disobedience Is Costly

Although it is comforting to know God gives second chances, we must understand that disobedience is serious. Jacob's sin against Esau forced him to flee his country and to be estranged from his brother. Jonah's disobedience almost cost him his life. Moses' murder of the Egyptian cost him forty years in the wilderness. David and Bathsheba's sin cost them the life of their son. The rich young ruler declined to obey Jesus and missed out on becoming His follower.

God wants to develop your character. He will let you proceed in your disobedience but not without discipline to bring you back. In your relationship with God, you may make a wrong decision, but the Spirit of God will help you recognize that you are going against God's will. He will guide you back to the right path and clarify what the Father wants. He may even take your disobedience and work it for good (see Rom. 8:28) as He corrects and teaches you His ways.

Even though God forgives and often gives second chances, the second chances are not guaranteed. When Aaron's two sons Nadab and Abihu were disobedient in offering unholy incense to the Lord, God struck them dead (see Lev. 10:1–7).

In front of all Israel, Moses struck the rock saying, "Listen, you rebels! Must we bring water out of this rock for you?" (Num. 20:10). Notice the word "we." God was the One who would bring water from the rock. Moses took God's glory, and God did not remove the consequences of that disobedience. He refused to allow Moses to enter the Promised Land. In that instance God gave no second chance.

Obedience Brings Future Blessing

Although obedience is costly, it is always worth the price. Whenever you think the cost may be too great, consider what it will cost you *not* to do the will of God.

While we were still a very small church with an attendance of less than fifty, we staffed and supported three mission churches, and we were asked to sponsor another mission in Winnipeg, Manitoba, more than five hundred miles from Saskatoon. Someone would have to drive this thousand-mile round trip in order to minister to them. At first, it sounded impossible for our little group.

I shared with our congregation that a faithful group of people in Winnipeg had been meeting for more than two years and they wanted to start a church. Since they had called on us to help, we had to determine whether this was God's work and whether or not He was revealing His activity to us. Was this our invitation to join Him in what He was doing? The church believed it was God's doing, and we knew we had to obey. We agreed to sponsor the new mission, then asked God to give us the strength and resources to do it.

I, along with others from our church, drove a number of times to Winnipeg to preach and minister to the people, and in a short time God provided a pastor—and a salary! The story did not end there, however. That church became the mother church to nine other mission churches and started an entire association of churches.

When our Richard finished seminary, this same church called him to be their pastor. Then our second son, Tom, was called to be on the staff as the associate pastor. Little did I know that one act of obedience—that at first appeared impossible—held such potential for future blessing for the kingdom and for my family as well. How grateful I am that we chose to obey God and start that church so far away from us!

Summary

Both major adjustments and costly obedience come before you experience God's presence and power. Many Christians and churches come to this moment of truth and decide the cost is too great. What they often do not consider is what it may cost them not to obey. When God gives you an assignment, the obedience may require sacrifice for you and for those around you. Nevertheless, obedience to Him is not an option—it is *required* of every servant. When you obey, God accomplishes what He purposed, and you will be overwhelmed with the experience of God's power and presence. You and those around you will come to a greater knowledge of God.

Experiencing God Today

Has God ever invited you or your church to join Him, and you refused because the price was too high? Ask God to reveal to you any disobedience in your past. If God brings something to mind, agree with Him by confessing your sin. Surrender your life afresh to His lordship and agree that you will obey no matter what the cost.

Whenever you sense obedience is too costly, that indicates you have misunderstood who you are and what you have. As a disciple of Christ, you have been bought with a price, and you are not your own. Everything you have belongs to God. You are a manager of God's resources. Since you belong to Him, renew your dedication to Him for His purposes. Pray and agree with God that anything He asks is reasonable. Commit yourself to pay the price to obey His will. Begin watching now for the first opportunity to obey what God asks.

QUESTIONS FOR REFLECTION

1. Consider a directive from God that you have recently obeyed. How did you experience God as you obeyed Him? Is there anything God had to teach you before you were prepared to obey?

2. How has your following God cost others? How has others' obedience to God cost you?

3. Have you ever suffered the consequences of not obeying God? If so, what were they?

19

God Accomplishes His Work

But anyone who lives by the truth comes to the light, so that his works may be shown to be accomplished by God. (John 3:21)

My plan will take place, and I will do all My will. . . . Yes, I have spoken; so I will also bring it about. I have planned it; I will also do it. (Isaiah 46:10–11)

Affirmation

When we experience God's invitation to join Him, some people insist on seeing some kind of sign. In essence they are saying: "Lord, prove to me this is You, and then I will obey." When Moses stood before the burning bush and received his invitation to join God in His great work, God promised to affirm the invitation in due time. He said, "This will be the sign to you that I have sent you: when you bring the people out of Egypt, you will all worship God at this mountain" (Exod. 3:12). In other words: "Moses, you obey, and I will deliver Israel through you. You will come to know Me as your deliverer, and you will stand on this mountain and worship Me."

God's affirmation that He had sent Moses would come *after* Moses obeyed, not before. This is most frequently the case in Scripture. The affirmation comes after the obedience. When Jesus invited Peter to get out of the boat to walk on the water, He did not assure Peter he would stay afloat! The Lord simply said, "Come!" (Matt. 14:28). Peter wouldn't know if he could walk on the water until he took his first step.

Because you love God, obey Him. Then you will so fellowship with Him that you will come to know Him intimately. His work through you to accomplish God-sized assignments will be a joyous time for you!

What if the "Door" Closes?

Suppose you sense the call of God to a task, a place, or a particular ministry, and when you set about to do it, everything goes wrong. Often people say, "Well, I guess that wasn't God's will."

Since God calls you into a relationship with Him, be careful how you interpret your circumstances. Many times, we jump to a conclusion that God is moving us in a particular direction. We make up our minds about what He is doing and when He is going to do it, according to what seems logical to us. We start following the logic of our own reasoning, but then nothing seems to work out. We have a tendency to neglect our relationship with God and take things into our own hands, but don't do that.

Usually, when God calls or gives you a direction, His call is not the thing He wants you to do. He is telling you what He is *about* to do where you are. For example, examine this record of the apostle Paul's ministry:

> They went through the region of Phrygia and Galatia and were prevented by the Holy Spirit from speaking the message in the province of Asia. When they came to Mysia, they tried to go into Bithynia, but the Spirit of Jesus did not allow them. So, bypassing Mysia, they came down to Troas. During the night a vision appeared to Paul: a Macedonian man was standing and pleading with him, "Cross over to Macedonia and help us!" After he had seen the vision, we immediately made efforts to set out for Macedonia, concluding that God had called us to evangelize them. (Acts 16:6–10)

God had already told Paul He would reach the Gentiles through him, but God—not Paul—would do the saving. Paul started in one direction, and the Spirit stopped him (see Acts 16:6–10). Then he began in another. Again, the Spirit prevented him. What was God's original plan? To reach the Gentiles. What was Paul's problem? He was trying to figure out what to do, and the "doors" of opportunity seemed to close. In fact, God was saying, "Listen to me, Paul. Go and sit in Troas until I tell you where to go."

While he was in Asia Minor, in the city of Troas, Paul received a vision to go to Macedonia and help the people there. God's plan was to carry the gospel westward toward Greece and Rome. He was at work in Macedonia and wanted Paul to join Him in that place.

When you begin to follow what you sense God wants you to do and circumstances seem to close the door of opportunity, go back to the Lord and clarify what God said. Better yet, always try to make sure on the front end exactly what God is saying. Remember, He is not calling you primarily to a task but to a relationship. Through that relationship, He will accomplish His purposes through your life.

Moses had to re-check Gods' directions constantly. He obeyed God, spoke to Pharaoh, and everything went wrong, but Moses didn't quit. He went back to the Lord to clarify what was happening.

God began to give him directions about the plagues He would bring on Egypt. Pharaoh seemed to be getting more and more obstinate. Moses daily sought God's directions and obeyed them. Later, Moses could look back and see God's handiwork in all that took place. God delivered Israel from the Egyptians in such a way that Israel, Egypt, and the surrounding nations knew God had done it. Pharaoh's stubbornness was not a sign that Moses misunderstood God's directives. Rather, it was the way God performed an even greater work than Moses could have imagined.

A Couple's Call to Student Work

I talked with a couple who said God was inviting them to Saskatoon to do student work. They initiated the process for assignment as missionaries, and the mission board turned them down. Their conclusion was: "We made a mistake."

I advised them not to jump to that conclusion but to go back and recall what God said when they sensed His call. They were canceling the whole plan of God because one detail did not work out as they thought it should. I asked them to spend time confirming God's will. Was He calling them to missions? Was He calling them to student work? Was He calling them to Canada?

Then I said, "Keep that sense of call in place, but watch to see how the God who is speaking is going to implement what He said. When God speaks a word of direction, He will bring it to pass. Just be careful you do not let circumstances cancel what God said."

This couple had to go to God and be sure they understood His directives. Perhaps He had a different city in mind for them. He may have wanted them to secure a different means of financial support. Or He may have wanted more time to prepare them for the assignment. As they awaited confirmation from God, I advised them to keep doing all they knew in obedience to Him.

If you're in a situation like this, what should you do?

1. Clarify what God said, and identify what may have been your "additions" to what He said.

2. Keep in place what God has said.

3. Let Him work out the details in His timing.

4. Do all you know to do.

5. Wait on the Lord until He tells you what to do next.

God is all-powerful. He can change your circumstances in a moment. What takes longer is for Him to work in our lives so we are prepared to be of service to Him. As this couple earnestly sought God's guidance and surrendered their wills fully to Him, God did guide them. They ultimately knew God was not leading them to Canada although in their hearts they had wanted to come. Instead, God led them in a different direction of ministry and has used their lives significantly ever since. God has also allowed them to make an important contribution to the work in Canada over the years as a result of the ministry positions they have held.

Slow Going

Does God seem to be working slowly in your life? Jesus had been with His disciples about three years when He said: "I still have many things to tell you, but you can't bear them now. When the Spirit of truth comes, He will guide you into all the truth. For He will not speak on His own, but He will speak whatever He hears. He will also declare to you what is to come" (John 16:12–13).

Jesus had more He wanted to teach the disciples, but they were unprepared to receive it. Jesus knew, however, that the Holy Spirit would guide these disciples into truth on God's timetable.

You may be saying, "God, hurry up and make me mature." Perhaps you are asking God to give you a new and larger assignment. But are you ready for it? God will lead you in His truth as you respond in obedience, step by step. If you feel God is slow to work in your life, ask yourself these questions:

1. Am I responding to all God is presently leading me to do?
2. Have I obeyed all I already know to be His will?
3. Do I really believe He loves me and will always do what is best in my life?
4. Am I willing to wait patiently on His timing and obey everything I know to do in the meantime?

Grass that is here today and gone tomorrow does not require much time to mature. A giant oak tree that lasts for generations requires much more time to grow strong. God is concerned about your life through eternity. Allow Him to take all the time He wants to shape you for His purposes. Larger assignments may require longer periods of preparation.

God Accomplishes His Work through You

The Holy Spirit will never mislead you about the Father's will. In order that you not miss the purpose God has for you, He has given His Spirit to guide you according to His will. The Spirit also *enables* you to do God's will. You are completely dependent on God for the knowledge and for the ability to achieve His purposes. You must be patient and wait until you hear a word from God about His will and His ways.

Jesus is our model. He never failed to know and do His Father's will. Everything the Father proposed to do through His life, the Lord Jesus did. Thus, Jesus could claim at the end of His life that He had completed everything His Father had given Him to do (see John 17:4).

What was the key to Jesus' perfect obedience? He was always rightly related to the Father. If you walk in a consistent relationship with God, then you should never come to a time that you do not know His will. There should never be a situation in which you are not enabled by the Holy Spirit to carry out God's will.

In Jesus, we have the picture of a perfect love relationship with the Father. Jesus consistently lived out that relationship. You and I quickly conclude that we are a long way from that, but Christ is fully present in us to help us know and do God's will (see Gal. 2:20). We need to adjust our lives to God and faithfully live out that relationship with absolute dependence on Him. He will never fail to draw us into the middle of His purpose and enable us to do it—as He did for people throughout Scripture.

Moses. Only through obedience did Moses begin to experience the full nature of God. We see a pattern of God speaking, Moses obeying, and God accomplishing what He purposed to do:

- God invited Moses to join Him in what He was doing to deliver Israel.
- God told Moses what to do.
- Moses obeyed.
- God delivered the Israelites from captivity in Egypt as He had promised.
- Moses and those around him came to know God more intimately.

When the people stood between the Red Sea and the oncoming Egyptian army, God told Moses to hold his staff over the sea and Moses obeyed. God parted the sea and the people crossed on dry ground (Exod. 14:1–25). Then Miriam led the people in a hymn of praise describing their new understanding of God.

When the people were thirsty and had no water to drink, they complained to Moses. God told Moses to strike a rock with the staff. Moses obeyed and God caused water to flow from the rock (Exod. 17:1–7). Whenever Moses obeyed what God told him to do, he and the people of Israel experienced the awesome power of God at work.

People of Faith. When Noah obeyed, God preserved his family and repopulated the earth. When Abraham obeyed, God gave him a son and built a nation. When David obeyed, God made him a king and greatly increased the power and prosperity of Israel. When Elijah obeyed, God displayed His astounding power by sending down fire from heaven. These people of faith came to know God by experience when they obeyed Him, and He accomplished His work through them.

The Disciples. Luke records a beautiful experience of Jesus' disciples. The Lord invited seventy of His followers to join Him in the Father's work. Jesus gave these people specific directions, telling them how to travel, what to preach, how to respond to receptive listeners, and how to handle rejection. They obeyed Him and experienced God working through them to heal people and cast out demons. Jesus praised the Father for revealing Himself to these followers (see Luke 10:21–22). Then Jesus turned to His disciples and said, "The eyes that see the things you see are blessed! For I tell you that many prophets and kings wanted to see the things you see yet didn't see them; to hear the things you hear yet didn't hear them" (Luke 10:23–24).

These disciples were blessed. They had been chosen by God to be involved in His work. What they saw, heard, and came to know about God was something even prophets and kings longed to experience but didn't.

You, too, will be blessed when God does a special, God-sized work through you. You will come to know Him in a way that brings joy to your life. When others see you experience God that way, they will want to know how they, too, can experience God as you do. So be prepared to point them to God.

If you are obedient, God will accomplish remarkable things through your life. You'll want to declare the wonderful deeds of the Lord, but you'll need to be careful that any testimony about what God has done gives glory to Him. Pride may cause you to want to tell your experience because it makes you feel important. However, you must avoid any sense of pride. "The one who boasts must boast in the Lord" (1 Cor. 1:31).

You Come to Know the Lord

Scripture shows us that when God did something through an obedient person or people, they came to know Him in new and more intimate ways. God revealed His name to Moses: "I AM WHO I AM" (Exod. 3:14). Jesus expressed Himself to His disciples by saying:

- "I am the bread of life." (John 6:35)
- "I am the light of the world." (John 8:12)
- "I am the door." (John 10:9)
- "I am the good shepherd." (John 10:11)
- "I am the resurrection and the life." (John 11:25)
- "I am the way, the truth, and the life." (John 14:6)
- "I am the true vine." (John 15:1)

Jesus identified Himself with the I AM of the Old Testament. Knowing and experiencing Jesus in these ways requires that you trust Him. For instance, when He says, "I am the way," what you do next will determine if you come to experience Him as "the way" in your own life. When you believe Him, adjust your life to Him, and obey what He says, you come to know and experience Him as "the way." This is true about everything God reveals to you. As you follow Him obediently, He works in and through you to reveal Himself to you and to those around you.

Summary

God is at work today reconciling a lost world to Himself through His Son Jesus Christ. God invites you to be involved with Him. When you obey, He accomplishes His work through you in such a way that you and those around you know God has been at work. When you experience God working in and through you, you come to know Him more fully. As Jesus said, "This is eternal life: that they may know You, the only true God, and the One You have sent—Jesus Christ" (John 17:3). You come to know Him as you experience Him in your life.

Experiencing God Today

God longs for you to desire Him and His ways. Read the following prayer from the psalmist and make it your own. Ask the Lord to lead and guide you in all His ways for His glory.

> Teach me, LORD, the meaning of Your statutes, and I will always keep them. Help me understand Your instruction, and I will obey it and follow it with all my heart. Help me stay on the path of Your commands, for I take pleasure in it. (Ps. 119:33–35)

QUESTIONS FOR REFLECTION

1. Are you presently waiting on the Lord to fulfill His word to you in some way? How do you spend your time waiting?

2. What is something God has accomplished through your life? How did people witness God's activity as He worked through you? How have you given glory to God for what He did?

20

Returning to God

*And let us be concerned about one another in order to promote love
and good works, not staying away from our meeting,
as some habitually do, but encouraging each other, and all the
more as you see the day drawing near. (Hebrews 10:24–25)*

Serving without Knowing

I was preaching one Sunday about how Christ's presence in our lives dramatically affects our daily living. At the close of the service, a man came forward weeping. The pastor asked him to share his story with the congregation. The man confessed that a decade earlier his wife had urged him to come with her to church. When he visited, he liked the people, enjoyed the worship, and decided to join the congregation. Later, he heard the church needed teachers in the children's Sunday school department, so he volunteered. Over the years, he served in numerous capacities in his church including being a deacon and a Sunday school teacher. Yet as I preached that morning, the Holy Spirit awakened him to the fact that he did not have a personal relationship with Jesus. This good man had been practicing religion without a genuine, life-changing encounter with Christ.

As I spoke of how the Holy Spirit walks with us to guide us each day, the man realized he was not hearing the Holy Spirit speak to

...ked of God's love for us, he saw that he served God but ...uly know God. To his and the church's surprise, this man suddenly recognized that, for all his service and attendance at church, he did not have an experiential relationship with God.

This man is not alone. If there is one comment I hear over and over from people who study *Experiencing God*, it is this: "I thought I knew what it meant to be a Christian and to walk with God. But after studying this material I realize that although I was a religious person, I did not really know what it meant to enjoy a personal relationship with God."

That is the heart of this book—to move you from merely being religious to having a vibrant, real, growing relationship with God.

Limitless Fellowship, Limitless Possibilities

John said to the believers in the first century, "What we have seen and heard we also declare to you, so that you may have fellowship along with us; and indeed our fellowship is with the Father and with His Son Jesus Christ" (1 John 1:3). Then he added, "We are writing these things so that our joy may be complete"(1 John 1:4).

Just as the apostle John wrote what he had seen and heard to encourage his fellow believers, so when I wrote *Experiencing God*, I was simply sharing what God had taught me as I walked with Him for many years. It was neither a theological treatise nor an exhaustive book on the Christian life. It was just a testimony of what God taught me as I experienced Him.

The result of sharing these truths with others has been unbelievable! It has led to opportunities for me to speak in 114 countries. It has allowed me to share God's truths in churches of every size and denomination. It has brought invitations to speak at the White House, the Pentagon, and the United Nations. It has led me to a ministry to Christian CEOs of many of America's largest companies. And most significantly for me, it has resulted in the testimonies of countless people who share that through the study they learned to experience God for the first time. What a joy for me to know that, as God walked with an ordinary person like me, He would do so much to encourage God's people around the world. My prayer is that you will never settle for less than all God intends to do through your life as He walks with you.

Restoring Broken Relationships with God

There are times in every Christian's life when one senses a clear loss of intimacy with God. Even the most zealous Christians can find their love for God has cooled if they are not careful. How does this happen? What are the signs, and how can we restore a relationship with God once it has been broken?

I see a pattern in Scripture of how God's people experience revival.[1] Although revivals often exhibit unique features, the following six characteristics generally occur when people fall away and then return to God:

1. God is on mission to redeem a world that does not know Him and is lost in its sin (see Rom. 5:8). We do not naturally seek after God. He pursues us (see Hos. 11:7–11).

2. God is the One who initiates a love relationship with us that is real and personal (see John 1:12).

3. Because of sin, our hearts tend to depart from this intimate relationship. We do this individually and also as God's people, collectively. This departure is devastating and will lead to spiritual death if it is not corrected (see Jer. 3:20–22).

4. Whenever we stray from God to any degree, He disciplines us in increasing measure until we return. God the Father loves us as His children, and He will correct us as our heavenly Father until we turn from our rebellion (see Heb. 12:5–11). He will continue to discipline us until we reach a moment of crisis at which we must make a serious choice. This decision is either to repent and return to God, or to perish in judgment (see Isa. 59:1–20).

5. We cry out to God in our distress and return to Him. Scripture promises that "if we confess our sins, He is faithful and righteous to forgive us our sins and to cleanse us from all unrighteousness" (1 John 1:9). In confession, you agree with God about the awful nature of your wrongdoing. Confession and repentance go together. When you repent of sin, you turn away from that sin and return to God. When your fellowship with God is broken because of sin, agree with Him about

your condition, and turn from it. Return to God, and He will forgive you and reestablish your relationship with Him. Christians often speak of "rededicating" their lives to God. But we must recognize that God does not call us to rededicate ourselves; He calls us to repent of our sin. When we want fellowship with God to be restored, we must acknowledge that it is our own sin that caused the breach in the first place. Second Chronicles 7:13–14 reflects on this point:

> "If I close the sky so there is no rain, or if I command the grasshopper to consume the land, or if I send pestilence on My people, and My people who are called by My name humble themselves, pray and seek My face, and turn from their evil ways, then I will hear from heaven, forgive their sin and heal their land."

God's prescription for restored fellowship with Him is humility, prayer, seeking His face, and repentance. He promises to hear, forgive sin, and bring healing. God loves us too much to allow us to stay where we are.

6. When we return to God (and not merely to religious activity), He returns to us in a fresh, close relationship and begins once again to fulfill His purposes for us (see Zech. 1:3; 2 Chron. 15:1–3). Spiritual revival occurs when the life of God returns to our souls. This can happen to an individual, a church, a denomination, or a nation. The way you know you are truly restored to God is when He returns to you (see James 4:8). If you merely give lip service to your need for reconciliation with God, He is not fooled (see Gal. 6:7). The joy of your salvation, the power of God, and His holy cleansing of your life will not occur until you sincerely return to God.

How do we lose intimacy with God? There are three parables of Jesus in Luke 15 that describe how this can happen.

The lost sheep (vv. 3–7). How do sheep get lost? They typically are drawn away by distractions. They don't consciously choose to wander from the rest of the flock. They simply follow whatever catches their interest at the moment. Going from one thing to the next gradually draws the sheep farther and farther from where it should be until it is hopelessly lost and in grave danger.

The lost coin (vv. 8–10). Valuable possessions are generally lost through carelessness. No one means to lose something precious, but by not taking precautions, we can misplace a treasured object. Nothing is more priceless than our relationship with God. Yet we can neglect it because of our preoccupation with daily concerns. In the busyness of life, we forget to pray and we cut short our times with the Lord. Then one day we discover God seems far from us. We have inadvertently lost the intimacy we once enjoyed with Him.

The prodigal son (vv. 11–32). In this story, the son chooses to leave home to indulge in a lifestyle that dishonors his father. Tragically, there are those who deliberately abandon their fellowship with Christ. Perhaps they decide they want to pursue worldly pleasures or they refuse to obey what God has clearly commanded—such as forgiving someone who has offended them. Some move far from where they once were with God. Only a willful, repentant choice to return to God can bring someone back who has moved far away.

Our departure from God may go unnoticed—at least at first. But before long, the fact that we are now far from the Lord becomes obvious to us and to those who observe us. There are at least four ways you can discern if you have drawn apart from God.

1. *You no longer hear from God* (see Deut. 30:17; Amos 8:11–12). Deuteronomy 30:17 says, "But if your heart turns away from God and you do not listen . . ." Scripture warns that disobedience to God inevitably leads to spiritual deafness. The longer we refuse to heed a word from God, the harder our hearts become toward Him. Eventually, we will have steeled ourselves against God's Word to the point that our heart becomes impervious to anything God says.

2. *You lose your joy* (see John 15:9–14). Jesus claimed He had given the disciples His teaching so "that My joy may be in you, and your joy may be complete" (John 15:11). Since the natural by-product of abiding in Christ is joy, a joyless Christian is a contradiction in terms. However, when we become so preoccupied with concerns and various tasks that we fail to abide in Christ, our joy in the Lord inevitably wanes.

3. *Your life does not produce spiritual fruit* (see John 15:1–8). The natural result of abiding in Christ is spiritual fruit. Galatians

5:22–23 identifies the fruit the Spirit produces in a Christian's life: love, joy, peace, patience, kindness, goodness, faith, gentleness, and self-control. The more such fruit there is in your life, the more like Jesus you will be. Spiritual fruit is not something you produce by your own effort. It is the outgrowth of an intimate relationship with Christ.

4. *You no longer experience spiritual victory in your life* (see Deut. 28:25). Scripture promises that if God is for us, nothing can stand against us (see Rom. 8:31). However, if God is not for us, then we will experience continual defeat. In Old Testament times, God cautioned His people that one clear way to measure if they were pleasing to God was whether or not they were victorious over their enemies. When God's people experienced defeat, according to Scripture, it was an incontrovertible sign that they were no longer pleasing to God. Experiencing such grievous defeats would often drive God's people back to Him (see this recurring cycle in the book of Judges). But eventually, God's people allowed their hearts to become so hardened that God allowed their total destruction as a people in A.D. 70 by the Roman armies.

Spiritual Warfare?

A former pastor once came to me and solemnly recounted the devastating defeats he had experienced in his life. His church had fired him. His wife had left him and filed for divorce. All of his children had departed from walking with God and were indulging in gross immorality. His finances were in shambles, and he could not meet his obligations. Finally, his health had broken from a series of stress-related illnesses. Grimly, he pleaded, "Pray for me, my brother. I am experiencing intense spiritual warfare!"

This man was in graver danger than he realized. He assumed that all of his problems were the result of Satanic attacks. Yet he did not take into account the fact that God was allowing him to experience these continual defeats. If this man's life was pleasing to God, would He allow him to undergo one terrible defeat after another? While God does allow those He loves to suffer—Job, Paul, and Jesus are examples of that—it is possible to go through illness or attacks and yet to do it victoriously. This man was being beaten on every front. He needed to draw near to God and ask God to search his heart to see if

Returning to God

there was any wickedness in him (see Ps. 139:23–24) causing God to remove His hand of protection from his life (see Isa. 5:4–5).

The safest thing to do as a Christian is to guard your relationship with God so you do not depart from Him in the first place. But how do you protect your relationship with God? You can do the following four things:

1. Proverbs 4:23 cautions: "Guard your heart above all else, for it is the source of life." The heart is the core of our being. It is the arena in which we experience our greatest spiritual victories as well as our most devastating defeats. We cannot afford to neglect it or to take its condition for granted. When we allow ourselves to be exposed to sin or we let unforgiveness and bitterness dwell within us, we will no longer enjoy the intimacy with God we once did. Only you can guard your heart. No one else can do that for you. It takes conscious, sustained effort to protect yourself from sinful, destructive thoughts and habits.

2. Proverbs 11:14 warns: "Without guidance, people fall, but with many counselors there is deliverance." Our hearts are desperately wicked, and they can easily deceive us (see Jer. 17:9). We might believe we are sharing a prayer request with others out of concern for someone when in fact we are merely gossiping. We may think we are relating a personal testimony at our church for the glory of God when in fact we are bragging. That is why surrounding ourselves with godly friends who feel free to voice their concerns to us is healthy. Such advisors rarely volunteer for this service in your life, however. You must enlist them and invite them to share any counsel with you they believe you need to hear. Having people around who care about you and who will alert you when they see your heart shifting away from God can save you much heartache.

3. Jesus said, "Love the Lord your God with all your heart, with all your soul, and with all your mind" (Matt. 22:37). That should be the gauge for your Christian life. Periodically meditate on your love for God. Ask, "Am I loving the Lord my God with *all* my heart, or have other affections begun crowding out my devotion to Him?" Then examine your soul: are the deepest parts of your life wholly devoted to God? Survey your mind. Are your thoughts entirely subjected to Christ and your love for Him? When you find you are not loving God as you should, immediately take action to return to your

love relationship with God. If you practice this personal evaluation regularly, you will find that you never drift far from Christ before you recognize it and address the necessary issues in your life.

4. Jesus also said: "Therefore, everyone who hears these words of Mine and acts on them will be like a sensible man who built his house on a rock" (Matt. 7:24). Loving God is a choice we make. Love is never merely a feeling or a thought. Love requires action. If you love God, you will put into practice God's commands found in Scripture. It is too late to begin trying to follow God's instructions when the storms of life assail you. Adopt a lifestyle of immediate obedience. Then when trials inevitably come, your life will be firmly grounded in God's Word, and nothing will be able to harm your relationship with Him.

If you find you are not as enthusiastic and devoted to God as you once were, take time to pray. Return to God and immediately begin to experience His presence returning in your life. If you have not departed from God, write a prayer of thanks and commit yourself to remain steadfast and true to Him.

Summary

Despite the glorious opportunity we enjoy to experience close fellowship with God, we all have a tendency to depart from that relationship in various ways: through worldly distractions, by carelessness in our spiritual lives, and by a deliberate choice to walk away from God. Evidence that we have drifted from God includes: not hearing from God anymore, a loss of joy, an absence of spiritual fruit in our life, and a loss of victory. To prevent this from happening, you should diligently guard your heart; surround yourself with people who will hold you accountable; fervently seek to love God with all your heart, mind, and soul; and make it a practice to immediately obey whatever God tells you.

Experiencing God Today

Reflect on your walk with God. Is it more vibrant and powerful now than it has ever been? Or has something been lost? If you sense you are not walking with God as closely as you once did, carefully re-read this chapter and ask the Holy Spirit to alert you to any areas where you have been guilty of departing from God. Return to Him quickly and wholeheartedly.

QUESTIONS FOR REFLECTION

1. Take a moment to consider any evidence in your life that you have wandered from your love relationship with God. Are you regularly hearing God speak to you? Is your life filled with the joy of the Lord? Are you seeing spiritual fruit in your life? Are you experiencing victory?

2. Are you presently loving God with all your heart, soul, mind, and strength? If you are not, what might you do today to rekindle your love for God?

3. Do you have people in your life who feel free to share their concerns with you when they see you departing from your love relationship with God? If not, what might you do to enlist a friend to help guard your heart?

---

1. You can find a full discussion of this pattern for revival in the book *Fresh Encounter: Experiencing God in Revival and Spiritual Awakening* (Nashville: B&H Publishing Group).

21

Experiencing God as Couples

To sum up, each one of you is to love his wife as himself, and the wife is to respect her husband. (Ephesians 5:33)

Marriage: A Gift from God

People often ask me: "Henry, how do you explain how God has used your life to accomplish so much for His kingdom?" My response is always twofold: First, I am an extremely ordinary person. I think God wanted to demonstrate what His incredible power could do in peoples' lives so He searched high and low for the most ordinary person He could find for His demonstration, and He finally came upon me! I can only say that I have sought with all my heart to surrender to God, and the results of that commitment have been incredible. But the second thing I quickly add is this: "When God intended to use an ordinary life like mine for His purposes, He chose in His great wisdom to match me up with the partner perfectly suited to me and to God's direction for my life."

I am by nature a shy, introverted person. My parents were British and brought me up to be reserved and to eat fried chicken at picnics with a knife, fork, and napkin! My wife, Marilynn, is an off-the-scale extrovert who was born and raised in Oklahoma. We could not be more opposite if we tried. Yet God had a purpose for both of us from the beginning.

Both of our families were active in their local churches. Our fathers were deacons. Both sets of parents helped start new churches. Having grown up in such homes, we both surrendered our lives when we were young to do whatever our Lord commanded and to go wherever He told us to go. Early on, we grew to love the local church and to have a heart for missions.

God's plans for me included learning to walk by faith through some extremely challenging times as a mission pastor in Canada and eventually traveling millions of miles around the world teaching others what God had instructed me. For me to fulfill God's will in these ways, I would require a life partner with a unique calling of her own. God brought Marilynn into my life, and what a joy it has been to experience God's will together for nearly fifty years!

God's Purpose for Marriage

For several years, Marilynn and I led "Experiencing God as Couples" conferences across the country. It was marvelous to invite husbands and wives to stand together before God to see what He intended for their marriage. Ultimately, a study course with videos was made of this teaching, and a large percentage of couples who attended our conferences felt called into Christian ministry through these events. Many marriages were restored. Once couples came to understand God's purpose for their marriage, they discovered an entirely new and exciting dimension to their lives together.

Jesus said of marriage:

> "Haven't you read, that He who created them in the beginning made them male and female. . . . For this reason a man will leave his father and mother and be joined to his wife, and the two will become one flesh? So they are no longer two, but one flesh. Therefore what God has joined together, man must not separate" (Matt. 19:4–6).

Marriage is God's joining together of a man and woman to create a union through which He can accomplish His purposes and be glorified. It is not merely a human contract or agreement but is, rather, a divine union, a new creation that did not exist before. God has a special purpose for each couple. He is absolutely committed to the sanctity of marriage and He hates divorce! (Mal. 2:16).

Just as God clearly guided Marilynn and me to marry, God has led you to your spouse. If you have not done this recently, take time to list the various ways you know God directed you to be joined with your spouse. At times during the busyness of daily life, we forget that God gave us a husband or wife as an expression of His love for us.

One Flesh

What does it mean to be one flesh? It means your life is not your own. If you are married, you and your life partner are not two separate individuals trying to coexist. You are one. For your wife to feel pain is for you to suffer too. For your husband to experience spiritual victory is for you to be successful as well.

When God has a plan for the wife, it means God's activity will affect the husband too. I have heard a person say, "I want to go forward with God, but my wife is unwilling. Should I go on without her?" My response is: "You are one flesh. You cannot leave your spouse behind." Others have said, "My wife clearly senses God wants us to be more involved in missions, but I haven't heard God say anything to me." My response: "You are one flesh. If God spoke to your spouse, He has just spoken to you!" Because you are one flesh, you need to adjust your life to a word God speaks to your partner.

That is why I always strongly advise couples coming to me for premarital counseling to consider carefully where God is leading their potential partner because, after they are married, God's directives to one directly affects the other. I have known people who had a clear sense of God's leading in their lives in one direction but, after they married, they set aside everything God had previously said to them because their spouse was not interested in those same things. When I asked Marilynn to marry me, I knew God had been working in her life long before we met. When Marilynn was five years old, she was gravely ill and almost died. After that, she had a strong sense that her life belonged to God. So I asked her, "Marilynn, what has God told you He intends to do through your life? What promises have you made to God? If I marry you, I promise to spend the rest of my life helping you keep every promise you made."

Do you know what commitments your spouse has made to God? Are you aware of his or her spiritual pilgrimage? Do you have a sense of where God is presently leading your spouse? Christians ought to be aware of these important questions concerning their life partner. How have you helped your partner respond to God's activity and to obey His will?

Spiritual Leadership in the Home

Marilynn and I have spoken to thousands of couples over the years. We challenge husbands to do everything they can to help their wives become all God intends. Likewise, wives ought to strive to help their husbands become men of God. Christian couples must make their mutual love and edification a top priority. If parents neglect their own walk with God, their children will be imperiled. The greatest thing you can do for your children is to support and encourage your spouse's walk with God.

Protecting Our One Flesh

Being spiritually one with your spouse is critical to hearing from God. That is why the apostle Paul warned believers not to marry unbelievers (see 2 Cor. 6:14). He said it's like trying to mix light and darkness. They cannot become one spiritually because they are opposite in their fundamental natures. The spiritual intimacy you have with your spouse will affect your walk with God. The apostle Peter said a husband who mistreats his wife will find his prayers hindered (see 1 Pet. 3:7). That is also why it is wise never to allow your anger or damaged relationship to remain unresolved (see Eph. 4:26).

Missionary Smocking

Marilynn worked with me in pioneer missions in Canada for eighteen years. She has also walked alongside me as I have been a writer and speaker. Over the last two decades, she has traveled with me to numerous countries as we encouraged God's people together. However, as she and I were having coffee together one day, she shared that as a young girl, she had always dreamed of doing international missions, and although she had traveled around the world with me, she had never actually gone on a formal mission trip. I sensed this was a passion God had placed in her heart and I knew I needed to help her fulfill it.

Soon afterward, Marilynn heard of some missionaries in Asia whose little girls did not have many nice clothes. Marilynn loves to smock little girls' dresses, so she and a friend sewed some beautiful dresses and mailed them to the missionaries. The missionaries were deeply grateful. They shared that there was dire poverty among the people with whom they worked and asked if there were any way Marilynn could come and teach the local women to smock. Then they could sew dresses to sell and earn an income for their impoverished families. When Marilynn mentioned the possibility to me, I could see the gleam in her eye, and I knew this was an opportunity for her to do some genuine mission work. Smocking for Jesus!

Marilynn began collecting materials, and by the time she left for the trip she had two large boxes brimming with supplies. She traveled to Asia with a medical missions team from our church. While everyone else carried stethoscopes and thermometers, she took along sewing needles and thread. Then for a week, she taught a group of ladies in Asia how to smock.

Marilynn loved it, the ladies were ecstatic, and plans were made to sell the clothes. Now our church's medical missions team has asked Marilynn to go with them to West Africa! Marilynn is a grandmother of fourteen. She has served with me faithfully in ministry for nearly half a century. But these are some of the most rewarding and fulfilling days in her life! I'm so glad that when I saw God working in her life, I was able to encourage her and see her experience the joy of the Lord as she responded to God's invitation.

JOINING IN GOD'S ACTIVITY IN YOUR SPOUSE'S LIFE

One of the most exciting things you can do is to look for where God is working in your partner's life and join Him! There are several ways you can do this:

1. *Pray regularly for and with your spouse*. God knows what your spouse is going through better than you do. He knows your partner's fears and insecurities. God knows what He intends to do through your spouse. Praying regularly for your life mate enables you to gain God's perspective. Couples can easily frustrate each other. If we look at our partner solely from a human perspective, we see his or her limitations, failures, and weaknesses. When we view our spouse from God's perspective, we see unlimited potential in the hands of God. As we pray, God can alert us that we need to take a specific action, or He can prompt us to share a particular word of encouragement.

God may show you abilities in your spouse he or she does not see. As I prayed for Marilynn, God affirmed that she has some wonderful insights into walking with God that could encourage many others. While I have been the "professional" speaker throughout our marriage, I felt impressed to encourage her to accept speaking invitations that came her way. I sensed Marilynn needed to be a steward of what God had taught her and that it would richly bless others. As you pray for your spouse, what have you sensed God saying?

2. *Regularly discuss spiritual issues with your spouse.* Some Christian couples never speak to each other about God's activity. They assume God is working, but they never talk about it. Ask each other questions such as: "What has God been showing you in your quiet times lately?" "Has God placed any particular burden on your heart as you have been praying?" "You seemed very intent during the pastor's sermon today; what was God saying to you?" I have found that my wife is the best person with whom to share God's activity in my life. As I relate what I have been hearing God say, Marilynn recognizes things I miss. Together, we hear more clearly from God than we do separately.

3. *Review your spiritual markers together.* As God leads couples through the years, there will be certain key moments when He speaks clearly and unmistakably. It is important to regularly recall these times together. This helps in two ways. First, it prepares you to understand where God is leading. When I came to my official age of retirement, I, like everyone else my age, had to decide what to do. Should I join a country club and buy a set of golf clubs? But as Marilynn and I reviewed what God had done in our lives as a couple, we realized that all of our married life had been preparatory for what God wanted to do next. We ultimately formed Blackaby Ministries International (www.blackaby.org) so we could respond to God's invitations around the world to continue ministering. When our son Richard sensed God leading him to join our ministry, we recognized again that this fit perfectly with the spiritual markers of our lives. More recently, God has led Tom to join the ministry as well. It is as if God has been working in our family all these years for such a time as this! Together, we can respond to each new invitation God gives us because we have a clear sense as a couple—and as a family—of how God has led us to this point. A second benefit of reviewing your spiritual markers is that it provides a wonderful opportunity to

celebrate God's activity in your lives! Marilynn and I have a regular time each morning when we have coffee and reflect on God's goodness to us over almost five decades! What joy that brings!

4. *Minister together as a couple.* God led you to your spouse for a reason. One purpose is to produce godly offspring (see Mal. 2:15). If couples look for God's activity together, they will discover unique ways God wants to use them to carry out His kingdom work. I know couples who regularly go on mission trips, coteach a Sunday school class, teach English to immigrants, intercede for others, host a home Bible study, take international students into their homes, work with single adults, or adopt foreign children. There are numerous opportunities for couples to find tremendous reward in ministering together as God leads. One couple had separate ministries for years. The husband served as a deacon and on the church finance committee while the wife went on international mission trips. After several years, the wife finally convinced her husband to go with her on a mission trip. The man was overwhelmed by the experience. In tears he confessed to his wife, "Now I understand what you have been talking about all this time!" They had been missing out on the privilege of serving their Lord together. What are some ways you and your spouse are presently joining in God's activity together? Prayerfully consider opportunities to do so.

5 *Give together.* Many Christian couples faithfully put their checks in the offering plate as it is passed each Sunday, but they have never tapped into the joy of giving together. God is at work in the world around you. He wants you to become involved both personally and financially. Marilynn and I have experienced great joy in determining together where God wants us to invest money back into His kingdom. We support our local church but also various ministries around the world. This involves far more than writing a check. It includes praying together and discovering how God wants us to invest our finances in His kingdom. Together, we are laying up treasures in heaven!

Summary

God has called all of us to be on mission with Him. One of the first places we must seek His activity is in the life of the person to whom we are most intimately related. If God has given you a life partner, you will want to be involved in whatever great work God intends to do in that man's or woman's life.

<u>Marriage is the most fundamental and intimate human relationship God has created.</u> It is God who brings a man and woman together, and He does so for a purpose. As God is active in your spouse's life, He invites you to join in His activity. Be alert to how God wants to involve you in His work in your spouse's life.

Experiencing God Today

Pause to reflect on how God brought you and your husband or wife together. Consider all God has done to bless your life because of the life partner He gave you. Take some time to visit with your spouse about the pilgrimage God has taken you on together, and praise Him for His goodness to you both.

QUESTIONS FOR REFLECTION

1. Do you and your spouse take time to regularly talk about God's activity in your family, church, and world? If not, how might you begin to do that?

2. What are some things you sense God is doing in your spouse's life? How might you become involved in that activity?

3. What is a ministry you and your spouse have been able to do *together*? What is a ministry you might be able to do together in the future?

4. How have you and your spouse determined your giving? How have you purposefully been investing in God's kingdom as a couple?

22

JOINING GOD'S ACTIVITY IN YOUR CHILDREN'S LIVES

I will bless those who bless you, I will curse those who treat you with contempt, and all the peoples on earth will be blessed through you. (Genesis 12:3)

CHILDREN AND GOD'S ACTIVITY

Marilynn and I were married in California in 1960. Those were turbulent times! We were in Los Angeles during the Watts riot. I was doing graduate work near Berkeley University during the student protests. The local schools regularly had air-raid drills to train school children what to do in case of a nuclear attack. Many people discouraged us from bringing children into such a dangerous and unsettled world. But I noticed that throughout Scripture when times were difficult, God's answer was often to send a baby into the world. Isaac, Moses, Samuel, Samson, John the Baptist, and, of course, Jesus were God's response to difficult times. Ultimately, Marilynn and I had five children—four boys and a girl. All five are serving in full-time Christian ministry, and now our grandchildren are beginning to sense God's call on their lives into ministry as well.

When Richard was born, I spent all night praying over him after we brought him home from the hospital. I believed God had given him to us for a particular purpose. I sensed God wanted to use him in Christian ministry when he grew up. I also knew that, being reared in a pastor's home, there would be many pressures on him from others to simply follow in his father's footsteps. So I never told him what I thought God wanted him to do. Instead, I asked God to show me how to help Richard learn to know and do God's will.

There were some difficult times along the way. Richard ran into some serious health issues as a child. During his teen years, he had to decide if he would go God's way or the world's. When he entered college, he began to make preparations to be a high school social studies teacher. But I knew he was sidestepping God's will. I continued to pray and sought to help Richard develop a walk with God in which he would obey what God told him.

Halfway through his freshman year, Richard walked down the church aisle one Sunday during the altar call. In tears, he explained that he knew God was calling him into Christian ministry and that he had been running from God. He didn't want to be a pastor just because his dad was or because everyone expected him to. Moreover, he had grown up seeing firsthand the challenges that come to a pastor and his family. But he would resist no longer. Standing at the front of the church, I smiled and for the first time told my oldest son I had known all his life God was calling him into ministry. With a startled look, he asked, "Well if you have known for so long, why didn't you tell me?" I replied, "I wanted you to hear it from God."

Richard went on to complete seminary and to serve as a pastor. Today, he is the president of our ministry! God gave us a similar opportunity in each of our children's lives to help them walk with God so they wouldn't miss out on anything God intended to do in their lives.

One of the most exciting and rewarding invitations God gives to us is the opportunity to join His activity in our children's lives. Scripture says:

> Sons are indeed a heritage from the LORD, children, a reward. Like arrows in the hand of a warrior are the sons born in one's youth. Happy is the man who has filled his quiver with them. Such men will never be put to shame when they speak with their enemies at the city gate.
> (Ps. 127:3–5)

Joining God's Activity in Your Children's Lives

While not everyone will be married or have children, for those who do become parents, children are a special assignment from the Lord. Wise parents understand God has a unique design for each child, and they should carefully watch to see where God is at work in each son's or daughter's life. Notice the significant purpose God had for these children in the Bible:

- Isaac (Gen. 17:19)
- Joseph (Gen. 37:5–11)
- Moses (Exod. 1:15–2:3)
- Samson (Judg. 13:1–5)
- Samuel (1 Sam. 1:11)
- David (1 Sam. 16:11–13)
- Jeremiah (Jer. 1:4–10)
- John the Baptist (Luke 1:13–17)

The psalmist declared:

> For it was You who created my inward parts; You knit me together in my mother's womb. I will praise You, because I have been remarkably and wonderfully made. Your works are wonderful and I know this very well. My bones were not hidden from You when I was made in secret when I was formed in the depths of the earth. Your eyes saw me when I was formless; all my days were written in Your book and planned before a single one of them began. God, how difficult Your thoughts are for me to comprehend; how vast their sum is! (Ps. 139:13–17)

Since God created every person, only He knows the maximum potential for each life. He knows what will lead to joy and fulfillment. He recognizes our shortcomings. He understands how our weaknesses can drive us to Him. By His grace and power, He can work even through our frailties. God has given us strengths, which, if submitted to the Holy Spirit's guidance, become powerful instruments in His hands. Each of us has a unique pilgrimage with special insights and sensitivities that God can use in significant ways for His kingdom. No success or failure in our lives is wasted with God. He does not squander any of our disappointments. He fashions the unique life to which He calls us, and then He is glorified when we live for Him. No life is ordinary when it is in the hands of our extraordinary God.

The apostle Paul gloriously identified God's eternal design for every person:

> For those he foreknew he also predestined to be conformed to the image of His Son, so that he would be the firstborn among many brothers. And those He predestined, He also called; and those he called, He also justified; and those He justified, He also glorified. (Rom. 8:29–30)

God's Eternal Purpose for Your Children

God's purpose for each of your children is that they become like Christ. From the beginning of time, God knew your children would dwell on this earth, and He intended for them one day to act and think like Christ. To accomplish this, God seeks to draw each of your children into a love relationship with Him. God will lead every child on a unique journey. He will speak to your children and allow circumstances in their lives so He can fashion them into Christ-likeness. Throughout the process, God invites you to participate in His work in your children's lives. Your influence as a parent is extremely significant. God wants you to:

1. *Pray for your children.* Prayer is not primarily for us to tell God what we want Him to do for our children. It is for God to adjust our lives so we can be His instrument in their lives. We don't always know what is best for our kids. We aren't aware of all they experience at school. We don't see all the temptations, criticisms, threats, or pressures they undergo. God does not make our children immune from difficulty, but He will alert parents so we can be God's spokesperson when our children need to respond to the circumstances of their lives. God also knows the potential of each child. As much as we love our children, we can't begin to imagine all God has in His heart for them (see 1 Cor. 2:9). We rob our children if we merely want them to meet *our* expectations. We need to be aware of God's agenda for our kids' lives so they experience the abundant life God intends for them (see John 10:10).

Parents often find themselves praying that their children never experience any pain or hardship. Yet God may allow various degrees of discomfort in your child's life to help him or her grow and learn. If God is seeking to bring maturity and Christ-likeness to our children through hardship, then it is counterproductive to pray away every difficult circumstance God allows in their lives. It is far better to ask God to help us understand what He is attempting to do through the circumstances our children experience. We tend to focus our attention on what is happening to our kids *today* while God knows what He is preparing them to be and do for *eternity*.

2. *Talk with your children about God's activity.* Parents talk to their children about numerous things, but no topic is as important as discussing God's activity in their lives. Deuteronomy 6:6–9 and 20–25 instructs parents to regularly talk to their children about God's activity. Parents should rehearse with their children the acts of God throughout their family history. They ought to recount how they met Christ personally, how God led them to be married, how God guided them in their careers, and how God has walked with them through the years. Parents should point out God's ongoing work in their own lives so the family learns to recognize God's activity.

As Marilynn and I reared our children, we constantly pointed out God's activity to them. When God provided for a financial need, we praised God as a family. When God answered our prayers, we helped our sons and daughter see the connection between what we prayed and what happened next. As a result, walking with God became a natural part of our children's lives.

I also asked my children God-centered questions. Instead of "What would you like to be when you grow up?" I asked, "What do you sense God wants you to do?" When my children came to me with a question, they learned to expect me to point them to God: "What do you think God wants you to do?" was my usual reply. If I had merely given my opinion every time they came for help, they would have learned to come to me for answers instead of to God. I wanted them to learn to habitually trust in God, not in their parents. As my children grew older, I regularly asked, "What has God been teaching you lately?" Such a question always provided opportunities to discuss important issues.

3. _Minister with your children_. One of the greatest joys we've had as parents has been ministering alongside our children. We often invited people to our home, and through those times our children learned to care for others. When I was a pastor, I often took a child with me when I went to speak at one of our mission churches. At times, I would take a child to visit a widow or someone in the hospital. Our family also served together in vacation Bible school and at youth camps.

I know families who go on a mission trip together every year. Some families openly discuss the family budget and decide together which causes—beyond the support of their local church—they will contribute to. Many of history's greatest missionaries and ministers were taught by their parents to be on mission with God.

As my children have grown, I've had the privilege of speaking and writing with all five of them. Last year, I had a new experience. I spoke at a men's conference along with Richard and *his* oldest son, Mike—three generations of Blackabys all ministering for the Lord together!

It's important to model for our children how to join in God's activity. Whenever we would hear of a new ministry opportunity from God, we would share it with our children and ask what they thought God wanted us to do. As our children grew, they began to recognize God at work around our family and they would suggest ways they thought we should become involved. As Marilynn and I watched our children mature, we realized that the greatest single contribution to God's kingdom we may have made during our lives is to teach our children to observe where God is at work and to join Him.

Summary

God created the family and intends that children grow to know and love Him. Parents must be sensitive to the Holy Spirit's activity in their children's lives. God knows what to do to bring our children into a love relationship with Him. We must constantly be alert to God's activity in our children's lives and be ready to get involved as God invites us.

Experiencing God Today

Take time to consider each child God has entrusted to you. It is an awesome responsibility. Praise God for His willingness to walk with you and to guide you as you teach your children to know and love Him. Be aware that, even when they reach adulthood, your sons and daughters still see you as a role model.

QUESTIONS FOR REFLECTION

1. Take a moment to think about each of your children. What are some things you see God doing in their lives?

2. How are you praying for your children? Are you merely praying your own agenda to God, or are you seeking God's agenda for your children?

3. How are you joining in God's activity in your children's lives?

23

EXPERIENCING GOD IN THE CHURCH

And they devoted themselves to the apostles' teaching, to fellowship, to the breaking of bread, and to prayers. (Acts 2:42)

GOD'S ACTIVITY IN THE CHURCH

When I was speaking once at a church, a young girl came to the front to pray during the altar call. No one from the congregation joined her, so I went over and stood beside her. I discovered she was praying for the salvation of her nine-year-old friend. It was a special and tender moment for me to hear her intercede for her friend.

That evening, I extended another altar call at the close of my sermon and noticed this same girl walk down the aisle with another little girl in tow. Sure enough, her friend was declaring her decision to become a Christian. At the close of the service, the pastor began to do what he always did—announce the girl's decision and ask the church to formally vote her into membership upon her baptism. I couldn't help myself! I spoke up and said, "Pastor! You're hiding the activity of God from your people!" Then I recounted for the congregation what had happened.

That morning, God had clearly spoken to the little girl about her friend's need for salvation. She had walked to the front of that imposing church auditorium and prayed for her friend. Then she had gone home and invited her friend to come back to the evening service with her. Now, just a few hours later, we were witnessing the miracle of someone's eternal salvation. Yet the congregation was responding by merely taking a formal, routine vote for someone to be added to the church roll. That pastor began to weep and to ask his people to forgive him. He realized he had been practicing religion but had not been helping his people recognize God's activity in their midst. God was powerfully working in the lives of some of that church's youngest members, and no one seemed to notice. As the congregation began to watch for God's activity in their midst, a completely new, exciting dynamic grew up within the church.

God created the church to be unlike any other human organization. It is a living body, created by Christ (see Matt. 16:18), and Christ is its Head (see Col. 1:18). Through the church, God intends to extend His kingdom throughout the earth. God's activity in the church, therefore, is crucial to every believer. It is essential that every Christian be an active member of a local church.

You'll notice that in Scripture, almost every mention of the church refers to a local congregation. Every congregation is important to Christ, and each one has a particular assignment from the Lord. The Scriptures tell us how believers ought to act toward one another:

- Accept anyone who is weak in faith, but don't argue about doubtful issues . . . Each of us will give an account of himself to God. Therefore, let us no longer criticize one another, but instead decide not to put a stumbling block or pitfall in your brother's way. (Rom. 14:1, 12–13)
- No one should seek his own good, but the good of the other person. (1 Cor. 10:24)
- Since each of you put away lying, speak the truth, each one to his neighbor, because we are members of one another. (Eph. 4:25)
- No rotten talk should come from your mouth, but only what is good for the building up of someone in need, in order to give grace to those who hear. (Eph. 4:29)

- Submitting to one another in the fear of Christ. (Eph. 5:21)
- Accepting one another and forgiving one another if anyone has a complaint against another. Just as the Lord has forgiven you, so also you must forgive. Above all, put on love—the perfect bond of unity. (Col. 3:13–14)

What do you notice as you read these Scriptures? Being a member of the church is a selfless act! The church does not merely exist for what you get out of it. It is your opportunity to invest in the lives of God's people and to join God's activity through His people. God knew that your church needed you. That's why God added you to that body (see 1 Cor. 12:18). Your involvement is part of the equipping of your church to carry out God's purposes.

Have you considered why God added you to the church He did? Are you functioning in that role?

We've already discussed hearing God speak through the church. However, I want to challenge you that as you seek to join God in His activity around you, one of the first places you should look is in your own congregation. At first glance, you may not see anything in your church that looks like divine activity. So you may need to ask the Holy Spirit to help you recognize what He is doing.

When I served as a pastor, one of the most important things I did was to help my people recognize when God was at work in our midst. At small or informal meetings, I often asked what the members had witnessed of God's activity that week. University students would tell how God had opened opportunities to share their faith with fellow students. Business people told about God's activity in the work place. Mothers would relate how God led them to establish a group of Christian mothers to pray for the public school. Seniors recounted how God led them to intercede for someone during the week. These informal times of sharing became wonderful opportunities to celebrate together God's activity in our midst.

God Works during a Time of Sharing

Every time we gathered as a church body, we watched to see what God would do. Sometimes it was at the close of the service when people would respond publicly to what God had called them to do. During our prayer meetings and evening service, we often invited people to share what God was saying to them.

One Sunday evening, a college student stood up during a sharing time and told the congregation God had been pursuing him and that he realized he needed to give his life to Christ and to follow Him in baptism. We stopped the service right then, and I asked the church to affirm him and receive him into our fellowship immediately. Then, seeing that God was at work that evening in a powerful way, I asked if there were others who sensed God wanted them to do something and who were ready to yield to His lordship right then. Person after person rose to tell how they were prepared to respond to what God asked of them. The service lasted for more than two hours, and many people made significant spiritual decisions. I never even preached the sermon I had prepared! Yet everyone sensed God had worked in a powerful way when we adjusted our service to His activity in our midst.

One Hurting Person

First Corinthians 12:26 indicates church bodies should be so united that if one member suffers, the rest of the congregation shares the pain. For churches to function this way, people must learn sensitivity to God's activity in the lives of other members. At times, God alerts one church member to what He is doing in another's life.

When I was a pastor, we had a beloved older couple in our church. One fall, the husband, Arthur, passed away leaving his wife, Marion, a widow. Marion was a petite, gracious, and humble woman from England who was mortified at the thought she might be a burden to her church family. She was especially worried that she would be unable to care for her house and yard now that her husband was gone. Yet she dreaded asking for help. So she prayed diligently.

Richard was a university student at the time, and one Sunday evening he entered the auditorium early and sat down to wait for the service to start. He glanced around as the auditorium was filling up and noticed Mrs. Clark sitting on the other side of the room. Richard thought to himself, "I wonder who cares for her yard now that Mr. Clark is gone?" Suddenly, he felt God asking him to go and find out the answer right then. Richard went to Mrs. Clark and said, "I was just wondering who is going to take care of your yard this year." Mrs. Clark's eyes filled with tears, and she struggled to keep her composure. "No one," she replied. Richard offered to stop by on the following Saturday to see what he could do. Mrs. Clark's relief was evident.

The next Saturday, when Richard arrived at Mrs. Clark's house, the yard was in shambles! He spent most of the day collecting fallen tree branches, raking leaves, and mowing the grass. As he was finishing up, he spied Mrs. Clark with a handful of money she intended to give him for his labor, but he adamantly refused. He explained that God had clearly told him to do what he had done and that it would be wrong for him to take her money when she had so little. "But" Richard added, "I *do* know you are a great baker. *Any* time you are baking something, it would be great if you wanted to make a little extra for me."

The next day when Richard entered the church foyer, he was met by the aroma of fresh baking. Mrs. Clark was waiting for him with two large bags filled with baked goods for him! This became a weekly tradition. My son mowed Mrs. Clark's lawn and returned with an armload of mouth-watering baked items.

Who would ever have thought a college student and an elderly widow could become special friends? God would. He designed the church for people of all ages and levels of spiritual maturity. He wants church members to be so closely aligned that when a senior citizen is hurting, a college student in the congregation will sense the burden and meet the need.

You need to prepare yourself before going to church so you're ready to join God in whatever work He may be doing in your congregation. Too often, church members attend services and merely seek out their friends. It never dawns on them that people may be there who are experiencing tremendous pain and hurt. There may be first-time visitors without anyone to offer even a greeting.

The Holy Spirit can guide you to someone who is hurting if you are sensitive to His leading. Perhaps as you enter the auditorium, the Holy Spirit will prompt you to sit in a different place than you normally do in order to talk with someone who needs encouragement at the close of the service. Allow the Holy Spirit to lead you to a visitor, and welcome that person to your church. The Spirit may encourage you to pray regularly for the single parent sitting in front of you who seems deeply moved by the sermon that day. Maybe the Spirit will inspire you to approach a teenager after the service to encourage him by saying you'll pray for him. Every week, the Spirit knows who is hurting or who is seeking answers from God or who desperately needs to know if God's people care. If you're sensitive to the Spirit's nudging, you can be God's instrument of healing and love right in your own church family.

Watch and Pray!

I mentioned earlier that my home church has a special time in the worship service when people are invited to the front of the auditorium to pray during the pastoral prayer. The pastor always tells us to close our eyes and bow our heads. I prefer instead to do what Jesus commanded His disciples—to *watch* and pray! I feel this could be a key time to see if there are hurting people around me. It is tragic that every Sunday people in our churches suffer terribly, but no one else is even aware of their pain.

One Sunday, I noticed a distinguished elderly woman who seemed downcast. During the prayer time, I slipped out of my seat and went over to her. I asked if there was anything I could do for her as she seemed quite sad that morning. She told me it was the one-year anniversary of the death of her husband and that this day had been extremely hard for her. She was not sure she could handle the grief. I asked if I could pray for her, and she readily accepted my offer.

I've prayed for many people over the years, but this one surprised me. I found myself asking God to do things in this dear woman's life I had never thought to ask for anyone before. I recognized that the Holy Spirit was helping me ask things that were on God's heart to provide for this woman (see Rom. 8:26). When I finished, she smiled and with a sense of peace told me she knew she would be all right.

Several weeks later was a holiday season. I know that recent widows and widowers have a particularly difficult time during the first holidays they spend without their spouses. Again I noticed the woman sitting near my wife and me, and again I slipped over to ask how she was doing. She smiled and said the Lord had been good to her and that she was doing very well. Whenever my wife and I are at our church now, we watch for this woman and try to encourage her. God has ministered to her in a special way.

On any given Sunday, there are numerous people in my congregation who are hurting and who long for assurance that God knows and cares about what they're going through. It has been my joy to enter church on Sunday with a prayer to God that I am available for the Spirit to lead me to the one who needs encouragement that day. How exciting this has made Sundays for me! I never know what God might ask me to do as I not only worship Him but serve Him among His people.

Scripture exhorts believers to "carry one another's burdens; in this way you will fulfill the law of Christ" (Gal. 6:2). God's Word also says, "So we must not get tired of doing good, for we will reap at the proper time if we don't give up. Therefore, as we have opportunity, we must work for the good of all, especially for those who belong to the household of faith" (Gal. 6:9–10).

Too many Christians have developed a self-centered attitude toward their church. They look upon church as something that exists to meet their needs and to deliver entertaining services each week. However, Jesus said we must deny ourselves (see Matt. 16:24). Our desire should not be that we are always ministered to but that we follow Jesus wherever He leads us. Rather than focusing on what our church is doing for us, we ought to be asking what God is seeking to do in our church *through* us.

A Men's Ministry

A businessman once told me he had grown disenchanted with his church. This man wanted to participate in a vibrant men's ministry to help him grow and to be accountable, but there was no such ministry in his church, and the staff had no immediate plans to begin one. "Should I leave my church and find one that believes in ministering to men?" he asked. I reminded him that God adds members to the body as it pleases Him (see 1 Cor. 12:18), and I suggested that if God added him to a church without a men's ministry, maybe God intended to begin one through him. This man was a successful businessman and had always been a leader. Why not offer those skills for the Lord's service and let God use him to make a positive difference in his church?

The man, half reluctantly, went to the staff of his church and told them he was willing to organize a men's event for the church.

The staff told him they, too, sensed a need for such a ministry, but they had needed someone to spearhead it. At the first event, men in his church came out of the woodwork to attend! It was such a tremendous success, everyone asked what they were going to do next. The numbers consistently grew until this man saw hundreds of men actively participating in this new ministry. Eventually, other churches contacted this man to ask if he could help them begin a men's work also.

He hosted several city-wide events, and men from across the city felt the impact. The man was overcome by how God had used his life to so dramatically impact people. He came to realize that when he sensed a need in his life, it was not so he could complain about it and abandon his church. It was the Holy Spirit prompting him to help transform his church into the body of believers God intended it to be.

Summary

God adds people to church bodies for a reason. He wants to use your life to make a positive difference among the people where He has placed you. You must be sensitive to the Spirit as He leads you to serve Him in your church. As you respond to the Holy Spirit, you'll find He uses you to bless the people in your congregation and to help your church become what God intends it to be.

Experiencing God Today

Recall how God guided you to join the church in which you are a member. How did you know that was where God wanted you? Review the ways God has ministered to you through your church and consider how God has used your life to bless others.

QUESTIONS FOR REFLECTION

1. Has the Holy Spirit alerted you to someone in your church who is struggling or in need? What might God want to do through you to minister to that person or family?

2. Has God made you aware of a problem or need in your church? How might God use your life as part of the solution to that problem?

3. When you attend church, are you alert to people who may need encouragement? If God has led you to some specific people, what have you done in response?

4. If you are not aware of people in your church to whom you could minister, why do you think that is? How could you be more spiritually prepared the next time you go to church?

24

Experiencing God in the Marketplace

So he reasoned in the synagogue with the Jews and with those who worshiped God, and in the marketplace every day with those who happened to be there. (Acts 17:17)

Divine Encounters in the Dentist's Chair

One day John, a good friend of mine who owns a large company, went to the dentist. A hygienist lowered John back in his chair and inserted various tubes into his mouth. While she was poking a sharp metal object in his mouth, she informed him that several years ago he had turned down her husband's job application. John suddenly felt extremely vulnerable!

Apparently, years earlier John had been notified that a job applicant had failed a mandatory drug screening test and could therefore not be hired, even though he showed great promise. The human resources director would normally have informed the job applicant of the disappointing news, but John felt God leading him to tell the young man himself. Certainly this was not something a company owner and CEO would relish doing, but John called the man into his office and explained to him that he was extremely impressed with his credentials. John indicated that the applicant was the kind of talented person his company was seeking, but he had failed the drug test. John was obligated to follow company policy and decline to hire him. John then looked the young man in the eye and reminded him that he was a newlywed with his first child on the way. John cautioned that if he continued to use drugs, he could lose his health, his wife, and his children. His family would experience enormous hurt if he did not make some major changes in his life.

"He really took your warning to heart," the hygienist concluded. "He came home shaken by what you said and got rid of his drugs. He eventually found a good job and has been very successful. He's become a great husband and father, and I know he would want me to thank you for taking time to talk to him in the middle of your busy day like you did. That brief talk changed my husband's life!"

John was just an ordinary Christian businessman who was invited one day to join God in saving a man's family and career. Every day holds limitless possibilities as God walks with people in the marketplace.

God Chooses Businesspeople

For too long, Christians have assumed that the activity of God occurs only on Sundays at church. In reality, the Scriptures show that God is continually at work in the marketplace. When God launched His great work to bring salvation to humanity, He called Abraham, one of the most successful businessmen of his day (see Gen. 24:35). Abraham's son Isaac also prospered in the marketplace (see Gen. 26:12–14). Likewise, Isaac's son Jacob became wealthy through his business acumen (see Gen. 30:43). Joseph served God, not as a preacher or missionary but as a grain administrator (see Gen. 41:37–57). Moses had a profound encounter with God while in the midst of his work (see Exod. 3:1–6). Elisha was invited to join God's activity while plowing a field (see 1 Kings 19:19–21). Amos declared he was not a prophet or the son of a prophet but a sheep breeder and a tender of sycamore trees (see Amos 7:14). Daniel served God as a government official.

Jesus was trained as a carpenter. When He set about to call the twelve people who would walk with Him as His disciples, He chose fishermen and other career people (Mark 1:16–20). Businesspeople are not intimidated by the world. That is the environment in which they live and thrive. Once these people experienced a life transforming encounter with Jesus, they were prepared to turn their world upside down! Joseph of Arimathea was a businessman who, although he feared religious leaders, had the courage to approach Pilate, the Roman leader, for Jesus' body (see John 19:38; Mark 15:42–43). Joseph used his business contacts and influence to provide Jesus a proper burial, and all four Gospels recount his story. Lydia, a businesswoman, was a key member of the church at Philippi (see Acts 16:14–15). Two strong supporters of apostle Paul's church planting ministry were Aquila and Priscilla, a couple who ran a business (see Acts 18:1–2).

The marketplace—not the church building—is where people spend most of their time. God does not wait to encounter them when they enter His house on Sundays. He goes to where people are and encounters them during their everyday lives. Sunday services are an opportunity for believers to worship God and to be equipped for their mission where they live and work during the week (see Eph. 4:11–12).

God Is at Work!

One of the greatest spiritual movements I see today is what God is doing in the business world. I work with a group of Christian CEOs of some of America's largest companies. These men and women have realized God placed them in their positions for a purpose. They impact tens of thousands of employees and control huge advertising budgets. They have access to world leaders that missionaries do not.[1]

One businessman's company produces power plants, and he provided one free to a village in Africa on the condition he could tell the people why he was helping them. By the time the power was turned on in that community, the chief and many of the villagers had become believers. The CEO was then invited by a top government leader to provide power plants to numerous other villages, all with the freedom to tell them he was doing it out of his love for Jesus Christ.

Another CEO has given Bibles to world leaders as gifts when he visits their countries on business. One businessman I know took early retirement, purchased a declining company, completely transformed it, and has been donating its profits to Christian ministries as his way of investing in God's kingdom.

Many people are discovering that God has placed them in a company so they can be a witness to their colleagues and clients. I could tell you numerous stories of people who led their coworkers to faith in Christ, and I know business leaders who lead Bible studies during lunch hour for their staffs.

Many people who meet Christ in their workplace would never have visited a church on Sunday. So Christ sends His servants to job sites where the people who need to hear about Him work. In the same way we pray over missionaries who travel to other countries to share the gospel, I believe churches ought to have commissioning services for those who go into the marketplace every Monday morning.

Jesus and Zacchaeus

Luke 19:1–10 tells one of the most encouraging stories of the Bible. As Jesus passed through Jericho on His way to Jerusalem and His appointment with the cross, word had spread that the great miracle worker and teacher was coming down Main Street. Crowds gathered quickly to catch a glimpse of Him. Zacchaeus, a businessman notorious for his unethical and ruthless practices, also felt an inner compulsion to see Jesus. Despite the man's tough exterior and hard-nosed reputation, God was pursuing him.

As Jesus passed by, many people shouted at Him to draw His attention. But suddenly Jesus spied the infamous tax collector in a tree. He knew His Father was at work in that man's life and called out, "Zacchaeus, make haste and come down, for today I must stay at your house." Scripture doesn't tell us how, but Jesus recognized that the Father was drawing Zacchaeus to Himself, and Jesus immediately joined Him.

God is at work among businesspeople around the world. There is a restlessness in many of their hearts as they realize reaching the top of the corporate ladder or achieving financial goals does not bring the peace and contentment they've been seeking.

Seeing Zacchaeus in the Workplace

One man was at work when the Holy Spirit drew his attention to a particular colleague. Although he didn't know the other man well, he felt impressed to ask the coworker to lunch. Over lunch, the man confessed that just that morning, he had left his wife. Before the day was over, the Christian had led this troubled coworker to place his trust in Christ and be restored to his wife.

A salesman was making his regular rounds through the community when he saw a house for sale. A few weeks later, he spied a moving van in the driveway of that house. Two weeks after that, he noticed a wheelchair ramp being installed by the front door. Every time this Christian drove by that home, he felt the Spirit nudge him to find out who lived there. Finally one day as he drove by, he felt strongly that he should pay a visit. So he stopped and rang the doorbell. The house was not far from the salesman's church so he decided to invite the stranger to church. A disabled man met him with a bitter, lonely story. He was deeply grateful someone had cared enough to come by. The man said he had noticed the church and wondered if its people were friendly or not. Now he knew.

Other businesspeople have discovered God has granted them prosperity so they can invest their wealth in the kingdom of God. Suddenly, rather than being absorbed in their work, these men and women have found a new world of God's kingdom activity open up to them. Some have begun using their resources to build church buildings around the world. Some have taken early retirement and gone to work for Christian organizations. Others have invested in Bible colleges and seminaries that are training people for Christian ministry. Businesspeople have supported orphanages as well as ministries to those suffering from hunger and disease. Jesus commanded those who would be His followers: "But seek first the kingdom of God and His righteousness, and all these things will be added to you" (Matt. 6:33). Jesus expects every disciple to make it his or her first priority to be involved in the building of God's kingdom and to trust God to provide for all other needs.

Revival

I believe God is going to bring revival to North America, and I suspect He may bring it through the marketplace. Why? For one thing, Christian businesspeople are interconnected across all denominations. Often, church leaders have little contact with people of other denominations or even other churches. But businesspeople work through networks of connections. They are also pragmatic and can be extremely creative.

Churches that learn to tap into the creative and administrative talents of their members in order to accomplish kingdom work will discover God is using their people to dramatically impact their community and world. Businesspeople know how important it is to communicate and to advertise. Many pastors are swamped with counseling and ministering to their members and have little time to take on administrative challenges. But I have found that if you want to get a meeting organized for a Christian event, ask a businessperson to organize it.

Businesspeople have access to people and places many church staff do not. They can contact government officials or other influential leaders. They are not intimidated by secular leaders, whereas some ministers are. They can even enter some countries that are opposed to Christianity and therefore closed to Christian missionaries. Today, thousands of Christian businesspeople are discovering that God has provided them with unique opportunities and resources that can significantly benefit the work of God's kingdom.

Summary

Throughout history, when God sought to accomplish a great work, He often did it through a businessperson. The marketplace is where people spend much of their time, and that is where God will go to encounter people and to meet their spiritual needs. He wants to work through Christian businesspeople in the marketplace to bring others into a saving relationship with Him. Christians must be alert to what God intends to do through their lives each day as they go to work.

Experiencing God Today

If you are a businessperson or a professional, take time to reflect on why God led you to your present place of employment. Think about the clients and colleagues you encounter each day. Has God placed you in a spiritually needy mission field? Ask the Lord to reveal how He wants to impact the people around you through your life.

QUESTIONS FOR REFLECTION

1. If you are presently involved in the marketplace, what have you seen God doing where you work? How have you been joining in that activity?

2. What skills, experiences, contacts, and resources has God given you that He wants to use for building His kingdom?

3. How have you been seeking God's kingdom first and then allowing God to add everything else to you?

4. How does the way you live reflect the fact you believe God is Lord of your career and over your company?

---

1. For further information, see Henry and Richard Blackaby, *God in the Marketplace: 45 Questions Fortune 500 Executives Ask about Faith, Life, and Business* (Nashville: B&H Publishing Group, 2008).

25

Experiencing God in His Kingdom

After John was arrested, Jesus went to Galilee, preaching the good news of God: "The time is fulfilled, and the kingdom of God has come near. Repent and believe in the good news." (Mark 1:14–15)

A World at the Doorstep

Speaking at a church a couple of years ago, I preached on Sunday morning from the book of John, using the story of the Samaritan woman at the well. I pointed out how Jesus took time to minister to a notorious woman with a tarnished reputation. Her life was so radically transformed that her entire town came to faith in Jesus (see John 4:39–42). Later, after Pentecost, many more Samaritans readily accepted the gospel (see Acts 8:4–25). It is likely that the conversion of the Samaritan woman laid the groundwork for a widespread work that occurred later.

I challenged the people in the congregation that they, like the woman at the well, might be a catalyst for the conversion of many people. I urged them to be willing for God to do a powerful work in their lives so they could impact others for Christ. During the altar call, many people came to pray, moved by what God had said to them. After the service, a long line of people waited to speak to me.

One woman said, "God told me I am to be the woman at the well for my country in Ghana." A man told me, "God told me I am to be the woman at the well for my people in Pakistan." Person after person told me God had invited them to be His instruments to impact their homeland for Christ. I had no idea there were so many different nations represented in this one church.

The pastor of the church was overwhelmed. He, like many pastors, had welcomed each new member into his church family with the perspective of what they could do for his church. Could they teach a Sunday school class? Serve on a committee? Sing in the choir? But he had never asked how God might be intending to impact the world through the people in his congregation. Was God adding them to his church so the pastor and people could equip them to go back to their countries and share the faith with their family and friends? Was God adding members to assist the church in sending mission teams into the new members' home countries?

God's Heart for the World

John the Baptist preached this message: "Repent, because the kingdom of heaven has come near!" (Matt. 3:2). Jesus preached, "Repent, because the kingdom of heaven has come near!" (Matt. 4:17). And when Jesus sent out His twelve disciples into the towns and villages, "He sent them to proclaim the kingdom of God" (Luke 9:2). Clearly, Jesus' ministry was to build God's kingdom.

The kingdom of God is the rule of God in the hearts of people around the world. Every church that follows Christ is part of the kingdom of God. If you are a true disciple of Jesus, you must obey His clear command to "seek first the kingdom of God" (Matt. 6:33). If we are to truly follow Jesus, God's kingdom must be our priority just as it is Christ's.

God always relates to you and your church with a world on His heart. As He speaks to you, He thinks of the masses around the world who do not yet know Him. Scripture explains that God *so* loved the *world* that He was willing to pay any price to bring salvation to those who were in danger of perishing (see John 3:16). You cannot love God without also loving what He loves. God cares for all the peoples of the world. He does not favor people from certain countries or nationalities or skin colors or political affiliations. He loves *people*, and He desires that *no one* perish. God knows the full, horrific extent of what it means to perish for eternity, and He does not want that to happen to anyone. Notice the heart of God as revealed in the Bible:

> "Go, therefore, and make disciples of all nations, baptizing them in the name of the Father and of the Son and of the Holy Spirit, teaching them to observe everything I have commanded." (Matt. 28:19–20)

> "Go into all the world and preach the gospel to the whole creation." (Mark 16:15)

> "But you will receive power when the Holy Spirit has come upon you, and you will be My witnesses in Jerusalem, in all Judea and Samaria, and to the ends of the earth." (Acts 1:8)

> I heard every creature in heaven, on earth, under the earth, on the sea, and everything in them say: "Blessing and honor and glory and dominion to the One seated on the throne, and to the Lamb, forever and ever!" (Rev. 5:13)

God's desire is that "every tongue should confess that Jesus Christ is Lord, to the glory of God the Father" (Phil. 2:11). God the Father was willing to go to enormous lengths to bring this about by sending His very Son to die on a cross for humanity's sin. Now, as He carries out His plan to redeem humanity, He has raised up the church as His instrument to bring a world to Himself.

God plans to use local congregations to make disciples of all nations. I'm pleased to hear of many churches who are sponsoring record numbers of mission trips around the world. International mission agencies are calling on churches to adopt people groups and to take responsibility for bringing the gospel to specific nations. We must keep in mind that God expects us to have the entire world on our hearts, just as He does.

The Great Commission is not a command to go into a *portion* of the world but into *all* the world. To aim for anything less is to be guilty of planned disobedience. You might argue, "But that's impossible for a church as small as ours!" To which my response would be, "Of course it is. But that does not make it any less binding on you." Jesus' command to "be perfect, just as your Father in heaven is perfect" is also impossible for you! But that does not make it any less obligatory. Clearly, you cannot carry out many of God's commands in your own strength or wisdom. You and your church will never be able to figure out how to impact a world for Christ. But God knows how to do that through you. He will lead your church to know what to do, where to go, and with whom you should partner to impact your world.

Be careful the moment you say, "That's impossible!" When you do, you are saying more about your faith in God than about the ability of your church. Never reduce a command of God to a level where you think you can obey it. When God asks you to do something that is impossible, rejoice!—because God is now going to bring you to a place where you'll experience His divine power working through you or else you will fail. That is a wonderful, exciting position to be in!

When the angel told teenage Mary that God was going to bring salvation to the world through her child, the angel had to reassure her, "For nothing will be impossible with God" (Luke 1:37). When Jesus commanded His followers to make disciples of all nations, He also promised, "And remember, I am with you always, to the end of the ages" (Matt. 28:20).

God knows better than we do what we are capable of doing. He continually works in our lives and our churches so we must depend upon Him with a faith that pleases Him (see Heb. 11:6). Moreover, in our weakness, His strength is manifested to a watching world (see 2 Cor. 12:9–10). The world will never come to faith in Christ because we developed a strong plan but because we faithfully obeyed an all-powerful God.

I have been delighted to watch God's people taking God at His Word and seeking to obey Him in whatever He leads them to do. Today, churches are taking the gospel into some of the most dangerous places in the world. People are using their vacations and going on mission trips to express God's love to those who have never met a Christian before. Churches are investing large portions of their finances in God's kingdom around the world.

Faithful in a Little

So how do you live a life that impacts the world and the kingdom of God? As I've said, only God can enable you to do that. But God has provided some biblical principles that show how He works in peoples' lives. One of these is the truth that if you are faithful in a little, God will entrust you with more. Jesus told the parable of the master who left his servants in charge of his possessions while he went on a distant journey. To one he allotted five talents; to another two talents; and to a third, one talent (a talent represented a large amount of money). Two of the servants did well with what they were given while the third did not. To the two who were good managers of what was left with them, their master replied: "Well done, good and faithful slave! You were faithful over a few things; I will put you in charge of many things. Share your master's joy" (Matt. 25:21).

The principle is clear: if you are faithful in the little assignments God gives you, God will trust you with more. I have seen this truth work in people's lives in every way imaginable. The regional manager of a large company once asked me if God had entrusted him with that position for a reason. I assured him God had. "But," I said, "this is not the end. If you are faithful to follow through with all God has for you in this role, God will give you a greater responsibility in His kingdom." Sure enough, he was later promoted to be the national CEO. "Is this what you meant?" he asked. "No, that's what God means. But this isn't the end. Be as faithful as you can in this assignment and then see what God has for you next." A while later, he told me he had been assigned responsibility for all of his company's international operations. Now he would be relating to world leaders and having a significant influence on entire nations.

I don't believe this man has yet seen the extent of what God intends to do through his life to bless His kingdom. His company does business in countries that have been closed or restrictive toward Christianity. I sense God is going to use this CEO and his influence to assist the expansion of God's kingdom around the world. He can talk with the national leaders of countries that would arrest Christian missionaries if they attempted to enter the country. As a businessman, he can represent Christ in ways and in places that would be impossible for most people. He has been entrusted with much, and God will be expecting much (Luke 12:48). There are no limits to what God will do when He has servants who are faithful in everything He gives them.

God knows how He can use your life to exert the maximum impact for His kingdom. He may not immediately give you a large, international assignment. But you can expect that He will have something for you to do. It may be a very ordinary task. It may not carry much prestige. However, if you faithfully do all God asks, then don't be surprised if God gives you something new that has greater ramifications. Always remember, though, that any assignment from God is more than we deserve. Don't be anxious to have larger and larger roles. Don't keep pushing and asking for greater tasks from God or lobbying with others for positions. Trust that when God is pleased with your faithful service, He will entrust you with more in His perfect timing.

Summary

God loves the entire world. He is constantly at work extending His kingdom. His kingdom includes every believer on earth. God looks for those who will make the pursuit and extension of His kingdom the chief aim of their lives. Those who are faithful in the assignments God gives will be entrusted with more.

Experiencing God Today

Take some time to study a map of the world. Examine each continent and look at the various countries. Which countries have you visited or gone to on a mission trip? Ask the Lord if you should make plans to minister in some way in a particular country. You may not be able to travel to that nation yourself, but you certainly can be praying for it and even sponsoring a mission effort there. Be sure to spend significant time this week interceding for those nations God places on your heart. Investigate various countries, and find out all you can about the kingdom of God in those nations.

QUESTIONS FOR REFLECTION

1. Are you seeking God's kingdom above everything else? What is the evidence?

2. How has God been using your life to impact another part of the world? What nation has God placed on your heart? How might you plan to be involved in missions soon?

3. Have you been faithful in what God has given you? What is the evidence?

4. Do you truly believe God can impact the world through your life and your church?

26

Continuing to Experience God

*Now to Him who is able to protect you from stumbling
and make you stand in the presence of His glory, blameless
and with great joy. (Jude 24)*

The Beginning, Not the End

Nearly two thousand years ago, two discouraged men were walking together to the town of Emmaus, roughly seven miles from Jerusalem (see Luke 24:13–35). They had chosen to follow Jesus and had been excited about all He had done and taught. But Jesus had been cruelly taken from them. Now, they were bewildered, not knowing what to do next. Suddenly, a stranger joined them and asked what they were talking about. They explained what had happened and how they could no longer follow Jesus as they had planned. During the next few hours, the stranger explained that the events surrounding Jesus' death were not the end but rather the beginning of an exciting new opportunity to walk daily with the Son of God. The stranger was the risen Christ Himself!

One thing we often hear from people who have studied this material is that there is a letdown after they finish—especially if they have been meeting regularly with a small group of people. Many tell us they hated to come to the end of the book because they feared their Christian lives might revert to patterns like before the study.

I want to encourage you that this does not need to be the case. Your encounter with Christ through this material has not been an end but a beginning.

I pray God has shown how you can experience a love relationship with Him that is real and fresh every day. I trust you have been challenged to see where God is at work and then to join Him. I hope you have made the adjustments in your life God has asked of you, and you are now obeying everything He told you to do. But all of this is only the beginning! There is far more God wants you to know and experience of Him. There are new truths He wants you to understand so they can set you free (see John 8:32). There is far more of God's nature, His purposes, and ways He still wants to reveal. This course should be the starting point for a whole new adventure in following Christ daily.

As you come to the end of this book, there are several important questions to think about: What are some things God has taught you about Himself as you've gone through this material? What has God revealed to you about your walk with Him? What are some commitments you have made to God through studying this material?

As you prepare to move on to the next stage in your walk with God, here are a few practices that will help you continue your spiritual growth:

1. *Stay regularly immersed in God's Word.* Remember God's instruction to Joshua: "This book of instruction must not depart from your mouth; you are to recite it day and night, so that you may carefully observe everything written in it. For then you will prosper and succeed in whatever you do" (Josh. 1:8). Make it a habit to be in God's Word daily. God has many truths to reveal if you will give Him the opportunity. Ephesians 5:26 gives the wonderful picture of Christ preparing the church to be His bride. Scripture says, "To make her holy, cleansing her in the washing of water by the word." As the church is immersed in God's Word, the Spirit of God uses Scripture to convict and cleanse God's people of sin and to become spotless before Him. Regularly spending time in Bible study allows the Holy Spirit to cleanse you of any sin and to increasingly make you like Christ.

2. *Remain intimately involved with a church family that will love and nurture you.* Hebrews urges us: "Not staying away from our

meetings, as some habitually do, but encouraging each other, and all the more as you see the day drawing near" (Heb. 10:25). God made believers interdependent. You cannot experience all God has for you apart from the rest of the body of Christ. Surround yourself with people who have a passion for Christ and His Word and who are willing to encourage you and to hold you accountable to the word God speaks to you.

3. *Pray regularly.* Daniel made it a habit to pray three times daily (see Dan. 6:10). As a result, he had a powerful prayer life in which God answered him the moment he began to speak (see Dan. 9:23). One of the best ways to prevent your heart from growing cold is to talk regularly with God. As you commune with Him, keep your focus on Him and remember to follow Him daily. Prayer is a two-way communication through which God also speaks to you. It is difficult to talk with God each day and continue to sin.

4. *Keep your promises to God.* Ecclesiastes warns: "When you make a vow to God, don't delay fulfilling it, because He does not delight in fools. Fulfill what you vow. Better that you do not vow than that you vow and not fulfill it" (Eccles. 5:4–5). Throughout this book, God may have spoken to you, and you've made commitments to Him in response. Remember that God takes our promises to Him extremely seriously. Take time to review this book and list the commitments you made. Keep that list in your Bible where you will see it regularly. Then be diligent to follow through with everything you promised God you would do. Keep in mind that a good intention is not the same as obedience. There are no substitutes for obedience.

5. *Process what God has done in your life as you've read this book.* God may have spoken to you many times, but if you don't let the truths soak into your heart and take root in your life, it will be like the seed that fell on stony ground and was soon taken away (see Matt. 13:20–21). Processing God's Word means allowing God to explain and apply all He has said to you. It is not enough to agree with what God said. You must also apply God's Word in your heart and life. This involves action.

If, for instance, God spoke to you about forgiveness, it is not enough to believe in forgiveness. You must ask God to examine your heart and relationships to see if there is anyone you have not truly forgiven. If God reveals someone, ask Him to show what action you must take to be reconciled. Then do what He says. Don't consider God's truth as doctrine to be believed but as a reality that must be lived and experienced. If God revealed some special truths to you during this study, don't let them be lost as you put this book on the shelf and go on with your activities. Identify all the truths God brought to your attention, and then meditate on them until you're sure you understand and experience everything God intended when He revealed the truth to you.

Closing Remarks

[I pray] that He may grant you, according to the riches of His glory, to be strengthened with power through His Spirit in the inner man, and that the Messiah may dwell in your hearts through faith. I pray that you, being rooted and firmly established in love, may be able to comprehend with all the saints what is the length and width, height and depth of God's love, and to know the Messiah's love that surpasses knowledge, so you may be filled with all the fullness of God. Now to Him who is able to do above and beyond all that we ask or think—according to the power that works in you—to Him be glory in the church and in Christ Jesus to all generations, forever and ever. Amen. (Ephesians 3:16–21)

In preparing this book, my prayer has been that you would come to know God more intimately as you experience Him at work in and through your life. Has God been speaking to you? Has He been teaching, guiding, or encouraging you? Has He been calling you into a love relationship with Himself? Has He invited you to be involved in His work? Can you identify what God has been doing in your life? I pray you can answer "yes" to these questions.

If God has been working in your life as you read, He has been preparing you for more intimate fellowship with Him and for assignments in His kingdom. I hope you have come to a deep sense of God's presence and activity in your life. What God has begun in your life He will bring to perfect completion: "He who started a good work in you will carry it on to completion until the day of Christ Jesus" (Phil. 1:6).

God has been gracious to allow me to join Him at work in your life. I thank God and praise Him for all He will do in and through your life in the days to come.

About the Authors

HENRY T. BLACKABY is founder of Blackaby Ministries International and former special assistant to the presidents of the following agencies of the Southern Baptist Convention: International Mission Board, North American Mission Board, and LifeWay Christian Resources. His father was a deacon and helped start churches in Canada as a lay pastor.

Henry is a graduate of the University of British Columbia, Vancouver, Canada, and Golden Gate Baptist Theological Seminary in Mill Valley, California. He has been granted four honorary doctoral degrees. He was the pastor of churches in the San Francisco and Los Angeles areas before serving as pastor of Faith Baptist Church in Saskatoon, Saskatchewan, Canada. Henry also served as a director of missions in Vancouver, British Columbia. He has spoken in 114 countries in churches and conferences. He counsels Christian CEOs of Fortune 500 companies and has spoken in the White House, Pentagon, and at the United Nations.

Henry has written numerous books including: *Experiencing God: Knowing and Doing the Will of God, Revised Edition*; *What the Spirit Is Saying to the Churches*; *Fresh Encounter*; *The Power of the Call*; *Called to Be God's Friend*; *Anointed to Be God's Servant*; *Chosen to Be God's Prophet*; *Prepared to Be God's Vessel*; *Experiencing God as Couples*; *A God-Centered Church*; *Called and Accountable*; *What's So Spiritual about Your Gifts?*; *Holiness*; *The Man God Uses*; *Experiencing Prayer with Jesus*; *Experiencing the Cross*; *The Ways of God*; *Worship: Believers Experiencing God*; *Experiencing the Resurrection*; and *Experiencing Pentecost*.

His wife is the former Marilynn Wells. They have five children: Richard, Thomas, Melvin, Norman, and Carrie. All five serve in full-time Christian ministry.

For further information about Henry Blackaby and his ministry, contact Blackaby Ministries International, P.O. Box 16338, Atlanta, GA 30321; phone: 770-603-2900; Web site: www.blackaby.org.

CLAUDE V. KING is the National Discipleship Specialist for LifeWay Christian Resources in Nashville. Claude worked with T. W. Hunt to develop *The Mind of Christ*. He is author or coauthor of twenty-one books and courses including *Experiencing God: Knowing and Doing the Will of God, Revised Edition; Made to Count Life Planner; Fresh Encounter; WiseCounsel; Come to the Lord's Table; Meet Jesus Christ;* and *Concentric Circles of Concern*. Claude serves as vice president on the board of directors for Final Command Ministries. He is a graduate of Belmont College and New Orleans Baptist Theological Seminary.

RICHARD BLACKABY is Henry's oldest son. He holds a B.A., M.Div., and Ph.D. in history as well as an honorary doctorate. He has served as a pastor and a seminary president and is currently the president of Blackaby Ministries International. He travels internationally speaking on the Christian life and spiritual leadership. He and his wife, Lisa, have three children: Mike, Daniel, and Carrie. Richard has coauthored a dozen books with his father including: *When God Speaks; Spiritual Leadership; Experiencing God: Day by Day; The Experience; God's Invitation; Hearing God's Voice; Called to Be God's Leader: Lessons from the Life of Joshua; Reality: Seven Truths from Experiencing God; Blackaby Study Bible; Discovering God's Daily Agenda; Experiencing God, Revised Edition;* and *God in the Marketplace: 45 Questions Fortune 500 Executives Ask about Faith, Life and Business*. He has also written *CrossSeekers; Putting a Face on Grace: Living a Life Worth Passing On;* and *Unlimiting God: Increasing Your Capacity to Experience the Divine*.

NOTES. In this book, Henry Blackaby is the primary author of content. Claude King was the primary editor for the original version. Richard Blackaby led in the revision and expansion in 2008.

The personal illustrations of the authors are written solely from their personal viewpoints. Others who were involved, if given the opportunity, could write a different and more complete account from diverse perspectives.

At times, monetary amounts are cited to describe how God met specific needs of His people as they prayed. Some of these events occurred in the 1970s when costs were much lower. Don't let the amounts God provided be the focus of your reading, but rather recognize that at that time, God's provision was significant and God's provision came in His perfect timing to meet our need.

Appendix

Names, Titles, and Descriptions of God

abounding in goodness and truth (Exod. 34:6)
acquainted with grief (Isa. 53:3)
Adam, the last (1 Cor. 15:45)
Advocate with the Father (1 John 2:1)
all (Col. 3:11)
Almighty, the (Job 5:17; 1:8)
Alpha (Rev. 1:8; 21:6)
Amen, the (Rev. 3:14)
Ancient of Days, the (Dan. 7:22)
anointed (Ps. 2:2; Acts 4:27)
Apostle and High Priest of our confession (Heb. 3:1)
author and finisher of our faith, the (Heb. 12:2)
author of eternal salvation, the (Heb. 5:9)
banner to the people, a (Isa. 11:10)
Beginning of the creation of God, the (Rev. 3:14)
Beginning, the (Rev. 21:6)
Beloved, My (Matt. 12:18)
Branch of the Lord, the (Isa. 4:2)
Branch, a (Isa. 11:1)
Branch, a righteous (Jer. 23:5)
Branch, the (Zech. 6:12)

bread from heaven, true (John 6:32)
bread of life, the (John 6:35)
breath of the Almighty (Job 32:8; 33:4)
bridegroom, the (Matt. 9:15)
brightness of His glory, the (Heb. 1:3)
brother of James, Joseph, Judas, and Simon (Mark. 6:3)
builder and maker (Heb. 11:10)
carpenter, the (Mark 6:3)
carpenter's son, the (Matt.13:55)
chief cornerstone, elect, precious (1 Pet. 2:6)
chief cornerstone, the (Matt. 21:42; Mark 12:10; Eph. 2:20)
Child Jesus (Luke 2:27)
chosen of God, the (Luke 23:35)
Christ, the chosen of God (Luke 23:35)
Christ Jesus my Lord (Phil. 3:8)
Christ of God (Luke 9:20)
Christ, the (Matt. 16:16)
comforter (2 Cor. 1:4)
Commander of the Lord's army, the (Josh. 5:15)
confidence of all the ends of the earth and . . . (Ps. 65:5)
Consolation of Israel, the (Luke 2:25)
cornerstone, a precious (Isa. 28:16)
Counselor, Wonderful (Isa. 9:6)
covenant to the people (Isa. 42:6)
Creator of Israel, the (Isa. 43:15)
Creator of the ends of the earth (Isa. 40:28)
Creator, a faithful (1 Pet. 4:19)
Creator, your (Eccles. 12:1)
crown of glory, a (Isa 28:5; 62:3)
Dayspring, the (Luke 1:78)
defender of widows, a (Ps. 68:5)
deliverer, my (2 Sam. 22:2; Ps. 18:2)
Deliverer, the (Rom. 11:26)
Desire of All Nations (Hag. 2:7)
diadem of beauty (Isa. 28:5)
diadem, a royal (Isa. 62:3)
door of the sheep, the (John 10:7)
door, the (John 10:9)

Appendix

dwelling place, our (Ps. 90:1)
dwelling, your (Ps. 91:9)
End, the (Rev. 21:6)
Excellent Glory, the (2 Pet. 1:17)
express image of His person, the (Heb. 1:3)
everlasting strength (Isa. 26:4)
Faithful and True (Rev. 19:11)
Father (Matt. 11:25)
Father of glory, the (Eph. 1:17)
Father of lights, the (James 1:17)
Father of mercies, the (2 Cor. 1:3)
Father of spirits, the (Heb. 12:9)
father to the fatherless, a (Ps. 68:5)
Father to Israel, a (Jer. 31:9)
Father who honors Me, My (said by Jesus) (John 8:54)
Father, Everlasting (Isa. 9:6)
Father, Holy (John 17:11; 20:17)
Father, My (John 8:54)
Father, our (Isa. 64:8)
Father, righteous (John 17:25)
Father, your (Deut. 32:6; John 20:17)
Fear of Isaac, the (Gen. 31:42)
fire, a consuming (Deut. 4:24)
fire, the devouring (Isa. 33:14)
first to rise from the dead (Acts 26:23)
First, the (Isa. 44:6; Rev. 22:13)
firstborn among many brothers (Rom. 8:29)
firstborn from the dead, the (Col. 1:18)
firstborn over all creation, the (Col. 1:15)
firstfruits of those who have fallen asleep (1 Cor. 15:20)
fortress, my (Ps. 18:2; 91:2)
foundation (1 Cor. 3:11)
foundation, a sure (Isa. 28:16)
fountain of living waters, the (Jer. 2:13)
friend of tax collectors and sinners, a (Matt. 11:19)
gift, indescribable (2 Cor. 9:15)
gift, the same (Acts 11:17)
glory, their (Ps. 106:20; Jer. 2:11)

glory, your (Isa. 60:19)
God (Gen. 1:1; John 1:1)
God of Hosts, the (El Sabaoth) (Ps. 80:7)
God of my salvation, the (Ps. 18:46)
God of your Salvation, the (Isa. 17:10)
God and Father of our Lord Jesus Christ (Eph. 1:3)
God and Savior Jesus Christ, our (2 Pet. 1:1)
God and Savior, our great (Titus 2:13)
God in heaven above and on the earth beneath (Deut. 4:39; Josh. 2:11)
God Most High (Gen. 14:18)
God my Maker (Job 35:10)
God my Rock (Ps. 42:9)
God of Abraham, the (Ps. 47:9)
God of Abraham, Isaac, and Israel (1 Kings 18:36)
God of Abraham, Isaac, and Jacob (Exod. 3:16)
God of all comfort (2 Cor. 1:3)
God of all flesh (Jer. 32:27)
God of all grace (1 Pet. 5:10)
God of all the kingdoms of the earth (2 Kings 19:15)
God of Daniel (Dan. 6:26)
God of David your father (2 Kings 20:5)
God of glory (Ps. 29:3)
God of gods (Deut. 10:17)
God of heaven (Gen. 24:3; Ps. 136:26)
God of heaven and earth (Ezra 5:11)
God of Israel (Exod. 24:10; Matt. 15:31)
God of Jacob (Ps. 20:1)
God of Jeshurun (the upright one) (Deut. 33:26)
God of mercy (Ps. 59:10)
God of my father Abraham (Gen 32:9)
God of my father Isaac (Gen 32:9)
God of my salvation, the (Ps. 51:14; 88:1)
God of my strength (Ps. 43:2)
God of Nahor (Gen. 31:53)
God of our fathers (Deut. 26:7)
God of our Lord Jesus Christ (Eph. 1:17)
God of our salvation (1 Chron. 16:35; Ps. 85:4)

God of peace (Rom. 16:20; 1 Thess. 5:23)
God of recompense (Jer. 51:56)
God of Shadrach, Meshach, and Abednego (Dan. 3:28)
God of the armies of Israel (1 Sam. 17:45)
God of the earth (Gen. 24:3)
God of the Hebrews (Exod. 5:3)
God of the living (Matt. 22:32)
God of the spirits of all flesh (Num. 16:22; 27:15)
God of the whole earth (Isa. 54:5)
God of truth (Ps. 31:5)
God of truth and without injustice (Deut. 32:4)
God of your fathers (Deut. 1:21)
God our Father (Eph. 1:2)
God our Savior (Jude 25)
God our strength (Ps. 81:1)
God over Israel (2 Sam. 7:26)
God the Father (John 6:27)
God the King of all the earth (Ps. 47:7)
God the Lord (1 Chron. 13:6; Ps. 85:8)
God who alone is wise (1 Tim. 1:17)
God who avenges (Ps. 94:1)
God who avenges me (Ps. 18:47)
God who does wonders (Ps. 77:14)
God-Who-Forgives (Ps. 99:8)
God who delivers me from my enemies, the (Ps. 18:47–48)
God-Who-Sees, the (Gen. 16:13)
God, a jealous (Deut. 4:24)
God, Almighty (El Shaddai) (Gen. 17:1)
God, great and awesome (Dan. 9:4)
God, Israel's (1 Chron. 17:24)
God, living (Jer. 10:10)
God, living and true (1 Thess. 1:9)
God, merciful and gracious (Exod. 34:6)
God, Mighty (Isa. 9:6)
God, my (Gen. 28:21; John 20:17)
God, my righteousness (Ps. 4:1)
God, O King (Ps. 145:1)
God, the Everlasting (Gen. 21:33; Isa. 40:28)

God, the faithful (Deut. 7:9)
God, great (Deut. 10:17)
God, the great and awesome (Neh. 1:5)
God, the true (Jer. 10:10)
God, your (John 20:17)
guarantee, a (2 Cor. 1:22; 5:5)
guide, our (Ps. 48:14)
habitation of justice, the (Jer. 50:7)
He who blots out your transgressions (Isa. 43:25)
He who built all things (Heb. 3:4)
He who calls for the waters of the sea (Amos 5:8)
He who comes in the name of the Lord (Ps. 118:26)
He who comforts you (Isa. 51:12)
He who declares to man what His thought is (Amos 4:13)
He who forms the mountains, and creates the wind (Amos 4:13)
He who makes the day dark as night (Amos 5:8)
He who makes the morning darkness (Amos 4:14)
He who raised Christ from the dead (Rom. 8:11)
He who reveals secrets (Dan. 2:29)
He who sanctifies (Heb. 2:11)
He who searches the heart (Rom. 8:27)
He who searches the minds and hearts (Rev. 2:23)
He who turns the shadow of death into morning (Amos 5:8)
He who was dead, and came to life (Rev. 2:8)
head of all principality and power, the (Col. 2:10)
head of the body, the church (Col. 1:18)
head of the church (Eph. 5:23)
head, the (Eph. 4:15; Col. 2:19)
heir of all things (Heb. 1:2)
help in trouble, a very present (Ps. 46:1)
help, my (Pss. 27:9; 40:17)
help, our (Ps. 33:20)
helper of the fatherless, the (Ps. 10:14)
Helper, another (John 14:16)
Helper, the (John 14:26)
He who has the seven Spirits of God (Rev. 3:1)
He who lives (Rev. 1:18)

Appendix

hiding place, my (Ps. 32:7)
High Priest forever (Heb. 6:20)
High Priest over the house of God (Heb. 10:21)
High Priest, a great (Heb. 4:14)
High Priest, a merciful and faithful (Heb. 2:17)
Him who is able to keep you from stumbling (Jude 24)
Him who is able to present you faultless before . . . (Jude 24)
Him who is from the beginning (1 John 2:13)
Him who is most just (Job 34:17)
Him who is ready to judge the living and the dead (1 Pet. 4:5)
Him who live forever (Dan. 12:7)
Him who lives forever and ever (Rev. 10:6)
Him who loves us and washed us from our sins . . . (Rev. 1:5–6)
Him who ought to be feared (Ps. 76:11)
Him who sits on the throne (Rev. 5:13)
Holy One (Luke 1:35; 1 John 2:20; Isa. 43:15)
Holy One and the Just, the (Acts 3:14)
Holy One of God, the (Luke 4:34)
Holy One of Israel (Ps. 71:22; Isa. 41:14)
Holy One who is faithful, the (Hos. 11:12)
holy Servant Jesus (Acts 4:27)
Holy Spirit, the (John 14:26; Ps. 51:11)
Holy Spirit of God, the (Eph. 4:30)
Holy Spirit, His (Isa. 63:10)
Holy Spirit, the promise of the (Acts 2:33)
hope in the day of doom, my (Jer. 17:17)
Hope of Israel, the (Jer. 14:8)
hope of Israel, the (Jer. 17:13; Acts 28:20)
hope of their fathers, the (Jer. 50:7)
hope, my (Ps. 71:5)
horn of my salvation (2 Sam. 22:3; Ps. 18:2)
horn of salvation (Luke 1:69)
Husband, my (Hos. 2:16)
husband, your (Isa. 54:5)
I am (Exod. 3:14; John 8:58)
I am who I am (Exod. 3:14)
image of God, the (2 Cor. 4:4)

image of the invisible God (Col. 1:15)
Immanuel (God with us) (Matt. 1:23)
immortal (1 Tim. 1:17)
inheritance, their (Ezek. 44:28)
intercessor, my (Isa. 53:12)
invisible (1 Tim. 1:17)
Jealous (Exod. 34:14)
Jesus (Matt. 1:21)
Jesus Christ (John 1:17; Acts 2:38)
Jesus Christ of Nazareth (Acts 4:10)
Jesus Christ our Lord (Rom 1:3)
Jesus Christ our Savior (Titus 3:6)
Jesus of Nazareth (John 19:19)
Judge of all the earth (Gen. 18:25)
Judge of the earth (Ps. 94:2)
Judge of the living and the dead (Acts 10:42)
judge, just (Ps. 7:11)
Judge, our (Isa. 33:22)
Judge, righteous, the (2 Tim. 4:8)
Judge, the (Judg. 11:27)
Just One, the (Acts 7:52)
King above all gods, the great (Ps. 95:3)
King from of old, my (Ps. 74:12)
King of all the earth, the (Ps. 47:7)
King of glory, the (Ps. 24:7)
King of heaven, the (Dan. 4:37)
King of Israel, the (Zeph. 3:15; John 1:49)
KING OF KINGS (Rev. 19:16)
King of kings (1 Tim. 6:15)
King of the Jews (Rev. 15:3)
King of the Jews (Matt. 27:11; John 18:39; 19:9)
King of the nations (Jer. 10:7)
King of the saints (Rev. 15:3)
King over all the earth, great (Ps 47:2)
King who comes in the name of the Lord (Luke 19:38)
King, everlasting (Jer. 10:10)
King, great (Ps. 48:2; Matt. 5:35)
King, my (Ps. 44:4)

King, our (Isa. 33:22)
King, your (Matt. 21:5; Isa. 43:15)
Lamb of God, the (John 1:29)
lamb without blemish and without spot (1 Pet. 1:19)
Lamb, a (Rev. 5:6)
Lamb, the (Rev. 5:8)
Lamb who was slain (Rev. 5:12)
lamp, my (2 Sam. 22:29)
Last, the (Isa. 44:6; Rev. 22:13)
Lawgiver, one (James 4:12)
Lawgiver, our (Isa. 33:22)
leader and commander for the people (Isa. 55:4)
life, eternal (1 John 5:20)
life, the (John 14:6)
life, our (Col. 3:4)
light (1 John 1:5)
Light, the true (John 1:8)
light of life, the (John 8:12)
light of men, the (John 1:4)
light of the world, the (John 8:12)
light to bring revelation to the Gentiles (Luke 2:32)
light to the Gentiles (Isa. 42:6)
light, a great (Isa. 9:2)
light, an everlasting (Isa. 60:19)
Light, true (John 1:9)
lily of the valleys, the (Song of Sol. 2:1)
Lion of the tribe of Judah (Rev. 5:5)
longsuffering, the (Exod. 34:6)
Lord (Luke 2:11)
Lord (Adonai) (Ps. 54:4)
Lord (Jehovah) (Gen. 15:6)
Lord and Savior, the (2 Pet. 3:2)
Lord and Savior Jesus Christ, the (2 Pet. 2:20)
Lord God (Gen. 2:4)
Lord God Almighty (Rev. 15:3)
Lord God of Gods, the (Josh. 22:22)
Lord God of hosts (2 Sam. 5:10)
Lord God of Israel (1 Chron. 29:10)

Lord God, the only (Jude 4)
Lord-Is-My-Banner, the- (Exod. 17:15; Num. 2:2)
Lord-Is-Peace, the- (Jehovah Shalom) (Judg. 6:24)
Lord Jesus (Luke 24:3; Acts 7:59)
Lord Jesus Christ (Gal. 1:3; James 2:1)
Lord Jesus Christ, our hope (1 Tim. 1:1)
Lord Most High (Ps. 7:17)
Lord my Rock (Ps. 28:1)
Lord of all the earth, the (Josh. 3:13)
Lord of both the dead and the living (Rom. 14:9)
Lord of glory, the (1 Cor. 2:8; James 2:1)
Lord of heaven and earth (Matt. 11:25)
Lord of hosts (Ps. 24:10)
Lord of kings (Dan. 2:47)
LORD OF LORDS (Rev. 19:16)
Lord of lords (Deu. 10:17; 1 Tim. 6:15; Rev. 17:14)
Lord of peace, the (2 Thess. 3:16)
Lord of the harvest (Matt. 9:38)
Lord of the Sabbath (Matt. 12:8; Luke 6:5)
Lord our God, the (Josh. 24:24)
Lord our Maker, the (Ps. 95:6)
Lord Our Righteousness, The (Jer. 23:6; 33:16)
Lord our shield (Ps. 59:11)
Lord over Israel (1 Chron. 28:5)
Lord who heals you, the (Exod. 15:26)
Lord who made heaven and earth (Ps. 115:15; 121:2)
Lord who sanctifies you, the (Exod. 31:13)
Lord-Will-Provide, the- (Gen. 22:14)
Lord your God, the (Lev. 11:44)
Lord your Maker, the (Isa. 51:13)
Lord, my (John 20:28)
love (1 John 4:8)
Maker of all things, the (Jer. 10:16)
Maker of heaven and earth, the sea, and . . . (Ps. 146:6)
Maker of the Bear, Orion, and the Pleiades . . . (Job 9:9)
majestic Lord, the (Isa. 33:21)
Majesty on high, the (Heb. 1:3)
Maker, his (Prov. 14:31)

Appendix

Maker, my (Job 32:22)
Maker, our (Ps. 95:6)
Maker, your (Isa. 54:5)
Man attested by God (Acts 2:22)
Man Jesus Christ, the (1 Tim. 2:5)
Man of sorrows (Isa. 53:3)
Man, a righteous (Luke 23:47)
Man, the second (1 Cor. 15:47)
Man, that just (Matt. 27:19)
Man, the (John 19:5)
Man, this (Mark 6:2)
Master (Luke 5:5; 2 Tim. 2:21)
Master in heaven, a (Col. 4:1)
Mediator, the (1 Tim. 2:5)
Mediator of a new covenant, the (Heb. 9:15)
Messenger of the covenant, the (Mal. 3:1)
Messiah, the (John 1:41)
Mighty One of Jacob, the (Ps. 132:2,5)
Mighty God (Isa. 9:6)
Mighty God of Jacob (Gen. 49:24)
morning star (2 Pet. 1:19)
Morning Star, the Bright and (Rev. 22:16)
Most High (Ps. 18:13; 92:1)
Most High over all the earth, the (Ps. 83:18)
Most Holy, the (Dan. 9:24)
Most Upright (Isa. 26:7)
Nazarene, a (Matt. 2:23)
offering and sacrifice to God, an (Eph. 5:2)
oil of gladness (Heb. 1:9)
Omega (Rev. 1:8)
only begotten of the Father, the (John 1:14)
One greater than Jonah (Matt. 12:41)
One greater than Solomon (Matt. 12:42)
One greater than the temple (Matt. 12:6)
one Lawgiver who is able to save and to destroy (James 4:12)
One who gives salvation to kings, the (Ps. 144:10)
One who is and who was and who is to be, the (Rev. 16:5)
One who remembered us in our low state (Ps. 136:23)

One you are to dread (Isa. 8:13)
One you are to fear (Isa. 8:13)
One you should hallow, the (Isa. 8:13)
One, My Elect (Isa. 42:1)
Passover, our (1 Cor. 5:7)
peace, our (Eph. 2:14)
Physician (Luke 4:23)
portion, my (Ps. 119:57)
portion in the land of the living, my (Ps. 142:5)
Portion of Jacob, the (Jer. 10:16)
portion of my inheritance, the (Ps. 16:5)
Possessor of heaven and earth (Gen. 14:22)
possession, their (priest's) (Ezek. 44:28)
Potentate, blessed and only (1 Tim. 6:15)
potter, the (Isa. 64:8; Rom. 9:21)
power of the Highest (Luke 1:35)
power of God, the (1 Cor. 1:24)
Power, the (Matt. 26:64)
praises of Israel, the (Ps. 22:3)
praise, your (Deut. 10:21)
priest forever according to the order of Melchizedek (Heb. 5:6)
Prince, the (Dan. 9:25)
Prince and Savior (Acts 5:31)
Prince of life (Acts 5:31)
Prince of Peace, the (Isa. 9:6)
Prince of princes, the (Dan. 8:25)
Prince of the hosts, the (Dan. 8:11)
Promise, the Father of (Acts 1:4)
prophet from Nazareth, the (Matt. 21:11)
Prophet who is to come into the world (John 6:14)
Prophet, the (John 7:40)
propitiation for our sins, the (1 John 2:2)
Rabbi (John 3:2)
Rabboni (Teacher) (John 20:16)
ransom for all, a (1 Tim. 2:6)
Redeemer from everlasting, our (Isa. 63:16)
Redeemer, my (Job 19:25; Ps. 19:14)

Redeemer, our (Isa. 47:4)
Redeemer, their (Ps. 78:35; Prov. 23:11)
Redeemer, your (Isa. 41:14)
refiner and purifier, as a (Mal. 3:3)
refuge and strength, our (Ps. 46:1)
refuge for the oppressed (Ps. 9:9)
refuge from the storm, a (Isa. 25:4)
refuge in the day of affliction, my (Jer. 16:19)
refuge in the day of my trouble, my (Ps. 59:16)
refuge in times of trouble, a (Ps. 9:9)
refuge, my (2 Sam. 22:3; Ps. 142:5; Isa. 91:2)
refuge, our (Ps. 46:7)
refuge of His anointed, saving (Ps. 28:8)
resurrection and the life, the (John 11:25)
reward, your exceedingly great (Gen. 15:1)
righteousness and sanctification and redemption, our (1 Cor. 1:30)
Rock of his salvation (Deut. 32:15)
rock of my refuge, the (Ps. 94:22)
rock of my salvation, the (Ps. 89:26)
rock of my strength and my refuge, the (Ps. 62:7)
rock of offense, a (1 Pet. 2:8)
Rock of our salvation, the (Ps. 95:1)
Rock of Israel, the (2 Sam. 23:3)
rock, my (Ps. 18:2; 92:15)
Rock, spiritual (1 Cor. 10:4)
Rock, the (Deut. 32:4)
Root and the Offspring of David, the (Rev. 22:16)
Root of David (Rev. 5:5)
Root of Jesse (Isa. 11:10; Rom. 15:12)
rose of Sharon, the (Song of Sol. 2:1)
ruler over the kings of the earth, the (Rev. 1:5)
Ruler, a (governor) (Matt. 2:6)
salvation, my (Exod. 15:2; Ps. 27:1)
salvation, Your (Luke 2:30)
sanctuary, a (Isa. 8:14)
Savior in times of trouble (Israel's) (Jer. 14:8)
Savior—Jesus (Acts 13:23)

Savior of all men, the (1 Tim. 4:10)
Savior of the body (Eph. 5:23)
Savior of the world, the (John 4:42)
Savior, my (2 Sam. 22:3)
Savior, the (Eph. 5:23)
Savior, their (Isa. 63:8)
Savior, your (Isa. 43:3)
Sceptre (Num. 24:17)
seal, a (Eph. 1:13)
seed, His (1 John 3:9)
seed, his (Abraham's) (Gal. 3:16)
Seed, the (Gal. 3:19)
servant to the circumcision (Rom. 15:8)
Servant, holy (Acts 4:27)
Servant, My (Matt. 12:18)
Servant, My righteous (Isa. 53:11)
seven spirits of God (the sevenfold spirit) (Rev. 5:6)
shade at your right hand, your (Ps. 121:5)
shade from the heat, a (Isa. 25:4)
shelter for His people, a (Joel 3:16)
Shepherd and Overseer of your souls, the (1 Pet. 2:25)
Shepherd of Israel (Ps. 80:1)
Shepherd of the sheep, great (Heb. 13:20)
Shepherd, one (Eccles. 12:11)
Shepherd, the Chief (1 Pet. 5:4)
shepherd, the good (John 10:11)
shield for me, a (Ps. 3:3)
shield, my (Ps. 18:2; 28:7)
shield, our (Ps. 33:20)
Son of Abraham (Matt. 1:1)
Son of David (Matt. 1:1; Luke 20:41)
Son of God (John 1:49; 1 John 4:9)
Son of Joseph (John 6:42)
Son of Mary (Mark 6:3)
Son of Man, the (Matt. 12:40; 24:27)
Son of the Blessed One, the (Mark 14:61)
Son of the living God (Matt. 16:16)
Son of the Most High God (Mark 5:7)

Appendix

Son, My beloved (Mark 1:11)
song, my (Ps. 118:14)
Spirit of adoption, the (Rom. 8:15)
spirit of burning, the (Isa. 4:4)
Spirit of Christ, the (Rom. 8:9)
Spirit of counsel and might, the (Isa. 11:2)
spirit of faith, the (2 Cor. 4:13)
Spirit of glory, the (1 Pet. 4:14)
Spirit of God, the (Gen. 1:2; Matt. 3:16)
Spirit of grace, the (Heb. 10:29)
Spirit of grace and supplication, the (Zech. 12:10)
Spirit of His Son (Gal. 4:6)
Spirit of holiness, the (Rom. 1:4)
Spirit of Jesus Christ, the (Phil. 1:19)
spirit of judgement, the (Isa. 4:4)
spirit of justice, a (Isa. 28:6)
Spirit of knowledge and of the fear of the Lord, the (Isa. 11:2)
Spirit of life, the (Rom. 8:2)
Spirit of our God, the (1 Cor. 6:11)
Spirit of the living God, the (2 Cor. 3:3)
Spirit of the Lord, the (Isa. 11:2; Luke 4:18)
Spirit of truth, the (John 14:17; 15:26)
spirit of wisdom and revelation, the (Eph. 1:17)
Spirit of wisdom and understanding, the (Isa. 11:2)
Spirit of your Father, the (Matt. 10:20)
spirit of wisdom, the (Deut. 34:9)
Spirit who bears witness, the (1 John 5:6)
Spirit who dwells in us, the (James 4:5)
spirit, a life-giving (1 Cor. 15:45)
spirit, a new (Ezek. 11:19; 18:31)
Spirit, the eternal (Heb. 9:14)
Spirit, His (Num. 11:29; Eph. 3:16)
Spirit, My (Gen. 6:3; Matt. 12:18)
Spirit, the (Num. 11:17; Acts 16:7))
Spirit, Your (Neh. 9:30)
Spirit, Your good (Neh. 9:20)
Star, a (Num. 24:17)
stone of stumbling (Isa. 8:14; 1 Pet. 2:8)

stone which the builders rejected (Matt. 21:42; Mark 12:10; 1 Pet. 2:7)
stone, a living (1 Pet. 2:4)
stone, a tried (Isa. 28:16)
Stone of Israel, the (Gen. 49:24)
strength of my life (Ps. 27:1)
strength to the needy in his distress, a (Isa. 25:4)
strength to the poor, a (Isa. 25:4)
Strength of Israel, the (1 Sam. 15:29)
strength of my heart, the (Ps. 73:26)
Strength, his (Ps. 59:9)
strength, my (Ps. 28:7; 118:14)
Stronghold, my (Ps. 18:2)
sun and shield, a (Ps. 84:11)
support, my (2 Sam. 22:19; Ps. 18:18)
surety of a better covenant, a (Heb. 7:22)
sword of your majesty, the (Deut. 33:29)
Teacher (Mark 9:17)
Teacher, the (Matt. 26:18)
teacher who has come from God, a (John 3:2)
tower from the enemy, a strong (Ps. 61:3)
trap and a snare, a (Isa. 8:14)
trust from my youth, my (Ps. 71:5)
truth, the (John 14:6)
vine, the (John 15:5)
vinedresser, the (John 15:1)
vine, the true (John 15:1)
voice of the Almighty, the (Shaddai) (Ezek. 1:24)
voice of the Lord (Ps. 29:3)
way, the (John 14:6)
wisdom from God (1 Cor. 1:30)
wisdom of God, the (1 Cor. 1:24)
witness to the people, a (Isa. 55:4)
Witness, Faithful and True (Rev. 3:14)
witness, my (Job 16:19)
witness, the faithful (Rev. 1:5)
Word of God (Rev. 19:13)
Word of life, the (1 John 1:1)

Word, the (logos) (John 1:1)
You who dwell in the heavens (Ps. 123:1)
You who hear prayer (Ps. 65:2)
you who judge righteously, testing . . . (Jer. 11:20)